D1251183

The Art of Interpretation in the Age of Computation

The Art of Interpretation in the Age of Computation

Paul Kockelman

OXFORD

UNIVERSITY PRESS

Oxford University Press is a department of the University of Oxford. It furthers the University's objective of excellence in research, scholarship, and education by publishing worldwide. Oxford is a registered trade mark of Oxford University Press in the UK and certain other countries.

Published in the United States of America by Oxford University Press
198 Madison Avenue, New York, NY 10016, United States of America.

© Oxford University Press 2017

All rights reserved. No part of this publication may be reproduced, stored in a retrieval system, or transmitted, in any form or by any means, without the prior permission in writing of Oxford University Press, or as expressly permitted by law, by license, or under terms agreed with the appropriate reproduction rights organization. Inquiries concerning reproduction outside the scope of the above should be sent to the Rights Department, Oxford University Press, at the address above.

You must not circulate this work in any other form
and you must impose this same condition on any acquirer.

Library of Congress Cataloging-in-Publication Data
Names: Kockelman, Paul, author.
Title: The art of interpretation in the age of computation / Paul Kockelman.
Description: New York, NY : Oxford University Press, [2017] |
Includes bibliographical references and index.
Identifiers: LCCN 2016032470 (print) | LCCN 2016056107 (ebook) |
ISBN 9780190636531 (cloth : alk. paper) | ISBN 9780190636548 (updf) |
ISBN 9780190636555 (ebook) | ISBN 9780190636562 (online resource)
Subjects: LCSH: Semiotics—Psychological aspects. |
Signs and symbols—Psychological aspects. |
Natural language processing (Computer science) | Ontologies (Information retrieval) |
Information technology. | Anthropological linguistics.
Classification: LCC P99.4.P78 K65 2017 (print) | LCC P99.4.P78 (ebook) |
DDC 006.3/5—dc23
LC record available at https://lccn.loc.gov/2016032470

P
99.4
.P78
K65
20A

For Mia, Zeno, Lara, and my Mom.

CONTENTS

LIST OF FIGURES

LIST OF TABLES

ACKNOWLEDGMENTS

Bill Maurer and Paul Manning gave me very valuable feedback on different parts of this manuscript at several junctures, and in different forums. Both were very strong supporters of the project from the very beginning, and offered detailed and constructive criticisms at key points. Each of them heavily influenced the organization and arguments of the final manuscript. I cannot thank them enough.

Four other key interlocutors for this project were Eitan Wilf, Miyako Inoue, Julia Elyachar, and Nick Enfield. Eitan and Miyako organized conference panels that influenced my thinking, and forced me to write key parts of this manuscript, and their own work on related topics has proven particularly simulating. And my conversations with Julia and Nick, on related topics, go back a long way, and were particularly important in regards to the fundamental themes of this book, such as lines and circles. Thank you.

Jack Sidnell read parts of Chapter 6, in an early form, and suggested key changes. Talbot Taylor and Giovanni da Col, in their editorial roles for the journals *Language and Communication* and *Hau: Journal of Ethnographic Theory*, and Paul Manning and Miyako Inoue in their editorial roles for the *Journal of Linguistic Anthropology*, were particularly helpful. I presented parts of Chapters 1 and 5 to the Yale Film and Media Department, and received very stimulating feedback from John MacKay and Francesco Casetti.

Other scholars who contributed to this project, as interlocutors and inspirations along the way, include Paul North and Gary Tomlinson, Gabriele Schwab and Tom Boellstorf, Asif Agha and Greg Urban, Miki Makihara and John Collins, Circe Sturm and Catherine Lutz, Laura Kunreuther and Tony Webster, Magnus Pharao Hansen and Danny Law, John Hartigan and Elizabeth Keating, Sandra Kurfürst and Martin Zillinger, Paja Faudree and Joseph Errington, Erik Harms and Doug Rogers, Brian Larkin and Antina von Schnitzler, Mike Cepek and Jessica Jerome, Nick Seaver and Chris Ball, Adam Leeds and Xenia Cherkaev, Andrew Carruthers and Maria Sidorkina, Chris Hebdon and Dina Omar. Thank you.

Thanks to Hallie Stebbins, my editor at Oxford University Press, and to two anonymous reviewers whose comments and suggestions helped finalize the architecture and arguments of the book.

And special thanks to Cepek, Faudree, and Jerome.

Four chapters of the book involve previously unpublished works. And three chapters partially incorporate and, in most cases, radically rework material taken from the following articles and chapters:

2013 "The Anthropology of an Equation: Sieves, Spam Filters, Agentive Algorithms, and Ontologies of Transformation." *HAU: Journal of Ethnographic Theory* 3(3):33–61.

2013 "Huckleberry Finn Takes the Turing Test: The Transformation of Ontologies and the Virtuality of Kinds." *Language and Communication* 33:150–154.

2013 "Information Is the Enclosure of Meaning: Cybernetics, Semiotics, and Alternative Theories of Information." *Language and Communication* 33:115–127.

2012 "The Ground, The Ground, The Ground: Why Archeology Is So 'Hard'." *Yearbook of Comparative Literature* 58:176–183.

2010 "Enemies, Parasites, and Noise: How to Take Up Residence in a System Without Becoming a Term in It." *Journal of Linguistic Anthropology* 20(2):406–421.

1

Lines Crossed and Circles Breached

1.1. Semiotic Practices and Computational Processes

This book is about media, mediation, and meaning. It focuses on a set of interrelated processes whereby seemingly human-specific semiotic practices become
automated, formatted, and networked. That is, as computation replaces interpretation, information effaces meaning, and infrastructure displaces interaction. *Or so
it seems.*

I ask: What does it take to automate, format, and network semiotic practices?
What difference does this make for those who engage in such practices? And what
are the stakes? Reciprocally: How can we better understand computational processes from the standpoint of semiotic practices? How can we leverage such processes to better understand such practices? And what lies in wait?

There are six core chapters. The even numbered chapters take up these concerns
directly. Chapter 2 focuses on the relation between infrastructure and interaction.
Chapter 4 focuses on the relation between information and meaning. And chapter
6 focuses on the relation between computation and interpretation. The odd numbered chapters take up such concerns more indirectly, acting as connecting linkages
between, and less linear approaches to, the concerns of those chapters. Chapter 3
focuses on the relation between secrecy, poetry, and freedom. Chapter 5 focuses on
the relation between materiality, virtuality, and time. And chapter 7 focuses on the
relation between ontologies and their algorithmic transformations.

As will be seen, rather than foreground—and, as is so often the case, fetishize—
the latest application, platform, or processing technology, this book stays very close
to fundamental concerns of computer science, as they emerged in the middle part
of the twentieth century. In this way, I try to account for processes that underlie, or
serve as the foundation for, each and every digital technology being deployed today.
And rather than use the tools of conventional social theory to investigate such technologies, I leverage key ideas of American pragmatism, a philosophical stance that
understands the world, and our relation to it, in a way that avoids many of the

1

Paul Kockelman. *The Art of Interpretation in the Age of Computation.* © Oxford University Press 2017

conundrums and criticisms of twentieth-century social theory. I put this stance in dialogue with certain currents, and key texts, in anthropology and linguistics, science and technology studies, critical theory, computer science, and media studies (broadly conceived).

The rest of this chapter lays out the key moves, and organizational logic, of the entire book. Section 1.2 takes up the notion of lines, and how to cross them. It argues that, rather than privileging mere 'relations', our analysis must foreground a particular ensemble of relations between relations if we are to properly understand the following modes of mediation: semiotic processes, semiological structures, agentive practices, environment-organism interfaces, communicative channels, social relations, and parasitic encounters. Perhaps the best image here is of the bridge that connects two banks (and the trolls that live beneath it).

Section 1.3 takes up the notion of circles, and how to breach them. It shows the ways such modes of mediation get enclosed through processes that automate, format, and network them, such that their meaningfulness and means-ends-fulness is made to seem relatively portable: applicable to many contents and applicable across many contexts. Perhaps the best image here is the wall that encircles a city (and the cracks that allow seepage).

Section 1.4 reviews and reworks several key ideas of Charles Sanders Peirce, the founder of American pragmatism. It uses these ideas to motivate the organizational logic of the entire book. This will prime readers for many of the arguments and connections that follow.

And section 1.5 summarizes each of the chapters. It highlights key themes, arguments, and interlocutors. Readers impatient to begin can read it now if they wish.

1.2. Lines (and How To Cross Them)

What is the relation between media, mediation, and meaning? To answer this question, it is useful to begin with an extended example. Suppose, for the moment, that we are in the cloud-forests of highland Guatemala. It is early morning, just after dawn. A woman is tending to a hearth fire in a one-room house with a thatch roof. In a bed near the fire are her three children. Two are still asleep, but the oldest, a five-year-old boy, is watching her from beneath the blankets. As the fire begins to blaze, and its light fills the room, the woman notices that one of her hens must have gotten in during the night and shat near the fire. *Chix* (ugh, yuck), she says, using an interjection in Q'eqchi', a Mayan language spoken by around one million people. The boy looks where she is looking, and sees what she is looking at. He crawls out of bed, slips his feet into his shoes, and walks to the other side of the room where his father's machete is leaning against the wall. He returns with it, and scrapes up the turd with its blade. Holding the machete horizontally, he walks carefully to the door of the house. He opens it with his free hand, and flings the turd out into the underbrush.

While not an everyday event, this was certainly a frequent kind of encounter during my fieldwork in this village (Kockelman 2003, 2010a, 2016). Indeed, broadly speaking, it is probably a common enough occurrence in any household anywhere: a seemingly affective and adverse reaction to 'dirt' as matter out of place, and a communicative means to mobilize others to put dirt in its place. To understand its particular relevance for this project, it is useful to step through some of its fundamental features—*the relations between relations* that underlie its unfolding.[1]

Foregrounded in my description is what Peirce would consider a *semiotic process*: a sign or 'message' (the interjection *chix*), standing for an object or 'referent' (the chicken turd), and giving rise to an interpretant or 'response' (the boy's change in attention). See part (a) of Figure 1.1.

Also present is what the Swiss linguist Ferdinand de Saussure would call a *semiological structure*, or code: the relation between this sign (or 'signifier') and its object (or 'signified') as contrasted with other signs and their objects—for example, interjections like *ay, eh, t',* and *uyaluy*, which indicate entities or events that are impressive, doubtful, unintended, or scary. See part (b) of Figure 1.1.

Such modes of significance (or 'meaning') are also caught up in modes of selection (or 'value'). Just as objects underlie signs and interpretants, agents underlie sensations and instigations. See part (c) of Figure 1.1. Moreover, what the woman, as an agent, instigated (expressing an interjection) in the context of what she sensed (seeing matter out of place) made 'sense' given the features of that object and her interests as an agent. See part (d) of Figure 1.1. These might be called *agentive practice* and *actor-environment interface*, respectively.

Crucially, any such object-agent interrelation, as grounded in signs and interpretants as much as sensations and instigations, is related to other object-agent interrelations through some kind of *channel*: what the woman instigated (uttering the interjection *chix*) could be sensed by the boy (hearing the interjection *chix*); and what the woman pointed out (using the sign) could be seen by the boy (through the sign). See part (e) of Figure 1.1.

Finally, all of this turned on a *social relation*: a relation between a signer and an interpreter (a mother and her son) mediated by a relation between a sign and an interpretant (her interjection and his reaction). See part (f) of Figure 1.1.

***

Framed as such, this encounter involves at least six *modes of mediation*: semiotic processes, semiological structures, agentive practices, actor-environment interfaces, communicative channels, and social relations. Crucially, each of these modes of mediation seems relatively 'immediate'. That is, the semiotic process seems relatively indexical as opposed to symbolic, and thus grounded in causality as opposed to convention, and so motivated as opposed to arbitrary. The semiological structure turns on interjections, signs that seem to lie on the edge of language, where human voice seems to come closest to animal sound. As to agentive practice, the movement

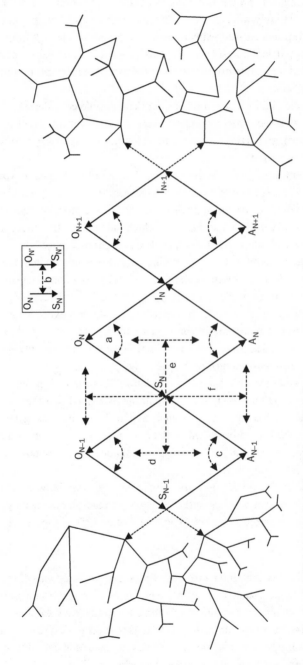

FIGURE 1.1 Relations between Relations, Modes of Mediation

from sensation to instigation seems minimally buffered, a reaction as opposed to an action. And the interface between an actor and an environment seems maximally transparent, or 'thin'; an agent confronts an object with minimal degree of remove. (And, indeed, the object indexed seems about as raw, as opposed to cooked, as can be.) The channel linking one agent to another is face-to-face, and hence seemingly direct and immediate. Each actor coexists in the same context, has access to the same contiguities, and so can see, hear, touch, and taste the same world. And the social relation seems primordial: mother and child, engaged in daily life in the privacy of their own home. Indeed, to some readers, the setting itself might seem premodern, or traditional—a peasant family living in the cloud-forest, with hearth fires and dirt floors, elbow to elbow with animals, several children to a bed, speaking a Mayan language, just at the break of dawn.

Such are some common stereotypes, anyway. A close examination of these practices (Kockelman 2003, 2010a, 2016) would show that there is extensive mediation all the way down. Indeed, the belief that each of these modes of mediation is relatively unmediated is itself a prejudice that is radically mediated—in this case, by assumptions that go back at least as far as Aristotle. In his *Politics* (of all places), Aristotle (2001a) made a series of tacit analogies that have long bedeviled anthropologists (if only unconsciously): as animals are to people, emotion is to reason, women are to men, children are to adults, animal cries are to human language, bare life (*zoe*) is to the good life (*bios*), pleasure and pain (as embodied feelings) are to good and evil (as reasoned judgments), violence is to law, slaves are to masters, body is to mind, and the household is to the *polis*. As may be seen, underlying these dichotomies is an entrenched set of presumptions regarding what is relatively immediate and what is relatively mediate, what is instinctive and what is instituted, what is natural and what is conventional, what is raw and what is cooked.

I don't use the word "bedeviled" lightly. On the one hand, anthropologists have rightly railed against such distinctions for decades, arguing that they are not just false but also harmful. Indeed, it is not difficult to show that what seems to be immediate is radically mediated, and that where we draw the line between the immediate and mediate is itself relatively mediated. And it is not difficult to show how pervasive and pernicious such assumptions are, insofar as they underwrite any number of harmful prejudices and practices, all the while being tacitly naturalized. On the other hand, anthropologists are repeatedly drawn to (what at first appears to be) the immediate—affect, animals, violence, bare life, the body, the private, the everyday, the traditional—if only to argue for its mediation. Indeed, methodologically, it is a discipline that prides itself on a kind of immediacy: the qualitative as opposed to the quantitative, ethnography as opposed to statistics, contextualism as opposed to formalism. Its central conceit goes something like this: I was there, and so saw it, heard it, and felt it, with minimal degree of remove—*so there*. (And just where was the anthropologist—that arch-parasite—when he watched these events unfold?) In short, anthropologists try to get close to what they deem is immediate, all the while decrying how far from that they really are, and how mediated it really is.[2]

Indeed, perhaps unsurprisingly, the opposite move has a very similar logic, and is made almost as often: to find immediacy in the relatively mediated. And so we have no end of scholarship that attempts to find the qualitative in the (seemingly) quantitative, the motivated in the arbitrary, the natural in the conventional, the analog in the digital, the affective in the cognitive, the indexical in the symbolic, the body in the mind, the concrete in the abstract, the materiality in the meaningful, the gesture in the symbol, the actual in the virtual. In both cases, scholars are drawn to one side of a distinction (the near or the far) and yet fight to dissolve the distinction (the near is far, the far is near)—and yet, simply in being drawn again and again to one position or the other, they instantiate the opposition.

Damned if you do; damned if you don't. And so there are also those who would focus on relations as opposed to relata, usually as part and parcel of the approaches just described. Perhaps the most famous move in this direction was made by Bourdieu (1992 [1977]), taking up an insight of Marx, itself reappraised in light of Heidegger: praxis, qua sensuous human activity, as lying between, and tying together, subjects (qua phenomenology) and objects (qua structuralism). As this story goes, praxis, as a power-laden process, is the real prime mover. And subjects and objects, or the immediate and mediate more generally, are really just the emergent precipitates of such a process—and thus effects, as much as conditions. That is, such poles are not preexisting relata that must be related; they are, rather, the emergent residue or trace of some more 'real', more 'sensuous', form of interaction. And indeed, as a more general sort of move, 'to the relations themselves' has been the catchphrase of several generations of theorists. But while this might seem to liberate us from the presumptions just described, it is all too easily reduced to them. Praxis (qua process or relation) becomes the near, or immediate; and its endpoints (the precipitates, or relata) become the far, or mediated. Framed another way, this approach has a two-stroke logic that might best be illustrated with a corporeal metaphor: first, postulate the neck as a solution to the mind-body problem; second, place yourself at the neck, such that it becomes the new immediate, and both body and mind become the new mediated. It sounds good, and it certainly is better; but, to some degree, it is simply a one-upping of prior approaches: a new immediate, a new mediate; a new center, a new periphery.

***

So what do we do in the face of such difficulties? Before we answer this question in full, it should be stressed that we framed our ethnographic event, our interactional unfolding, not in term of relations, but rather in terms of relations between relations. This wasn't done without reason. Everything is related to everything else somehow, and so to invoke 'relationality' per se is no help. Relations between relations, in contrast, underlie just about every useful move ever made in our understanding of meaning or value. For example, Peirce's understanding of semiotic processes; Saussure's understanding of semiological structure; Darwin and Veblen's understanding of natural selection and social distinction; Marx and Evans-Pritchard's understanding of value and social relations; Shannon and Serres's understanding of enemies, parasites, and noise; Aristotle's account of justice; and much else besides (Kockelman 2005, 2011a, 2013a). To understand praxis, to make sense of such interactions as they unfold, requires making principled reference to such relations between relations: for these are the grounds relative to which any practice (process, event, entity, action, relation, etc.) must be figured.

(Indeed, even the example offered above hardly delved into these. For such relations between relations did not just underlie the woman's uttering of *chix* [as a sign], and the boy's turning to look [as an interpretant]. They also underlay the women's seeing matter out of place [as a sign] and her saying *chix* [as an interpretant]; and the boy's seeing what his mother was showing [as a sign] and his undertaking an action to correct it [as an interpretant]. And they did not just organize that, but also the anthropologist's seeing of all of this [whatever the degree of remove], and his social relation to them. And they organized his writing up of what he saw, as well as your social relation to him. And so on, and so forth. In other words, such relations between relations are *recursively reticulated*. They embed and enchain indefinitely, as may be seen in Figure 1.1. And they may be infinitely recentered and rescaled, depending on the interests of the analyst.)

With these overarching commitments in mind, here are some of the key moves that must be made if we want to understand such processes and resolve such difficulties. First, rather than focusing on 'media' (qua relatively reified products), we will focus on mediation (qua underlying processes that give rise to such precipitates). We are not just interested, then, in particular kinds of media per se, and certainly not just interested in 'media' as traditionally understood (e.g., gramophones, film, typewriters), but rather in the conditions and consequences of such modes of mediation—understood materially, conceptually, socially, affectively, economically, morally, politically, and beyond.

Second, rather than focusing on mediation as a kind of relation, we will focus on mediation as a relation between relations. What we mean by this, and our reasons for it, were outlined above; and all this will be carefully illustrated, and argued for, in what follows.

Third, rather than focus on mediation in a narrow sense—say, as 'representation' or 'translation'—we will focus on many different modes of mediation, in their criss-crossings and co-presence. Many of these were exemplified above, and foregrounded in Figure 1.1.

Fourth, rather than focus on a particular ensemble of relations between relations, we will attend to the fact that such interrelations embed and enchain indefinitely. Shift, then, from the center of Figure 1.1 to any part of its periphery; and shift to our ability to shift per se.

Fifth, in the face of this potentially infinite recursive reticulation, we will reflexively foreground the framing processes that necessarily underlie any analytic choice: which relations between relations do we pursue, how far along them do we go, and in what directions, such that only some interrelations—but hopefully very important interrelations—come to the fore in our analyses (Goffman 1974; Kockelman 2011a). Indeed, Figure 1.1, as a kind of figuring, is precisely such a framing. In short, instead of just focusing on what is within the frame, we will foreground the framing itself, and its relation to those who frame (where those who frame may include the actors so framed as much as any analyst seemingly outside the frame).

Finally, while such commitments could be deployed to understand any particular form of media, or mode of mediation, we will tack back and forth between two stereotypically opposed modes of mediation: face-to-face interaction (as illustrated above) and computer-mediated interaction (broadly understood).[3] The point here is not to oppose these seemingly disparate, and erroneously separated, modes of interaction. Rather, it is to foreground, on the one hand, their radical entanglement and, on the other hand, their radical similarity. One and the same theory should be able to explicate both individually (their differences, their similarities); as well as their intersection (their co-constitution through entanglement); as well as widespread theories, or sensibilities, regarding why they should be opposed, or why they must be collapsed.

***

But that is not enough. The distinction between immediate and mediate, when properly understood, is not entirely without merit. Different modes of mediation (different semiotic processes, different semiological structures, different interfaces, different modes of selection, different kinds of agency, different channels, different social relations, and so forth), and hence different media per se (as particular concretizations of such modalities), should be distinguished—certainly by degree, and often in kind.

For example, media may be distinguished in regards to the distances (spatial, temporal, personal, modal) they bridge, the scales they bring together, and the worlds they entangle. They are different in regards to the sensations and instigations they open up, or close off, through their bridging—what they make accessible to experience, and consequential to action. They are different in regard to the senses of intimacy and formality that they foster—what should be meant by privacy or propinquity, what constitutes a safe enclosure for disclosure, to how wide a public can one connect. They are even different in regards to the sense of the possible (or necessary) that they make possible (or necessary)—what can be done, and what should be done; what can be hoped, and what should be feared. They are different in regards to the kinds of losses they forestall or hasten (say, through spoilage, noise or interception). They are different in regards to the degrees and kinds of agency they foster; the way they make particular agents more or less flexible or fixed in regards to what they say or do, think or feel, create or destroy. They are different in regards to the units of accountability they constitute—who and what, however distributed or individualized, can be held accountable; who or what can be counted, or counted on; and who or what comes to count, or is allowed to recount? They are different in regards to the parasites they foster—the ways they can break down or falter, generate the unexpected or new, as well as the ways they can be hacked or exploited, privatized or enclosed, opened or tinkered with. They are different in regards to the degree and scale to which they regiment our behavior, and the ease with which they may be noticed, celebrated, vilified, inaugurated, uprooted, or overthrown. They are different in regards to their degree of inalienability (e.g., eyes and hands versus glasses and gloves). They are even different in regards to how they mediate our very sense of mediation—what we deem near or far, fixed or fluid, rooted or portable, old or new, essential or superficial, genuine or spurious, material or immaterial, durable or ephemeral, necessity or luxury, fast or slow, small-scale or large-scale, actual or virtual.

How, then, do we handle all these differences, be they real or imagined? How do we account for such effects when such modes of mediation are always in transformation and contestation? And finally, what are the particular stakes of such differentiated effects in the wake of *that medium which seems to be the most mediated*, and thus *seems to herald the end of media*—the digitally rendered (such that information effaces meaning), the pervasively networked (such that infrastructure displaces interaction), and the technologically automated (such that computation replaces interpretation)?

1.3. Circles (and How To Breach Them)

As illustrated in the last section, the exemplary instance of *disclosure* is joint attention: pointing out something to another, such that both of you can attend not just to the same object, but also to your shared attention. More broadly, disclosure turns on showing as much as stating, implicating as much as explicating. It is a mode of sharing that has as both its roots and fruits a *semiotic commons,* a *phatic commons.*[4] We must share something—if only a channel, medium, or contact—in order to come to joint attention; and, having jointly attended, we come to share something. Stereotypically, this something that we share is some kind of perspective, value, resource, or good: a sense of a significant intersection or commons, if not a shared glimpse of the good, the just, or the true. But, if not that, at least we might come to share a sense of how our senses of the significant differ. While such values may be made explicit in formal encounters (the polis, a public, etc.), or stereotypically mediated encounters (mass media, reading publics, etc.), they are more often implicit, and grounded in encounters of the everyday quotidian kind, of the close kind—simply by sharing a story, shooting the shit, or interjecting the chicken shit, a shared sense of significance comes through.

To be sure, disclosure has other, related senses: making public the private, revealing a secret, uncovering a truth. For example, a dream discloses, as does a symptom, as does a text; as does the agent who interprets the dream, diagnoses the illness, or offers an exegesis of the text. As such, disclosure is often a key site of *reflexivity*, where we gain some degree of control over the self (e.g., a piece of us that is unruly), or become more conscious of the self (e.g., a part of us that is enigmatic). Finally, disclosure is often understood in bittersweet terms: gaining knowledge about, or power over, not just significant objects per se, but also gaining knowledge about, and power over, other subjects and, in particular, their sense of what is significant.

***

One stereotypic condition for disclosure is the existence of some kind of clearing, some kind of *enclosure*—a place and time in which the words and deeds, or gestures and symbols, of two or more actors are open to each other, such that some kind of interaction can unfold. A code is shared, a channel is open, a gaze is met, some object of attention is jointly attended to. This metaphor, which goes back to Heidegger at least, is woodsy: as if most of the forest is densely packed trees, such that there are no open lines of sight, such that there are wild animals on the prowl, such that we must keep moving. Only when we arrive at such a clearing, where the woods are sparse, where a fire can be built and the animals kept at bay, can we begin to disclose. We have a public (those within the clearing) that is kept private (to those outside it). Like the disclosure it enables, this stereotypic enclosure is bittersweet. And so it always has its marginal characters, the figures that can flit in and out of the clearing: taking part, perhaps taking apart, but always partially taking. From will-o'-the-wisps to anthropologists, from enemies to parasites, from hackers to spies, from ninjas to noise, from Google to Facebook, from wolves to chickens, from secret agents to the NSA.

***

But this potentially punctured circle is but one kind of enclosure, one condition for disclosure. Just as there are many ways to open, there are many ways to close. As will now be shown, while enclosure has many interrelated meanings, it prototypically involves processes of objectification, formatting, stabilization, and containment (and sometimes even ways of escape). And just as many such enclosures are a condition for disclosure, disclosure itself is often a condition for such enclosures.

The most often invoked kind of enclosure is the historic one, following scholars from Bacon and Marx to Polanyi and Foucault. First, there is that process whereby common lands were turned into private property, and peasants became proletariat. And second, that process whereby such doubly 'freed' persons—from both masters and means of production—were brought into disciplinary institutions, from the workhouse to the asylum.[5]

Following Benjamin (1968a), there is enclosure as shell, niche, skin, home, environs, or aura. The condition for something to keep its distance, no matter how close one comes. Ironically, there is *mind* as that which encloses (with its categories) and that which is enclosed (in our imaginary). Gell (1998), for example, showed that a remarkably widespread cultural imaginary of the mindful is that which is inherently concentric and containing. Related to this understanding of mind is enclosure as black boxing (Serres 2007): something that secures a secret, or keeps its inner workings obscure. Conversely, something that may be opened, hacked, jammed, exploited, understood, or exposed.

There is enclosure in the thermodynamic sense: a three-dimensional system surrounded by a two-dimensional surface that permits or prohibits different kinds of exchanges across its boundary (Reif 1965). Crucially, our social imaginary has similar enclosures: legal, normative, and causal boundaries that allow, or prohibit—and thereby filter or sieve—the movement of particular entities (and not just matter, information and energy, but also ideas, goods, and people). There is polis-ization (Fustel de Coulanges 1955 [1873]): the art of making a wall, be it symbolic or material, that encloses a body politic, such that values on the inside of the wall, in confrontation with those on the outside, seem relatively shared—a language, a morality, an economy, a technology, a system of weights and measures, a structure of feelings, a sovereign, a secret.

There is the closure of technical objects, as laid out by Simondon (1980 [1958]) in his discussion of concretization: when a system is bounded in such a way that its causes and effects are relatively localized within it, as opposed to spilling outside of it. Such a concretized object is internally coherent in such a way that it can do without an artificial environment, like a laboratory or workshop. It becomes independent of context, insofar as it incorporates that context into itself through its own functioning. Latour (1988) made much of this idea, with his account of extending networks: creating the conditions for scientific objects to reproduce their effects outside the laboratory. Relatedly, there is the notion of bubbles in cybernetics (Clynes and Kline 1960): the environmental envelopes we might put around human organisms to push them into space, such that they might take what is essential to their niche with them. And there is the fear that such bubbles might all too easily burst.

Crucial to the definition of language automata, or artificial languages, there is the notion of *recursive closure*: a set of elements is closed under some operation if that operation applied to any such element returns an element that is still in the set

(Sipser 2007, 45).[6] Such a definition is essential for developing an intuition for the scope or power of such languages, the way they bootstrap themselves into higher and higher degrees of complexity. From computer science, there is enclosure in the sense of a coming to a close, of ceasing or halting. For example, Alan Turing (2004 [1936]) famously argued that no program can always determine whether another arbitrary program, with a particular input, will finish running (and thereby 'halt'), or simply run on forever insofar as it is unable to 'make a decision' in regards to that input—for example, whether it is true or false, acceptable or rejectable, wheat or chaff.

There are the closed worlds described by Edwards (1996) in his account of computers and Cold War America. As developed by Mirowski (2001), these centers of control and surveillance were constituted by various kinds of enclosures: not just thermodynamically isolated and all-seeing, such 'clean rooms' also had the air of a quarantine, a prophylaxis, or a tomb. And there are envelopes more generally—that which protects against interlopers; and that which forestalls development.

There is Nietzsche's classic statement, in *On the Genealogy of Morals* (1967), that the stress of man's enclosure in society was a condition for him to succumb to bad conscience—itself a kind of illness that arises when one's prior instincts are suspended by the introduction of a new medium. Marshall McLuhan (1996 [1964]) made much of this point is his discussion of Narcissus and autoamputation. Relatedly, there is the closure of sense ratios, as introduced by Blake, and taken up by McLuhan: the displacement of perception that arises from our adaptation to new media, understood as any extension of ourselves. As Blake put it: "If perceptive Organs vary, Objects of perception seem to vary; If perceptive organs close, their objects seem to close also."[7]

In Saussure (1983 [1916]), we have the notion of a systemic totality (however projected, artificial, or imagined) within which the analysis of a semiological structure unfolds. Only inside this hermeneutic enclosure can a given element be assigned a specific value, or identity. Conversely, there is Freud's (1999 [1899]) notion of the impossibility of interpretive closure: "the dream-thoughts we come upon as we interpret cannot in general but remain without closure, spinning out on all sides into the web-like fabric of our thoughts." He famously called that part of a dream that "must be left in the dark," the "dream's navel, and the place beneath which lies the Unknown" (341).

***

While many of these modes of enclosure seem to offer a kind of 'objectivity' (when positively valenced) or a kind of 'objectification' (when negatively valenced), far more interesting than such modernist ontological presumptions (turning, as they do, on 'subjects', 'objects', and their interrelations and denigrations) is that such enclosures hold the promise of *portability* (Kockelman and Bernstein 2012). That is, many such modes of enclosure are conditions for making the meaningfulness and means-ends-fulness of particular media seem relatively applicable to many contents and in many contexts.[8] As Kockelman (2016, 7) puts it: To be applicable to many contents does not mean so much that any such medium is preternaturally primed for the contents of any domain it should encounter, but rather that it has the capacity to assimilate such contents to itself, or accommodate itself to such contents, on the fly or after the fact. Relatedly, to be applicable in many contexts does not mean so much that any such medium is independent of context, but rather that the context the medium is dependent on can be recovered from the medium, transported with it, or established wherever it is found.

It is useful to return to the semiotic processes exemplified in the last section, in order to highlight some of the properties that make various media highly portable.[9] For example, the sign (medium, system of signs, etc.) can be transported across time (it lasts), space (it travels), iteration (it copies), media or format (it converts), scale (it may be made big or near, loud or bright, etc.), composition (it can incorporate other signs or be incorporated by other signs), and agent (in regard to its formal properties, and against the background of a particular environment, it is relatively sensible, manipulatable, memorable, salient, etc.).

The objects that signs stand for (or the possible objects that signs from a particular system could stand for) are ontologically broad. That is, almost any entity or event, practice or process, qualia or quantia could be represented by, produced by, or regimented through, such signs. Overlapping with this last point, the event of representation (qua sign-token, and its accompanying context) and the event so represented (qua object-token, and its accompanying context), understood as distinct events with different participants, can be displaced from each other in time, space, person, and possibility (as broadly, or as narrowly, as can be).

An interpreting agent can get from the sign to the object in a wide variety of contexts, or can interpret almost any sign (or 'input'). That is, whatever is needed to decode the sign, or learn about the object through the sign, may be found (brought, bought, or built) wherever such an agent goes.[10] This agent can be displaced from the signifying agent (the one who produced the sign), along dimensions like space, time, person, and possibility. And finally, the interpretant generated—itself usually a sign with its own object, able to give rise to its own interpretant in turn—should itself have all the foregoing kinds of qualities (it lasts, it copies, it travels, etc.). This ensures that, if the medium/message cannot get from here to there (or me to you, or us to them, or now to then, or input to output) in 'one go', at least it can get there in several. And so it goes . . . for, as we saw above, such semiotic processes can embed and enchain indefinitely.[11]

***

Such interrelated properties are one way to characterize the *relative* contextual independence and scope of applicability of a given medium, mode of mediation, or semiotic technology. They are a condition for such technologies, and their users, to deal with any kind of content in any kind of context. With such crisscrossing dimensions and overlapping issues in mind, we may make some qualifications and highlight some conundrums.

Firstly, all such issues thereby affect intervention as much as representation, cognition as much as communication, and feeling as much as thinking. For example, various media allow us to act at a distance as much as describe at a distance, think at distance as much as talk at a distance. And they allow us to see and touch, and think and feel, at a small distance (a proximity) as much as at a large distance, the intra-atomic as much as the interstellar.

Secondly, such definitions have as much to with 'materiality' (in the sense of concreteness) as they do with 'objectivity' (in the sense of abstraction). Indeed, they run roughshod over such simplistic divisions.

Third, portability is necessarily a multi-dimensional, frame-dependent, and by-degrees notion. It has less to do with the qualities of a medium per se, than with the qualities of a medium in relation to not just an ensemble of agents, infrastructures, institutions, and imaginaries, but also other media that are, by comparison, less portable. It is thus necessarily relative and relational. The affordances of a particular medium (what it can and cannot do, what function or resource it offers or withholds, what hope or possibility it opens or forecloses) are judged relative to the affordances of other media—often prior media—by those who are accustomed to residing amid particular assemblages of media.

Fourth, in many situations the foregoing kinds of features are tightly tied to agency, be it practical (e.g., ways of residing in the world) or theoretical (e.g., ways of representing the world). In some sense, and with many caveats, the more portable a system, the more agency it affords its users (Kockelman 2007a, 2013a). Framed another way, it is often the case that agents who stand at the center of the most portable systems have a radical distance from all systems: they can represent other worlds, and others' worlds, without having to reside in them themselves. At least, so it seems.

Finally, nonportability (and a set of related distinctions, such as incommensurability, concreteness, context-boundedness, and immateriality) is just as important and, in some sense, already theorized as the converse of the above characterizations. To return to the concerns of the last section, one way of reframing and retheorizing the 'immediate' and the 'mediate' is as the 'non-portable' and the 'portable'. And so all the caveats introduced there should be echoed here: portability is an impulse more than an achievement; a process as much as a precipitate; something imagined more often than instantiated; the potential object of promises and fears as much as an actual characteristic of entities or events. There will always be hopes for (and fears of) *universal media*, or seemingly highly portable semiotic processes—be these weights and measures, languages and currencies, standards and protocols, laws and conventions, interfaces and algorithms, governments and disciplines, religions and weapons.

***

To be sure, just as there are many ways to close, there are also many ways to forestall such closure. We will take up many of these in this book—not just enemies, parasites, and noise, but also symptoms, exploits, hacks, and spies. Indeed a key anti-figure of some of the most stereotypic enclosures is that which is 'free-as-a-bird' (*vogelfrei*). This term was famously used by Marx [1967 [1867]]) to describe peasants en-route-to proletariats: they were free from lords, but also freed (in the sense of fleeced) of everything but their labor-power, and so forced to work in the factory. As we saw above, they were pushed out of one enclosure (the lands they once held in common) and pulled into another (the factory, the asylum, the prison, the clinic). Nietzsche (1967 [1887]) also used this term, which in nineteenth-century German referred to one who had been banished from the city, from the collective enclosure: no longer bound to its laws (and hence free), he was longer protected by its laws (and hence able to be killed without punishment). This book is, in some sense, precisely about such bittersweet freedoms.

1.4. The Semiotic Stance

Charles Sanders Peirce (1839–1914), the founder of pragmatism, was an American philosopher, mathematician, and logician. He is perhaps best known for his semiotic, or theory of meaning, with its focus on logic and causality, and the ways in which this theory contrasted with Saussure's semiology, with its focus on language and convention. In particular, he foregrounded iconic and indexical relations between signs and objects, theorizing the way meaning is motivated and context-bound. And he foregrounded inferential relations between signs and interpretants, highlighting the role of hypothesis and induction over deduction, and thus the role of imagination and experience over logic or 'code'.

   We first saw Peirce in our opening discussion of interjections, and he will be a central touchstone and springboard in later chapters. He is particularly relevant in the context of information science for a number of other reasons. For example, fifty years before Claude Shannon's famous masters thesis (1937), Peirce had seen the connection between Boolean algebra and electrical circuits (Chiu et al. 2005, 22). Writing between the eras of Babbage and Turing, Peirce had thought about logical machines (1887; and see Mirowski 2001, 31–43). As early as 1868, he had offered a compelling definition of virtuality (1902; and see Skagestad 1998). Like Shannon and MacKay, and other information scientists, Peirce was interested in the statistical nature of information, and measurement more generally, being the first to put confidence intervals on a proper philosophical footing (Hacking 2001, 266). Peirce's notion of thirdness was eerily similar to Michel Serres's (2007) notion of the parasite, which itself was derived from Shannon's ideas about enemies and noise. And before Shannon's mathematical theory of information, Peirce had developed a complementary theory of information, which itself was a small part of his broader theory of semiosis, or 'meaning'.

Rather than explore all of these fascinating connections here, the rest of this section will simply delve a little deeper into his understanding of *semiotic processes*, which were used to articulate several key claims made in the last two sections. For readers new to Peirce, this will constitute a brief introduction to the architecture of his thought, as it will be developed and deployed in later chapters. For readers who already know about him, this will show which of his ideas will be taken up at length, as well as how such ideas will be perturbed and transformed.[12] And for both sets of readers, this will allow us to sketch the conceptual organization of the rest of this book, and thereby bridge a wide range of otherwise disparate ideas, eras, literatures, and disciplines.

***

For Peirce, a semiotic process has three components: a *sign* (whatever stands for something else); an *object* (whatever is stood for by a sign); and an *interpretant* (whatever a sign creates so far as it stands for an object); see Figure 1.2. These components easily map onto more familiar terms, such as message (sign), referent (object), and response (interpretant); but, as will be shown below, they are much broader in scope and nuanced in detail. They also map onto Warren Weaver's latter distinction, in his famous introduction to Shannon's *Mathematical Theory of Communication* (Shannon and Weaver 1949, 4), between three levels

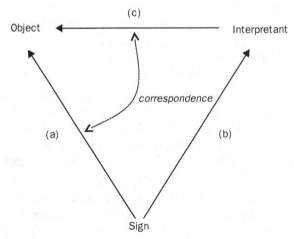

FIGURE 1.2 Peirce's Semiotic Process

of communication: the technical level (qua reproduction of signs); the semantic level (qua signification of objects); and the effectiveness level (qua creation of interpretants).[13]

While Peirce's distinction between sign and object can be mapped onto Saussure's more famous distinction between signifier and signified (with many caveats), Peirce's real contribution for the current argument is his foregrounding of the interpretant, and how it relates to the sign-object relation. In particular, any semiotic process relates these three components in the following way: a sign stands in relation to its object on the one hand, and its interpretant on the other, in such a way as to make the interpretant stand in relation to the object corresponding to its own relation to the object (Peirce 1955a, 99–100; and see Kockelman 2005). What is at issue in meaningfulness, then, is not one relation between a sign and an object (qua 'standing for'), but rather a relation between two such relations (qua 'correspondence'). The logic of this *relation between relations* was already shown in part (a) of Figure 1.1, which itself was shown to be just one part of the much broader account of meaning and mediation that will be developed in this book.

As we saw in section 1.2, *interjecting* is a semiotic process. When the boy turned to look at what his mother was responding to, there was an interpretant (the child's change of attention), an object (what his mother was looking at, or responding to), and a sign (the mother's direction of attention, and her uttering of the interjection). As Mead argued (1934), any *interaction* is a semiotic process. For example, when I hear my laptop beep (sign), I might plug it in (interpretant), insofar as I take the beep to be a warning that the battery is nearly drained (object). Generalizing interaction, conversational moves are patterned as semiotic processes: a first pair-part (question, command, assessment, etc.) relates to a second pair-part (answer, undertaking, agreement, etc.) as sign to interpretant, where the object is just the propositional content and illocutionary force, however elliptical or implicit, of the first pair-part (Sacks et al. 1974; Goffman 1981b).

Indeed, even *commodities* may be understood as semiotic processes (Kockelman 2006): the sign-component is a use-value (some quantity of qualities, such as a bushel of wheat, or a byte of data); the object-component is a value (understood as socially necessary labor time, incorporated effort, relative desirability, or marginal utility); and the interpretant-component is an exchange-value (some other use-value that might be exchanged for the first use-value, including a sum of money).

More generally, the constituents of so called 'material culture' are semiotic processes (Kockelman 2005, 2013a, 2015). For example, as inspired by Gibson (1986), an *affordance* is a semiotic process whose sign is a relatively 'natural' feature, whose object is a purchase, and whose key interpretant is an action that heeds that feature, or an instrument that incorporates that feature, insofar as the feature 'provides purchase'. (More canonically, an affordance is any possibility for action (cognition, imagination, interrelation, or affect) that is latent in an environment and open to an organism.) For example, when a cat climbs a tree, or avoids climbing a metal pole, such actions are interpretants of the purchase (or lack of purchase) provided by the features of bark and metal and claws (as affordances), insofar as such behaviors heed the traction of bark, or the slipperiness of metal, in the context of having claws. Indeed, as developed in Kockelman (2006b, 2011c), claws themselves are phylogenetic interpretants of the environments cats (and proto-cats) evolved in.

Relatedly, an *instrument* is a semiotic process whose sign is a relatively 'artificed' entity, whose object is a function, and whose key interpretant is an action that wields that entity, or another instrument that incorporates that instrument (insofar as it 'serves a function'). For example, a computer keyboard (as an instrument) is an interpretant of the function served by plastic (as an instrument), as well as the purchase provided by fingers (as an affordance), insofar as such a tool incorporates the hardness, lightness, and 'plasticity' of plastic, and takes into account the size, shape, and strength of fingers. For Peirce, much like Heidegger (1996 [1927], and see Kockelman 2015), meaning is as much embedded and embodied (in the people and things around us, and their relations to each other), as it is encoded and enminded.

As used here, then, affordances relate to instruments as fords relate to bridges: while each enables a traveler to cross a river (undertake an action, or achieve a goal, more generally), fords are happenstance bridges, just as bridges are intentional or artificed fords. Also, at least prototypically, affordances relate to instruments as parts to wholes, or features to entities. And thus, while we distinguish them here for analytic purposes, their separation is often a question of perspective. More important for our purposes is the fact that both affordances and instruments enable and constrain different kinds of actions (as well as affects, imaginaries, social relations, and so forth); they do this differently, and more or less transparently, depending on the capacities and propensities of the actor, and the context of the action; and they are regimented by physical causes as much as by social norms, and much else besides (price and protocols, instinct and infrastructure, etc.).[14] As will be seen, these issues—when generalized—are central to various understandings of media, whether these undergird 'virtual' environments or 'real' environments, whether they pertain to 'digital culture' or 'material culture'. Finally, and happily, while the ford, or bridge, relates to our discussion of lines, the fjord relates to our discussion of circles. If I may be allowed just one pun, 'afjordances' as much as affordances will be of interest in what follows.

In light of all these issues, in the chapters that follow, we will usually use the term *affordance* in an unmarked way, such that it can capture the meaning of 'instruments' as much as 'affordances', understood in these ideal typic and interrelated ways.

As we saw in section 1.2, just as an interpretant in one semiotic process can be a sign in a 'subsequent' semiotic process, a sign in one semiotic process can be an object in a 'higher' semiotic process. Semiotic processes both embed and enchain. So there is no need to constantly invoke a 'meta' level—that bugaboo of twentieth century theories of language and mind. As we also saw, an interpretant is not the 'interpreter' (the agent that offers an interpretation), nor is it necessarily or even usually something like a 'mental state'. It is simply that which a sign brings into being insofar as it stands for an object to such an interpreting agent. So there is no need to constantly invoke 'performativity'—that bugaboo of twentieth century theories of language and society. Semiotic processes, when properly understood, are inherently three-fold and so both such levels are built right in, and recursively so. Just as every interpretant is, in effect, a 'meta-sign'; every interpretant is, in effect, a 'doing to' the world.

***

Table 1.1 shows most of the core categories of Peirce's framework insofar as they will be deployed in this book. The top row shows the kind of relation in question. For example, not just semiotic process, but also semiotic ground, information content, logical relation, and so forth. The middle three rows show various modalities of such relations, famously organized as sets of threes. For example, not only sign, object, and interpretant (as components of semiotic processes); but also iconic, indexical, and symbolic (as modalities of semiotic grounds). Most readers will probably be familiar with some of these terms. And the last row shows which chapters will develop such relations and modalities at length.

As should be clear from the discussion of various other relations between relations noted in section 1.2 (social relation, semiological structure, actor-environment interface, and so forth), and other theorists and intellectual heritages surveyed in section 1.3 (from Saussure and Foucault to Marx and McLuhan), Peirce's ideas are just a small—albeit crucial—piece of the puzzle. In what follows, I simply want to show how semiotic processes per se relate to the overarching structure of this book, as introduced in section 1.1.

Very broadly speaking, chapters 2 and 3 will focus on the relation between signers (agents that produce signs) and interpreters (agents that produce interpretants). Just as the mother related to the son in our opening example, a speaker can relate to an addressee, and a Twitterer can relate to her followers. Chapters 4 and 5 will focus on the relation between objects and signs. Just as the chicken shit related to the interjection *chix* in our opening example, states of affairs can relate to assertions, and user attributes can relate to bit strings. And chapters 6 and 7 will focus on the relation between signs and interpretants. Just as the interjection gave rise to the boy's actions, a blog post or YouTube video can give rise to a comment, and an input to an algorithm can give rise to an output. Finally, as such examples should show, each of these three relations can (seem to) be more or less mediated, disciplined, or enclosed. In particular, the signer-interpreter relation can be subject to more or less 'networking'; the object-sign relation can be subject to more or less 'formatting'; and the sign-interpretant relation can be subject to more or less 'automating' (broadly construed). As promised in sections 1.2 and 1.3, we will tack back and forth between both extremes, focusing not just on their practical entangling but also on their ontological obviation.

TABLE 1.1
Some of Peirce's Key Categories

Semiotic Process	Meta-Categorical	Information Content of Word or Term	Information Content of Sentence or Message	Interpretant, or Effect of Sign	Semiotic Ground, or Sign-Object Relation	Kinds of Signs, or Modalities	Logical Relations
Sign	*Firstness* ('mediation')	*Connotation* ('sense')	*Rheme* ('focus')	*Affective* ('moods')	*Iconic* ('qualities')	*Quali-Sign*	*Abduction* ('hypothesis')
Object	*Secondness* ('intermediary')	*Denotation* ('reference')	*Theme* ('topic')	*Energetic* ('habits')	*Indexical* ('causes, contiguities')	*Sin-Sign* ('token')	*Induction*
Interpretant	*Thirdness* ('mediator')	*Information*	*Argument* ('reason')	*Representational* ('beliefs')	*Symbolic* ('conventions')	*Legi-Sign* ('type')	*Deduction*
Chapters 1–7	Chapter 2 and 6	Chapters 3, 4, and 6	Chapter 4	Chapter 4	Chapter 5	Chapter 5	Chapter 7

One reason to organize the book this way is because it allows readers to connect Peirce's ideas to those of John von Neumann and Alan Turing, key architects and theorists of the computer; and, through them, to those of Friedrich Kittler, a key theorist of digital media. In particular, Kittler (1996 [1993]) characterized information in terms of storage (in a message), transmission (along a channel), and processing (by an addressee). In some sense, he was trying to understand what he took to be the essence of information from its material instantiation in a modern digital computer wherein a single number, or bit string, can be read as a value (some kind of data), as an address (some place to put data), or as a command (some operation undertaken on the data located at an address).

Another reason to organize the book this way is because it allows readers to connect Peirce's ideas to Leonhard Euler, whose celebrated paper of 1736, "The Seven Bridges of Koenigsberg," laid the foundations for graph theory—the abstract study of edges and vertices, or relations and nodes, that underlies modern understandings of networked infrastructure (Dorogovtsev and Mendes 2003), computational automata (Sipser 2007), and so much else besides. In particular, the lines and circles highlighted in the last two sections, and the relations and relata in my diagrams, not only relate to the 1's and 0's of bit strings and Boolean algebra, they also relate to such vertices and nodes, or 'bridges' and 'banks'; see Figure 1.3.

Phrased another way, semiotic processes and graph theory are connected (!) by a particularly powerful metaphor: the path that connects an origin to a destination (such as a signer to an interpreter, an object to a sign, or a sign to an interpretant), where any point along the path may itself be parasitically subject to inference or interception, and thus become the origin or destination of other paths. See Figure 1.4.

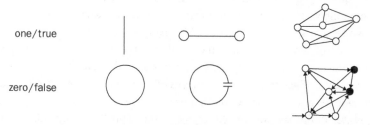

FIGURE 1.3 1's and 0's, Lines and Circles, Relations and Nodes, Networks and Algorithms

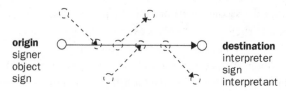

FIGURE 1.4 Relations and Relations to Relations

1.5. Overview of Chapters

Chapter 2, *Enemies, Parasites, and Noise*, is designed to burn bridges as much as build them. It begins by outlining some common properties of channels, infrastructure, and institutions. It connects and critiques the assumptions and interventions of three influential intellectual traditions: cybernetics (via Claude Shannon), linguistics and anthropology (via Roman Jakobson), and actor-network theory (via Michel Serres). By developing the relation between Serres's notion of the parasite and Peirce's notion of thirdness, it theorizes the role of those creatures who live in and off infrastructure: not just enemies, parasites, and noise, but also pirates, trolls, and internet service providers. And by extending Jakobson's account of duplex categories (shifters, proper names, meta-language, reported speech) from codes to channels, it theorizes four reflexive modes of circulation that any network may involve: self-channeling channels, source-dependent channels, signer-directed signers, and channel-directed signers. Such modes of circulation will allow us to theorize and interrelate a wide range of otherwise disparate entities and agents, such as logic gates and turnstiles, editors and amplifiers, relays and passports, filters and switches, catalysts and censors, transducers and erasers, couriers and wormholes. Finally, the conclusion returns to the notion of enclosure, showing the ways that networks are simultaneously a condition for, and a target of, knowledge, power, and profit.

Chapter 3, *Secrecy, Poetry, and Being-Free*, asks two questions: What are some of the secrets of networks? And what might constitute their poetics—an aesthetic means of revealing their secrets? To answer the first question, it leverages the relation between codes and channels introduced in chapter 2, delving into two topics that link them: degrees of freedom and secrets. By degrees of freedom, is meant the number of independent dimensions needed to specify the state of a system. Such a notion, along with related ideas like frames of relevance and scales of resolution, is shown to be essential not only to highly analog systems but also to digital ones, and to underlie physicists' understanding of materiality as much as philosophical understandings of the uncanny. This chapter argues that even relatively commensurate systems, which have identical degrees of freedom, can have different secrets, understood as inherent symmetries that organize their sense-making capacities. In some sense, all this is a way of reinterpreting the Sapir-Whorf hypothesis (that is, the idea that the language one speaks affects the way one thinks); and it is a way of generalizing such a hypothesis such that it can be usefully applied to media more generally (i.e., interfaces, applications, programming languages, channels, and so forth). To answer the second question, this chapter reviews different understandings of secrets, and shows how channels as well as codes can have inherent secrets (in addition to their ability to keep and reveal secrets in more stereotypic ways). By extending the notion of poetics, it shows how such systems can be made to reveal their secrets. Priming the reader for chapter 5, it points to the fundamental relation between poetics as such, and phenomena which are often labeled as 'virtual'. And the conclusion draws out the relation between Heidegger's understanding of references, Agamben's notion of *homo sacer*, and Google's page rank algorithm.

Chapter 4, *Meaning, Information, and Enclosure*, carefully reviews and further develops some overlooked theories of information. It highlights the ideas of Donald MacKay in relation to those of Claude Shannon, and it foregrounds the semiotic framework of Charles Sanders Peirce in relation to core ideas in cybernetics and computer science. Working with MacKay and Shannon, it describes and perturbs the concepts of selective information, structural information, and metrical information. Building on Peirce, it offers two alternative definitions of information, one focusing on interaction (topic, focus, reason) and the other focusing on institutions (denotation, connotation, information), that effectively mediate between relatively quantitative theories of information and relatively qualitative theories of meaning. It highlights the relation between Shannon's quantification of information and Marx's understanding of modes of production, Whorf's understanding of ontological projection, and McLuhan's account of media in relation to scale. And it exemplifies such ideas by showing how they apply to databases, user accounts, and social network websites. The conclusion argues that Gilles Deleuze's famous claim that we have moved from a society of discipline to a society of control radically misses the mark because his notion of enclosure only takes into account Foucault's disciplinary formations. Instead, this chapter argues that information is a species of meaning that has been radically enclosed, such that the values in question seem to have become radically portable: not so much independent of context, as dependent on contexts which have been engineered so as to be relatively ubiquitous, and hence ostensibly and erroneously 'context-free'; not so much able to accommodate all contents, as able to assimilate all contents to its contours, and hence ostensibly and erroneously 'open content'.

Chapter 5, *Materiality, Virtuality, and Temporality*, is in part about the relation between preservation and presumption. It focuses on the relation between that which is lost and that which is preserved, where the latter is understood as a trace of the former. And it focuses on the nature of the presumptions that ground such understandings: what must an interpreting agent assume about a given environment in order to infer a cause from an effect, or link a sign to an object more generally. This chapter is also, in part, about the relation between meaning and materiality. It focuses on various kinds of durability that allow particular materials to last, and thereby preserve meaning, by leaving relatively enduring traces. And it focuses on various ways this durability is imagined and utilized in particular media, and in particular understandings of mediation. In offering such an archeology of media, its focus is entropy as opposed to information, death as much as life, psychoanalysis as much as astrophysics. Such ideas are then used, in conjunction with the notions of secrets and singularities introduced in chapter 3, to review key understandings of the virtual: Deleuze, so far as he is taken up by later media theorists; and Peirce, so far as his theory of the meaningful is, by design, a theory of the virtual. Returning to the concerns of chapter 3, this chapter focuses on how we develop intuitions for the (otherwise secret) sense-making capabilities of highly complex systems. Along the way, we revisit and reevaluate Freud's theory of dreams, Grice's theory of non-natural meaning, Chomsky's notion of generativity, and Benjamin's notion of aura.

Chapter 6, *Computation, Interpretation, and Mediation*, shows that the sieve, as both a physical device and an analytic concept, is of fundamental importance not just to anthropology, but also to linguistics, biology, philosophy, and critical theory more generally. It argues that computers, as both engineered and imagined, are essentially text-generated and text-generating sieves. It inquires into the computational tasks asked of sieving devices and their relation to politicized notions like labor, work, and action, as well as their relation to highly romantic notions like creativity, contemplation, and communication. And it demonstrates the various ways that computation may be understood as the enclosure of interpretation, thereby delving deeply into the nature of such 'universal media machines' and their ontological relation to earlier notions like universal languages, steam engines, and world money (not to mention world spirits). To make these arguments, it reviews some of the key concepts and claims of computer science (language, recognition, automaton, transition function, Universal Turing Machine, and so forth) and shows their fundamental importance to the concerns of linguistic anthropology (and to the concerns of culture-rich and context-sensitive approaches to communication more generally). In relating computer science to linguistic anthropology, this chapter also attempts to build bridges between long-standing rivals: face-to-face interaction and mathematical abstraction, linguistic relativity and universal grammar, thirds (or 'mediators') and seconds (or 'intermediaries'). In some sense, then, this chapter opens up the black box of computational automata, and shows the space of virtual paths that lies inside. As in the case of codes and channels, such paths constitute key secrets of computation. Just like the secrets of channels and codes, their inherent symmetries lend themselves to different sensibilities. And like all generative mechanisms, there are ways of bringing them and the potentialities they enable (more or less) into intuition.

Chapter 7, *Algorithms, Agents, and Ontologies*, details the inner workings of spam filters, algorithmic devices that separate desirable messages from undesirable messages. It argues that such filters are a particularly important kind of sieve insofar as they readily exhibit key features of sieving devices in general, and algorithmic sieving in particular. More broadly, it describes the relation between ontology (assumptions that drive interpretations) and inference (interpretations that alter assumptions) as it plays out in the transformation of spam as a kind of message style. It focuses on the unstable processes whereby identifying algorithms, identified styles, and evasive transformations are dynamically coupled over time. This chapter then walks readers through Bayes's Equation, a mathematical formulation that lies at the heart of not just spam filters, but a wide range of other powerful computational technologies (data-mining tools, diagnostic tests, predictive parsers, risk assessment techniques, and mathematical reasoning more generally). It shows the limits of mathematical formulations through the formulations themselves by foregrounding some of the aporia of sieves. Along the way, it theorizes various kinds of ontological inertia, showing how certain assumptions are 'deeper' and so more difficult to historically transform. Concomitantly, it highlights various kinds of algorithmic ineffability, showing how certain processes are more difficult to mathematically capture. More generally, this chapter foregrounds the ways ontologies are both embodied in and transformed by such algorithms, and thus acts as a bridge between the concerns of machine learning and historical ontology. And it reinterprets classic ideas from computer science and artificial intelligence in light of these concepts and commitments—most notably, the Turing Test and the sabotaging of sieves. Above all, this inquiry demonstrates how equations and algorithms can simultaneously be subject to and contribute to anthropological analysis. It is meant to stand as a case study of many of the core concerns outlined in earlier chapters.

2

Enemies, Parasites, and Noise

2.1. The Burning of Bridges

Classic theories of channels, infrastructure, and institutions are eerily convergent. Each is understood as a kind of bridge that delimits a landscape, facilitates a passage, and forestalls a loss. For example, channels relate speakers to addressees, enabling the interpretation of meaning as much as its signification (Malinowski, Shannon, Jakobson). Infrastructure relates producers to consumers, enabling the realization of value as much as its creation (von Thünen, Marx, Marshall). Institutions relate selves to others, enabling the recognition of identity as much as its performance (Hegel, Mead, Goffman). Facilitating passage, each allows displacement in space, through time, between persons, and across possible worlds. Delimiting landscape, each helps constitute the poles so related: speakers and addressees, producers and consumers, selves and others. Finally, forestalling loss, each ensures that some medium endures—that words won't fade, that goods won't spoil, that personas won't wither. See Figure 2.1.

Within the confines of such traditions, the subjects so related (or the banks so bridged) are themselves split into different modalities: the virtual confronts the actual, constraints confront configurations, potential confronts performance. For example, speakers stand between *langue* and *parole*, or grammatical structure and discursive practice (Saussure). Producers stand between labor-power and its exercise, or an aggregate of mental and physical capacities and any action that taps those abilities (Marx). And selves stand between status and role, or ensembles of rights and responsibilities and any behavior that acts on those rights or according to those responsibilities (Linton). Virtualities, from such a vantage, stand at the intersection of freedom and necessity: *langue* involves creativity as much as constraint; labor-power involves sapience as much as strength; status involves entitlement as much as commitment. Finally, actualities are grounded in the very same affective and interactional immediacy that the original facilitation of passage was designed to overcome, or mediate: here, now, among us, in this world. And they are

Paul Kockelman. *The Art of Interpretation in the Age of Computation.* © Oxford University Press 2017

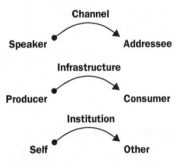

FIGURE 2.1 Channels, Infrastructures, and Institutions

generative of exactly those media that were channeled (messages), infrastructured (goods), or instituted (personas) in the first place. See Figure 2.2.

In short, these three terms (channel, infrastructure, institution) have been traditionally conceptualized by means of a single trope: the metaphor of a bridge that gathers the banks of a river around it (Heidegger 1977 [1954]). This is somewhat ironic because nothing seems to fit this metaphor more perfectly than codes, and representations more generally—those cognitive, social, and technological bridges that gather together what otherwise seem to be the most ontologically unbridgeable of banks: signifier and signified, sign and object, mind and world, word and referent, experience and event. Framed as such, channels and codes, or circulation and interpretation more generally, seem to partake of the same substance.

***

Taking off from Roman Jakobson, and working through theorists like Claude Shannon and Michel Serres, all in light of Charles Sanders Peirce, this chapter develops the consequences of this trope, while simultaneously undermining its presumptions. Broadly speaking, it has two goals. First, it brings the channel, and communicative infrastructure more generally, back into focus within the disciplines of linguistics and anthropology, as well as critical theory and political economy. Second, in so doing, it shows the tense relationship between Jakobson's framework, Shannon's mathematical theory of communication, Serres's theory of the parasite, and Peirce's theory of thirdness. In this way, it uses the foundational texts of four paradigms to map out some hidden passageways (and pitfalls) lying

	Virtuality	Actuality
Channel	*Structure*	*Practice*
Infrastructure	*Power*	*Exercise*
Institution	*Status*	*Role*

FIGURE 2.2 Virtualities and Actualities of Poles

between cybernetics, linguistic anthropology, actor-network theory, and American pragmatism.

More narrowly speaking, and perhaps more suggestively, by showing the similarities between Serres's notion of the parasite and Peirce's notion of thirdness, this chapter carefully theorizes the menagerie of entities who live in and off infrastructure: enemies and noise, meters and sieves, pirates and exploits, tolls and trolls, ninjas and skaterats, catalysts and assassins. And by extending Jakobson's notion of duplex categories (shifters, reported speech, proper names, meta-language) from code-sign relations to channel-signer relations, it describes four reflexive modes of circulation that any channeling, infrastructuring, or instituting system may involve: source-dependent channels, signer-directed signers, self-channeling channels, and channel-directed signers.

In some sense, then, this chapter is about two kinds of translation (or 'mediation') that may be loosely characterized as material translation (or channeling between signers and interpreters, qua circulation) and meaningful translation (or coding between signs and objects, qua interpretation). That is, just as codes relate signs to objects (or messages to referents), channels relate signers to interpreters (or speakers to addressees). As will be seen, Jakobson, Shannon, and Serres share a set of assumptions regarding the need for, and difference between, both kinds of translation. As will be argued, each is an attempt to see relations between relations, or thirdness proper, in terms of two analogous, but otherwise distinct, relations. This chapter highlights this tension. It shows some of the ways these thinkers creatively circumvent it, and some of the ways they get stymied by it. In so doing, it builds bridges (or, at least, finds fords) between them, and the kinds of scholarship they inspired, using each to extend the insights of the others.

2.2. Channel, Infrastructure, and Institution

Jakobson (1990a) famously argued that any speech event involves six constituent factors: speaker, addressee, message, referent, code, and channel. Moreover, each of these factors, when foregrounded, gives rise to a particular function: expressive (focus on the speaker); directive (focus on the addressee); poetic (focus on the message, or signifier); referential (focus on the referent, or signified); metalinguistic (focus on the code, or the relation between the signifier and the signified); and phatic (focus on the channel, or the relation between the speaker and addressee).[1] Finally, any given utterance may differentially focus on multiple factors of the speech event, and thereby simultaneously serve different kinds of functions.[2] See Figure 2.3.

Interjections, for example, are often treated as highly *expressive* signs insofar as they seem to foreground the affect or emotion of the speaker—whether they are disgusted, surprised, angry, or afraid of the object before them. As we saw in chapter 1, however, they are also often highly *referential*, insofar as they draw another's attention to the object itself through highly symbolic modalities. Indeed, as detailed

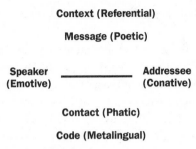

FIGURE 2.3 Jakobson's Factors (and Functions)

in Kockelman (2003), an interjection like *chix* can also be used as a negative impera-tive to a child: *do not touch that (yucky object)!* In this way, they can be highly *direc-tive*. And one can use this same interjection while listening to another tell a story, or describe an experience, indicating that one is not just listening to the other, but also that one is engaged in what that other is saying. In this way, interjections are highly *phatic*, serving as back-channel cues. As Malinowski would say, they func-tion to affiliate as much as inform—indeed, they function to disaffiliate as much as affiliate (that is to say, *alienate*), serving to both evince and establish a wide vari-ety of social relations.[3] Perhaps because interjections are often phonologically and morphologically marked, and can occur alone, they are often the focus of attention in regards to their sensual properties: not what do they stand for per se, but rather how do they sound, and in particular how is their sound related to what they stand for in allegedly iconic ways. In this way, interjections are caught up in the *poetic* function of language. Finally, they are caught up in reported speech and transla-tion. For example, once during my fieldwork in that village, when a man turned his head in disgust from the carcass of a rotting deer, his son interpreted his reaction using this interjection: *chix, chan a'an*, or 'he went, yuck'. In this way, interjections serve *meta-linguistic* functions.

We will return to Jakobson's distinction between the poetic function and the meta-linguistic function in chapter 3; and the rest of this chapter is, in effect, about the phatic function of media in a greatly expanded sense. For present purposes, it is helpful to introduce five interrelated shifts to Jakobson's schema. First, we may abstract away from speech events per se to semiotic events, or 'media moments', of any kind. In this way, we may focus on the following six factors: signs (whatever stands for something else); objects (whatever is stood for by a sign); codes (whatever relates a sign to an object); signers (whatever expresses a sign); interpreters (what-ever interprets a sign); and channels (whatever relates a signer to an interpreter, such that a sign expressed by the former may be interpreted by the latter).[4]

As argued in the introduction, and made ethnographically visible in the work of scholars like Elyachar (2010), Larkin (2004, 2008), Star (1999), and von Schnitzler (2008), channels are usually inseparable from infrastructure and insti-tutions. To go back to our opening example of the bridge, and our discussion of semiotic processes in chapter 1, the three components of a semiotic process (sign, object, interpretant) map onto entities as seemingly diverse as identities (role, status, attitude) and commodities (use-value, value, exchange-value), among other things.[5] Bear in mind, then, that 'messages' (and intentional communication per se) are at best the tip of a semiotic iceberg. In short, the fact that channels, institutions, and infrastructure are eerily similar as to their facilitating, delimiting, and forestalling functions is, in part, a simple consequence of the generality of semiotic processes.

Whereas Jakobson understood channels as turning on physical conduits and psychological connections, they should also be understood as turning on social conventions. As an example, we may turn to what is perhaps the most emblematic of semiotic events: joint-attention, or looking where another looks (or points). Such an event has three key components: a sign (your gesture that directs my attention); an object (whatever you are pointing to—say, that pen over there); and an interpretant (my change in attention). Within such a framing, an object is simply that to which we can jointly attend—however vague it is, or misaligned we are. In some sense, the figure is the object, qua information (in the sense of what I am directing your attention to, or informing you of), and the ground is the channel (infrastructure and institution) that allows you and I, as signer and interpreter, to intersubjectively relate in this way (by relating to this object) within a relatively isolated event. In part, this channel turns on a physical contact (e.g., a transparent medium in an illuminated enclosure, with open lines of sight, itself grounded in the sensory and instigatory capacities and sensitivities of the semiotic agents themselves). In part, it turns on a psychological connection (e.g., I treat your movement as an intentionally communicative gesture, I desire to know what you desire to make known to me). And, in part, it turns on a social convention (e.g., who is normatively permitted to direct whose attention, in what kinds of contexts, to what kinds of objects). As we saw in chapter 1, with our example of the interjection, such a process is perhaps the originary form of objectification. Within a particular kind of clearing, or enclosure, something is disclosed.[6]

Whereas Jakobson focused on speakers, a signer (or interpreter) may be understood as a semiotic agent (Kockelman 2004, 2005, 2007a): anything that can—to some degree—control the expression of a sign (determine where and when it is produced); compose a sign-object relation (determine what object is stood for, or what sign stands for it); or commit to an interpretant of this sign-object relation (determine what effect the expression of the sign will have so far as it stands for the object).[7] In particular, a given semiotic agent may have greater or lesser degrees of freedom or ability along any one of these dimensions (greater capacities to, or opportunities for, control, composition, and commitment), and thus often greater or lesser degrees of accountability for the effects of its actions. As will be discussed at length in chapters 6 and 7, such agents may be persons as well as things, animals and algorithms as well as tools and machines, and anything outside or in-between. And they are usually radically distributed, and hence both incorporating of, and incorporated by, other agencies. Indeed a given semiotic technology, or medium, usually turns on a more or less complicated assemblage of such agencies, themselves not just personified, but imagined with complex and contentious sociopolitical identities, participating in a complex division of semiotic labor. Such imaginaries of infrastructural agencies are often just as important to interaction as the actual workings of the infrastructures in which that interaction is situated.

Finally, as grounded in these abstractions and extensions, we may return to the fundamental symmetry of Jakobson's system: just as codes relate signs to objects, channels relate signers to interpreters. Both kinds of translation may be understood as paths (or bridges, as per the introduction) that lead from an origin to a destination. See Figure 2.4. But before we exploit this symmetry, by developing its repercussions in relation to Jakobson's duplex categories, we should undermine this symmetry—and indeed, undermine the notion of a channel (institution or infrastructure) as a bridge between banks, a relation between relata, an edge between nodes, or an action between agents.[8] In what follows, then, we first move backwards from Jakobson to a more famous model of communication, that of Shannon. We then move forward to an alternative reading of Shannon provided by Serres. Next, we return to Jakobson and generalize his duplex categories from sign-code relations to signer-channel relations. And finally, we link these concerns to more traditional senses of infrastructure, circulation, and value.

To foreground one arc of the following argument, note from our example of joint-attention how difficult it is to distinguish codes and channels (in their traditional sense) from each other, or to separate them from semiosis per se, or to isolate a solitary sign event from the hurly-burly of interaction in the first place. In a Peircean idiom, we might say that classic understandings of codes and channels take a mode of thirdness (qua relation between relations), itself artificially isolated from a nexus of thirdness (qua interrelationality per se), and reduce it to one of two simple relations, or modes of secondness. In particular, framing thirdness from the standpoint of actions or products, the relation between signs, objects, and

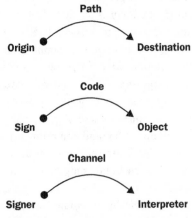

FIGURE 2.4 Path, Code, and Channel

interpretants gets reduced to a relation between signs and objects (qua meaningful translation, or 'interpretation'). And framing thirdness from the standpoint of actors or producers, the relation between signers, objectors, and interpreters gets reduced to a relation between signers and interpreters (qua material translation, or 'circulation'). Contrast Figure 1.1, for example, and all the details of the interjectional interaction it was used to illuminate. One key theme of this chapter is the conditions for, and consequences of, such reductions.

2.3. Shannon and Jakobson

Along with Norbert Wiener, Claude Shannon was a central figure in the cybernetics movement, and his contributions still form part of the backbone of computer science and information theory. In the *Mathematical Theory of Communication* (1948), his most influential work, Shannon offered a diagram that showed five key elements of any communicative event: a *source* of messages (e.g., a speaker producing an utterance); a *transmitter* of signals (e.g., a telephone that takes in the sound waves produced by the utterance and puts out electrical pulses); a *channel* along which signals are sent (e.g., the wires linking one telephone to another); a *receiver* of signals (e.g., another telephone that takes in electric pulses and puts out sound waves); and a *destination* for messages (e.g., an addressee listening on the other line). See Figure 2.5.

This model is very close to Jakobson's model, with a few key differences. First, note the difference between messages (whether spoken or heard) and signals (whether transmitted or received). Relatively speaking, messages are designed by and for some human mind; whereas signals are designed by and for some mechanical apparatus. Second, the transmitter is essentially an encoding device (message to signal); and the receiver is essentially a decoding device (signal to message). While both such devices involve inputs and outputs, the crucial function served by each is a kind of translation, qua mapping, between the signs in one code (say, English) and the signs in another code (say, Morse). And finally, the signal sent by the transmitter is not necessarily identical to the signal received by the receiver, for there is another element (not numbered, but named) in Shannon's diagram: *noise*. In particular,

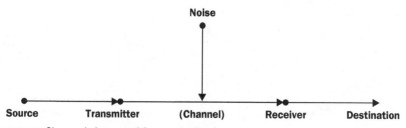

FIGURE 2.5　Shannon's Account of Communication

noise *relates to the relation between* the transmitter and receiver (which itself mediates between the source and the destination). It interferes, such that what is received is not the same as what was sent. Note that one reason it is not presented as its own element in Shannon's exegesis is because it is very possibly the key element. In particular, *the channel may be defined by, or understood in terms of, its capacity to fail, in the sense of introducing noise into the system, and thereby interfering with the signal and garbling the message.* This is probably the key movement from Shannon's mathematical theory of information to actor-network theory, via a famous text by Michel Serres, *The Parasite,* to which we will return below.

In his *Communication Theory of Secrecy Systems* (circulated in 1946, but only declassified in 1949), Shannon offered a similar diagram. Again there is a message source and message destination; and again there is a channel. However the transmitter and receiver are replaced by an encipherer and a decipherer, and the notion of a signal is replaced by the notion of a cryptogram—that is, an encipherer takes in a message and turns out a cryptogram (by means of some code), and a decipherer takes in a cryptogram and turns out a message (by means of some inverse of that code). See Figure 2.6. Finally, there is again an element that relates to the relation between the encipherer and decipherer (which itself mediates between the source and destination); but here it is labeled 'enemy cryptanalyst' instead of noise.[9] As Shannon explains in a footnote, "The word 'enemy,' stemming from military applications, is commonly used in cryptographic work to denote anyone who may intercept a cryptogram" (Shannon 1946, 657). In some sense, then, *the enemy is precisely that which the system is designed for (or rather against).* Though less important to Serres's analysis, the enemy, no less than noise, is both parasite on (relating to a relation), and aporia of, such communication systems. (Recall the anthropologist's relation to the mother-son relation in chapter 1.)

Notice, then, that a central issue for Shannon was efficient encoding and safe encryption given the presence of noise and enemies; and hence turned on the capacities and limits, or functions and failures, of channels. That is, it was proper encoding or encryption (think meaningful translation or 'interpretation') that led to proper channeling (think material translation or 'circulation'). Such encoding and encryption is, to be sure, a kind of translation in a very particular sense. It is not a relation between sign and object, or between message and referent, as it

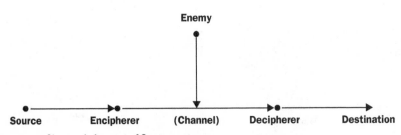

FIGURE 2.6 Shannon's Account of Secrecy

was in Jakobson. Nor is it even a relation between a sign and an interpretant, as mediated by an object, as in semiosis proper (recall the example of joint-attention). Rather it is a relation between a sign in one code (say, that of English) and a sign in another code (say, that in Morse, ASCII, or even Enigma), understood as a formal mapping, or function, that transforms a domain into a range. In short, just as Jakobson tried to account for sign-object relations without reference to interpretants (a reduction that is mitigated, as we will see below, by his introduction of duplex categories), Shannon tried to account for sign-interpretant relations without reference to objects. Thus while both theorists were interested in codes and channels, or meaningful and material translation, they each conceptualized codes in different ways. Nonetheless, in the terms introduced at the end of the last section, both engaged in a similar kind of reduction.[10]

As will be further discussed in chapter 5, Freud's psyche is really the internalization of a very simple speech chain, along with a very simple social relation: the id is the sender, the ego is the receiver, and the superego is that which intercepts or interferes with the message/idea/wish being sent.[11] Nowadays we are arguably caught up in much more complicated communicative infrastructures and social-moral imaginaries, so one might imagine our psyches are more complicated as well. In any case, to return to our discussion of agency in the last section, note how easy it is to 'personify' any agency along and outside a channel, and to 'internalize' a whole network of such 'personalities', 'identities', or 'voices'.

To conclude this section, several small ironies should be noted. For Shannon, the channel was the key condition for, and limit on, information. And his central theorem was about the information capacity of a channel (given a particular encoding). In contrast, Malinowski's (1936) understanding of the channel (which, in large part, Jakobson incorporated) emphasized affiliation (or social relations) over information. Indeed, for Jakobson, the referential function (focus on referent, or object) was the locus of information; whereas the phatic function (focus on channel) was the locus of psychological connection and physical contact between speaker and addressee. Similarly, as will discussed in chapter 4, Shannon's model is often criticized for focusing only on messages and signals (that is, signs), and thereby eliding meaning and referents (that is, objects), as well as eliding the receiver's response to such meaning-referent relations (that is, interpretants in the strict sense). However, what led to information in Shannon (the separation of forms from their meaning) gave rise to precisely the poetic function in Jakobson (with its focus on the sensual properties of signs). Indeed, one of Jakobson's alternative characterizations of the poetic function is closely related to Shannon's notion of *redundancy*—in particular, the text-internal repetition of tokens of a common type, as exemplified in metered verse (a topic we'll return to in chapter 3). In short, Jakobson's approach simultaneously takes up and undercuts Shannon's model, showing how the very same ideas (channel and message) can be theoretically framed in different ways. *With the tiniest of perturbations, then, mathematics morphs into aesthetics, information changes to affiliation, and redundancy becomes poetry.*

2.4. Serres and Peirce

In *The Parasite* ([1980] 2007), Serres begins by noting the multiple meanings of the word parasite in French: biological parasite, social parasite (in particular, the guest/host relation), and noise. From such humble beginnings, he goes on to theorize more lofty topics, with a scope comparable to Hobbes's *Leviathan*: the origins of society, the nature of evil, the essence of work, the conditions for value, the location of sovereignty, the foundations of property, a theory of networks, and beyond. Serres's work has been enormously influential in sociology and science and technology studies. Indeed, it is tempting to make the analogy that, as *The Parasite* is to *Leviathan*, so actor-network theory is to classical sociology.

The rest of this section will focus on Serres's theory of the parasite—as a relation to a relation, itself derived from Shannon's account of enemies and noise. Such a theory introduces a host of caveats to classic understandings of the channel, many of which resonate with Peirce's definition of thirdness. Only by incorporating such caveats, exploring such a resonance, and offering a range of critiques, can a more robust account of channels, and infrastructure more generally, be provided. What follows, then, is a concise and analytic overview of this work, so far as it bears on the concerns introduced above.

***

First, rather than focus on channels in the stereotypic sense, Serres opens up the analysis to relations more generally. Returning to section 2.2, such relations should be understood as psychological connections and social conventions as much as physical contacts. Returning to section 2.1, such relations should be understood as infrastructure and institutions as much as channels. More generally, returning to chapter 1, we might think of such relations as actions between agents, edges between nodes, bridges between banks, or mediation per se. Indeed, generously read, it may be argued that Serres's real interest is Peirce's notion of thirdness in its multiple guises. This resonance is so great that it is worth quoting both authors at length. As Serres puts it:

> I mean the intermediary, the milieu. A trunk, the tail, and the head: the trunk of the relation between head and tail. The milieu, the mediate. What is between, what exists between. The middle term. The means and the means to an end. The means and the tool; the tool and its use; the means and the use (2007 [1980], 65).

As Peirce put it, one hundred years before:

> By the third, I mean the medium or connecting bond between the absolute first and last. The beginning is first, the end second, the middle third. The end is second, the means third. The thread of life is a third; the fate that snips it, its second. A fork in the road is a third, it supposes three ways; *a straight*

road, considered merely as a connection between two places is second, but so far as it implies passing through intermediate places it is third (1955b, 80; italics added).

For Serres, any relation between two beings (or any edge between two nodes) is itself part of a larger whole, or system, composed of many interrelations among many beings. "Stations and paths together form a system. Points and lines, beings and relations" (10). In comparison, the schemata of Shannon and Jakobson focus on a part at the expense of a whole, or two nodes and one relation at the expense of the system. On the one hand, this critique is technical: communication rarely employs fixed, point-to-point channels. Rather, in addition to broadcast, most modern channels are networked, with various topologies: daisy chains (rings and lines), stars, mesh, and far beyond. On the other hand, this critique may be understood in (post)structuralist, or even Boasian terms: the part (qua node) gets its value in relation to the whole (qua network), even if only through the projection of an imagined totality. (Readers who balk when they hear the word 'system' are advised to just substitute the word *assemblage*—which would be in keeping with the spirit of Serres.)

Any relation between two beings, or edge between two nodes, or bridge between two banks, is itself a whole that may be decomposed into parts. So our designating it a basic unit, what Serres termed a 'black box', with relatively predictable relations between inputs and outputs, is grounded in our own ignorance of its inner workings. Indeed Serres calls such systems 'fractal' (73): when any part is looked at closely, it too turns out to be a system composed of relations and beings. We consider something a simple relation only when we are ignorant of its inner workings, or when it works so perfectly that it disappears from view. Both ignorance and knowledge may thereby reduce a third to a second, a ground to a figure, or a mediator to an intermediary. Serres is again worth quoting at length:

> I thought that the exchangers were intermediaries, that interference was on the fringe, that the translator was between instances, *that the bridge connected two banks*, that the path went from the origin to the goal. But there are no instances. Or more correctly, instances, systems, banks, and so forth are analyzable in turn as exchangers, paths, translations, and so forth. The only instances or systems are black boxes. When we do not understand, when we defer our knowledge to a later date, when the thing is too complex for the means at hand, when we put everything in a temporary black box, we prejudge the existence of a system. When we can finally open the box, we see that it works like a trace of transformation (2007 [1980], 73; italics added).

While we may think of a channel as that which translates material across space and time from one node to another, the channel may also be understood as a translator which takes in some kind of input (say, a sign) and puts out some kind of output (say, an interpretant). Thus, Serres is just as interested in nodes that link two relations as in relations that link two nodes. In the broadest sense, then, the relations that interest Serres are not just things like channels, infrastructure and institutions, but also the selves and others, producers and consumers, speakers and addressees—or semiotic agents more generally—who stand at the ends of such conduits, or at the banks of such bridges. Phrased another way, he is interested in both senses of translation: on the one hand, material translation along a relation between two nodes, qua signer and interpreter; on the other hand, meaningful translation by a node situated between two relations, qua semiotic agent transforming signs into interpretants. Serres, like actor-network theory after him, and Geertzean anthropology before him, takes Hermes to be its key figure (Serres 2007 [1980], 43; and see Crapanzano 1992). Recall that, with some caveats addressed in the last section, this is precisely the symmetry we found in Jakobson and Shannon between circulation and interpretation, or channel and code.

The essence of a channel, as a relation between two beings, it really a relation to this relation. As Serres puts it, "The parasite has a relation with the relation and not with the station" (2007 [1980], 33). That is, the channel should be understood in terms of its capacity to fail, in the sense of being subject to a variety of parasites (e.g., interference and interception, among other things). Thus, to go back to Shannon, the fact of enemies and noise was the condition of possibility for the design and functioning of the channel. In some sense, this may be the key point of Serres's system, and for some perhaps the most startling claim of the book: "Systems work because they do not work. Nonfunctioning remains essential for functioning" (Ibid., 79). Here it is worth recalling Peirce's description of paths, or channels, as secondness (merely a connection between two places) or as thirdness (as a series of potential places). As Serres puts it, "Every relation between two instances demands a route. What is already there on this route either facilitates or impedes the relation" (Ibid, 150). Serres, then, managed to treat channels, or material translation more generally, as thirds rather seconds.

Given this idea that the channel's function is defined by its failure, and given one key designation of the parasite as failure, the parasite can be much wider in scope than simple noise and enemies. The parasite is any *perturbation* of a relation: whatever deflects the achievement of an aim, for better or for worse, and whatever disturbs a third, no matter how large or small in magnitude. As Serres puts it, "The parasite bring us into the vicinity of the simplest and most general operator on the variable of systems. It makes them fluctuate by their differential distances" (2007 [1980], 191).

What counts as channel and parasite, or information and noise, or relation and relation to relation, is a function of position or perspective. In some sense, it may be argued that what Serres is really doing here is extending Mary Douglas's (1966) famous insight: just as dirt is matter out of place, we may say that *noise is information out of place.*[12] Phrased another way, the parasite is really a joker, or wild-card, who takes on different values depending on its position in a system.

This means that the relation between relations is really a triad, with each node able to play the role of parasite to the relation between the other two nodes. As Serres puts it, "In the system, noise and message exchange roles according to the position of the observer and the action of the actor, but they are transformed into one another as well as a function of time and of the system. They make order or disorder" (2007 [1980], 66).

Because of its joking nature, the parasite can be positive as much as negative. The exemplary parasite may not be noise or an enemy, but perhaps a catalyst that drives an otherwise slow reaction. Indeed, Serres goes so far as to see the parasite as both the stochastic process that generates variation (think interfering noise), as well as the sorting process that drives selection (think intercepting enemies). In this way, Serres also sees the parasite as a source of life, and at the inception of complex systems more generally. Looking ahead to chapter 6, we might extend this to think of the parasite as including both sieving and serendipity.

***

Having summarized some of the key claims of Serres's essay, several critiques are now in order. First, the joker metaphor is too powerful: by making the parasite a wild-card, the parasite is, by definition, everything: signal and noise, friend and enemy, edge and node, part and whole, life and death, code and channel. And so it is no surprise that Serres finds it lurking everywhere: a prime mover who just happens to be puny.

To say that we only understand function in the context of failing to function is just as much a commonplace of critical theory as it is to say that we only recognize the existence of the system when it breaks down, or the operation of a rule when it is violated. In contrast, Heidegger (1996) seemed to have a sense that the kind of consciousness or comportment that arises in the context of failure leads to a misrecognition of the nature of the 'functioning' that was there before the failure (for example, residence in the world gets erroneously refigured in terms of representations of the world).[13]

The trivial sense of the parasite is akin to negative reciprocity as Sahlins (1972) defined it. More generally, it is simply that which takes without giving; that which 'lives on' by 'living off'. And thus to argue for its fundamental importance is about as convincing as treating generalized reciprocity or balanced reciprocity as the fonts of all things modern, human, or true. Think, for example, of all the scholars who want to take the gift as exemplary of human sociality, where their emphasis is all too often a reaction to all those who want to take the commodity as exemplary of human sociality. All things economic, and intimate, are far more complicated (Kockelman 2007b, 2016).

Serres focuses on 'a relation to a relation', but insofar as most forms of meaning and value are really relations between relations (as shown in chapter 1), the parasite—insofar as it is, in one key guise, oriented towards capturing such values— is really a relation to relations between relations.

Finally, despite his repeated invocations of Hermes, and despite a sophisticated understanding of the varieties of translation, Serres spends very little time on interpretation (or code), focusing his efforts on circulation (or channel) instead. And so, while he usefully brings something like thirdness to circulation, his understanding of interpretation stays close to secondness in a way that is reminiscent of Shannon's mappings between messages and signals (or cryptograms). If Serres had done for the sign-interpretant relation (via the notion of an object—if only in the role of an 'objection' or 'obstruction') what he did for the signer-interpreter relation (via the parasite), the ramifications of the text would be much greater.[14]

So in the spirit of extending his insights to include the menagerie of beasts who live in and off interpretation (or 'codes/representations') as much as circulation (or 'channels/infrastructure'), as well as material culture more generally; in the hopes of foregrounding the relation between parasites and thirdness, or the ideas of Serres and those of Peirce; with an awareness of the foregoing critiques; and with the aim of succinctly theorizing what may be called, somewhat paradoxically, 'the parasitic function'; let me end this section with the following definition:

> *An instrument (action or sign) considered as a means to an end (or infrastructure considered as a path to a destination) is a second (or intermediary), but insofar as it implies (embodies or indexes) other ends it might be diverted to serve, or indeed implies any way it may fail to serve an end (whether original or diverted), it is a third (or mediator).*

The parasite is whatever inhabits such implications.[15]

2.5. Jakobson and Serres

In some sense, then, Serres capitalized on—or parasited—an insight that was latent in Shannon (and explicit in Peirce): the idea that the channel, as a relation, was itself best understood in terms of a relation to this relation (enemies, noise, and disturbances more generally). We might say that he used Shannon to overcome Shannon. Jakobson did something similar with Saussure. In particular, while he inherited a Saussurian model of the code (qua sign-object or signifier-signified relation), he also managed to use Saussure's categories to overcome Saussure. In particular, through his notion of duplex categories, and his focus on the speech event more generally, he brought context and history, or parole and diachrony, into a theory of signs—and thus understood language, as an ensemble of sign-object relations, in terms of practice as much as structure, transformation as much as stasis, context as much as code. Or, in the idiom of actor-network theory, which will be more thoroughly discussed and dismantled in chapter 6, Jakobson understood language as mediator as much as intermediary. In the rest of this key section, we review his arguments concerning such categories and extend them from codes to channels, thereby bridging some of the distance between Serres and Jakobson.

As part of his celebrated essay on grammatical categories in Russian (1990b; see also Lucy 1993), Jakobson theorized the relation between four seemingly unrelated kinds of signs: reported speech (e.g., 'John said, 'I'll go''), meta-language (e.g., "mutt' is a pejorative synonym for 'dog''), shifters (e.g., 'I', 'here', 'now'), and proper names (e.g., 'Jake', 'Mt. Rushmore'). See Figure 2.7. To understand such 'duplex categories', he systematically related messages (M) and codes (C), understood in their most general Saussurean sense as *parole* (token, practice, context, utterance) and *langue* (type, structure, convention, sentence). In particular, reported speech is a message that makes reference to a message (M/M), and meta-language is a message that makes reference to a code (M/C). Here 'makes reference to' (/) means 'stands for' or 'refers to'—that is, such messages (or signs) have as their referents (or objects) messages or codes.[16]

The other two duplex categories are a little more complicated. In particular, proper names are codes that make reference to codes (C//C), and shifters are codes that make reference to messages (C//M). Here 'makes reference to' (//) is best understood as 'decoded using' or 'interpreted with'—that is, the interpreter cannot get from the message to the referent without knowing something about either the message (qua sign token) or the code (qua relation between sign type and object type). In the case of proper names, for example, one cannot figure out who the name 'Mary' refers to without knowing who it referred to in the past (i.e., 'Mary' means that woman over there [in this sign event] because 'Mary' has meant that woman over there [in past sign events within this semiotic community, and such events are connected to each other by long indexical chains]).[17] Similarly, in the case of shifters, one cannot interpret a sign like 'I' or 'now' without knowing something about the speech event in which it was uttered: in particular, who said 'I', or when 'now' was said.[18]

M/M   **(Reported Speech)**
S/S   **(Signer-Addressing Signer)**

M/C   **(Meta-Language)**
S/Ch   **(Channel-Addressing Signer)**

C//C   **(Proper Names)**
Ch//Ch   **(Self-Channeling Channel)**

C//M   **(Shifters)**
Ch//S   **(Source-Dependent Channel)**

C = Code, M = Message, Ch = Channel, S = Signer
/ = 'Stands for' (C, M) or 'Addressed to' (S, Ch)
// = 'Decoded with' (C, M) or 'Guided by' (S, Ch)

FIGURE 2.7 Duplex Categories Revisited

Jakobson's original characterization of such duplex categories was important not only because it provided a unified account of four important kinds of signs (proper names, reported speech, meta-language, and shifters), but because—with the benefit of hindsight (and from the standpoint of his predecessors)—it identified four functions that all signs serve to some extent. With Kripke and Putnam, for example, we learn that all words are a little bit like proper names. With Bahktin and Goffman, we learn that all utterances are a little bit like reported speech. With Peirce, we learn that all symbols have an indexical component, and so are shifter-like. And with Mead and Austin, we learn that all signs are a little bit self-grounding and world-transforming. The ramifications of these facts for our understanding of the relation between language, social relations, and critical theory have been enormous. This is what we meant above when we said that Jakobson used Saussurian categories (code and message, or *langue* and *parole*) to move past Saussure's categories. His actual understanding of codes, and thus interpretation, was thus much more nuanced than his original message-referent schema would suggest.

***

If we move from codes (as relations between signs and objects) to channels (as relations between signers and interpreters) we may derive four new duplex categories, which may be loosely described as signer-directed signers, channel-directed signers, self-channeling channels, and source-dependent channels. And, as with Jakobson's categories, the point is not to identify four kinds of channels per se, but rather to identify four reflexive functions that any channel may serve—or, better, *four reflexive modes of circulation that any channeling, infrastructing, or instituting system may involve*. Such categories are thus to circulation what Jakobson's categories are to interpretation.

In particular, many signs are oriented to channels (or infrastructure more generally), and thereby open up or close off the possibility for other agents to engage in semiosis (channel-directed signers). Many signs are oriented to interpreters that are themselves signers, or are immediate means to more mediate ends (signer-directed signers). Many signs, by traversing certain paths, enable subsequent traversals of similar paths (self-channeling channels). And many signs only get where they're going as a function of where they begin (source-directed channels). After carefully defining and exemplifying these functions, we will conclude this section by comparing them to Serres's understanding of the parasite. In particular, while the first of these is similar to the parasite, the others also constitute beasts that live in and off of infrastructure.

As will be seen, all of these agencies—signer-addressing signers, channel-addressing signers, self-channeling channels, and source-dependent channels—may be understood as *controlling communication* and *communicating control* in the classic cybernetic sense (Bateson 1972; Shannon and Weaver 1963 [1949]; Wiener 1948), albeit in a radically transformed way. More broadly, through the signers and channels of one semiotic process, the signers and channels of other, more distal semiotic processes may be disciplined (governed, exploited, controlled, dominated, or enclosed). Such agencies, then, serve not only to *displace discipline* (across time, space, person, modality, impact) but also to *discipline displacement*.[19]

***

As with Jakobson's duplex categories, these four categories break up into two pairs, depending on how the phrase 'in reference to' is interpreted. See Figure 2.7. First, there are signers that make reference to signers (S/S), and signers that make reference to channels (S/Ch). For these two categories, the phrase 'makes reference to' (/) may be understood as 'addressed to' or 'directed towards'. (Compare 'refers to' in the case of Jakobson's original duplex categories.) The focus, then, is on the interpreter or destination: not how a sign gets somewhere, but where it is going.

A *signer-directed signer* (S/S) addresses another agent (or directs signs to it more generally) because of that agent's capacity as a signer. (Compare reported speech, or M/M.) Loosely speaking, one speaks to another in order to control what is subsequently said; or one causes an effect that is itself a cause of further effects. Signer-directed signers are thus oriented to interpreters who are themselves signers (be they persons, things, or anything outside or in between), such that the second agent's interpretants of the first agent's signs are themselves signs, but of a different nature, and thus with different powers than the first agent could have produced on its own. That is, one directs one's signs to another so that they will live on in the interpretants of the other, precisely because of how this transforms or preserves their efficacy as signs.

For example, such addressed others may function as relays (transporting signs into new domains of space, time, person, and possibility); amplifiers (transforming the quantity or intensity of the original sign's qualities); stabilizers (reducing the disorder of a sign, such that they may last longer); editors (improving a sign's legibility, grammaticality, felicity, and so forth); filters or sieves (sorting and transforming signs by reference to their form and content); ciphers (recoding signs); remediators (converting signs from one media into another); couriers (carrying signs along different routes at different speeds); erasers (removing the traces of signs, such that they are no longer detectable to some agent); and transducers (converting a signal in one form of energy into a signal in another form of energy), among other things.[20] Many interesting questions arise as to the reversibility and predictability of such processes: the degree to which one can recover the original sign given the interpretant, or predict the subsequent interpretant given the sign. As for prediction, recall our discussion of the commitment dimension of semiotic agency in section 2.2: a key dimension of power, following Hobbes (1994 [1668]), is being able to anticipate the future effects of present actions. As for recovery, irreversible processes (and simply difficult to reverse processes) project an inexorable historicity onto semiotic practices. Such modes of address (S/S) may therefore enable not so much the disclosure of value, as the foreclosure of return. Indeed, friction—or entropy more generally—is the quintessential parasite: Serres's essay is really just an extended riff on the Second Law of Thermodynamics, that arrow of time.

A *channel-directed signer* (Ch/S) addresses another agent because of that agent's capacity as a channel. (Compare meta-language, or M/C.) Loosely speaking, one speaks to another in order to control who is subsequently spoken to; or one directs the effects of a cause that one did not effect. In particular, channel-directed signers are oriented to interpreters who are themselves channels, such that the second agent's interpretants of the first agent's signs are transformations in the paths taken by other signs (themselves expressed by other signers). Working at the origin, they may transform the signs that are sent: capping and refracting. Working at the destination, they may transform the signs that are received: shielding and deflecting. And working anywhere along the path, they may transform the signs that are moving: routing, bridging, bifurcating, dead-ending.

As famously theorized by Nietzsche in *The Genealogy of Morals* and Freud in *The Interpretation of Dreams*, for example, the blockage of any message-qua-impulse often leads to a rerouting (through other channels) and an enciphering (through other codes) of the message.[21] Indeed, such unintended effects of controlling channels are often more interesting than the control of the channel per se. In some sense, then, channels, infrastructure, and institutions are themselves subject to dreams, obsessions, and parapraxes (qua 'slips of/on the path'). As will be discussed later in this chapter, this function is closest to Serres's parasite.[22] And as will be discussed in chapter 4, this function is closely related to MacKay's account of meaning, and Peirce's understanding of ultimate interpretants: the 'meaning' of a sign is the effect it has on an agent's beliefs or habits, understood as their propensity to subsequently 'channel' particular signs into particular interpretants.

***

Next, there are channels that make reference to channels (Ch//Ch), and channels that make reference to signers (Ch//S). For these two categories, the phrase 'makes reference to' (//) may be understood as 'guided by'. (Compare 'interpreted with' in the case of Jakobson's original duplex categories.) The focus, then, is on the channel or route: not where a sign is going, but how it gets there.

A *self-channeling channel* (Ch//Ch) leads to a certain destination, or takes a certain route, only because it has led to a certain destination, or taken a certain route. (Compare proper names, or C//C.) Loosely speaking, a signer has access to an interpreter because a signer has had access to an interpreter; or a message arrives at its destination because similar messages have arrived at similar destinations. Pathways, when understood as channels (moving signs and objects) as much as infrastructure (moving people and things) are famous for having this property

(Bourdieu 1977). Indeed, we might characterize the essence of the phenomenon as follows: *past movements leave indexical traces which channel future movements in iconic ways: from footprints to river banks, from wheel ruts to wormholes.*[23] As an embodied phenomenon, habits are the exemplary site of this process (as understood by scholars from Hume to Peirce)—especially habits that condition the conveyance of signs so far as they were conditioned by the conveyance of signs. More generally, any technique of the body (mind, self, ear, or tongue) may partake of this process insofar as it plays a role in the transmission of a message and persists because of the transmission of messages.

The classic image for this process (Simon 1996) is a simple-minded organism (say, a beetle) moving through an easily-modified environment (say, a sandy plane). However simple the imagined beetle's cognitive apparatus (e.g., it takes its next step as a function of the sand's contours in its immediate environment), it may engage in incredibly complex travels so far as it is coupled with its environment (e.g., each step it takes disturbs the sand's contours). In the case of channels and institutions, rather than sandy infrastructure, the analog is as follows: the movements of signs (or signers) through a medium leave traces in that medium; and these traces may, in turn, affect the movements of signs (or signers) through that medium. When this is done in an iconic or convergent fashion, we get self-channeling channels; when this is done in a chaotic or emergent fashion we get source-dependent channels. We will return to this idea in chapter 6, when such an environment-organism coupling will be shown to be (more or less) equivalent to a Turing Machine.

As with proper names (Kripke 1980, Putnam 1975), self-channeling channels have baptismal events, and a performative dimension more generally. For example, just as one can coin a term (or rather coin a code by establishing a relation between a sign and an object), one may forge a bond (or rather forge a channel by establishing a relation between a signer and an interpreter). Usually coining codes and forging channels go hand in hand: that which is coined circulates along that which is forged. Moreover, all the usual issues present in the coinage of codes (such as standardization), and top-down versus bottom-up regimentation (e.g. 'state' versus 'market', 'cathedral' versus 'bazaar', 'superego' versus 'id'), have their doppelgängers in the forging of channels.

A *source-dependent channel* (Ch//S) leads to an interpreter because of where it begins. (Compare shifters, or C//M.) Loosely speaking, where one departs from determines where one arrives at; or whoever interprets a sign is determined by whoever expresses a sign. In a narrow sense, source-dependent channels are like passports (in the context of messengers traveling along infrastructure) and spam-filters (in the context of messages traveling through channels): such entities may be permitted or prohibited from going certain places because of where they have come from (or what address or agency originally sent them).

In this regard, there are two complementary ways for the channeling agent to know where signs have come from, such that it can use this information to permit or prohibit future passage. First, the signs can be tracked or surveilled: their movements and positions, senders and peregrinations, can be logged in some way. (And this is itself directly related to what might be called a *critique of semiotic reason*: what are the limits of what can be known about the paths of signs and the processes of semiosis, and how does this affect the possibilities of governance?) And second, one may infer where a sign has been by its current properties. In other words, the features of a sign may themselves be indexical signs that point to the origins or history of the sign—who sent it, where it's been, and how it got there. The issue here is not using signs to engage in forensics or surveillance, but the need for a forensics and a surveillance of signs per se. That said, if we remember that most channels consist of people (at least at the nodes, if not along the paths, qua messengers) who not only send and receive signs, but also interpret and resignify—and thus both affect and are affected by the signs they send and receive—then few signs, as it were, can ever travel the same channel twice. In other words, channels may be transformed by their channeling, such that these forms of regimentation become utopian.[24]

***

To return to Serres, both signer-directed signers and channel-directed signers turn on a relation to a relation. In particular, one agent relates to a relation between two other agents. In the case of signer-directed signers, the first agent is 'in line with' the other two agents. In the case of channel-directed signers, the first agent is 'orthogonal to' the other two agents. In either case, whatever action the first agent undertakes (e.g., expressing a sign) has an effect on the relation between the other two agents (e.g., their modes of signification and interpretation). See Figure 2.8, top half.

In particular, signer-directed signers are fundamentally system-internal agents who leverage their position within a system. Woven directly into a system of agents and actions, or entities and relations, they act locally (expressing a sign to be interpreted by a nearby agent) in order to have extralocal effects (so far as the interpretant of the nearby agent will itself be a sign to a more distal agent). In contrast,

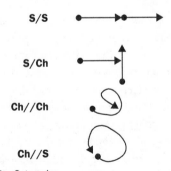

FIGURE 2.8 Topology of Duplex Categories

channel-directed signers are fundamentally system-external agents who are well positioned outside a system. Standing outside of a system of agents and actions, or entities and relations, they make and break (strengthen and weaken, conduct and obstruct) already existing relations between nodes in order to control flows (which signs go where to what effect). Relatively speaking, if the first are immanent to an assemblage, the latter are transcendent.

Above, we identified channel-directed signers as closely akin to parasites. In some sense, however, Serres's parasite stands between both these functions. While his focus was on system-external agents, he was aware that what is external to a system can quickly become internalized (via ideas like perturbation and invitation). And he was aware that what is internal to a system can quickly become externalized (via ideas like excrescence and banishment). Indeed, in some sense, these two functions relate to each other as signal and noise, in that one and the same agent may be framed as one or the other function depending on the scale at which a system is examined.

The remaining functions, source-dependent channels and self-channeling channels, have no obvious analog in Serres. Indeed, they do not turn on the relation between a (signifying and interpreting) agent and a relation between two other such agents. Rather, source-dependent channels turn on the relation between the second part of a journey and the first part. That is, where something has just been mediates where it will now go. More generally, the channeling of this sign depends on how it has been channeled. And self-channeling channels turn on the relation between the current journey and prior journeys. That is, where things like this have gone mediates where this thing will go. More generally, the channeling of this sign (token) depends on how this sign (type) has been channeled. See Figure 2.8, bottom half.

In some sense, both these functions turn on something like memory, history, habit, or disposition—whether grounded in the habitus or memory of an individual, in the culture of a group (qua intersubjectively held habitus or memory), or in the regimenting environs of individuals and groups (qua affordances, laws, protocols, waste-products, and so forth). Relatively speaking, if the first two functions were spatial; these two functions are temporal. If the first two deal with being-assemblage, these two deal with becoming-assemblage. And roughly speaking, if the first two have technological emblems (logic gates, computers, and internets), the latter two have biological emblems (neurons, nervous systems, and populations).

One may speculate on the reasons for this elision in Serres, and the repercussions of it. Indeed, one may wonder whether the relatively anti-Durkheim (and anti-Mauss and anti-Bourdieu) stance of actor-network theory is, in part, a reflection of this bias: individual bodies (habit) and collective histories (culture) are arguably two of the most reviled enemies of this paradigm. Or, framed another way, by making the parasite a 'wildcard' (able to be anything anywhere anytime), and making the hurly-burly a 'system' (composed of nothing but an endless stretch of endlessly swappable and scalable nodes and edges), Serres did away with most forms of traceable identity (or self-channeling channels, qua proper names) and grounded locality (or source-dependent channels, qua shifters).

2.6. The Proliferation of Parasites

In short, just as Jakobson built on Saussure to overcome Saussure, Serres built on Shannon to overcome Shannon. Each exploited insights that were latent in the systems of their predecessors. And just as Jakobson thereby produced a more nuanced notion of codes (via his understanding of duplex categories), Serres produced a more nuanced understanding of channels (via his understanding of parasites). Each thereby transformed what seemed to be a second into a third; and each thereby recovered some of the richness that existed prior to an otherwise widespread reduction.

Moreover, in extending Jakobson's notion of duplex categories from the relation between codes and signs to the relation between channels and signers, we have seen that Serres's system had something like metalanguage (the parasite per se), and perhaps even reported speech (the parasite when perturbed), but nothing like proper names and shifters. Finally, just as we used Jakobson's extension of Saussure (regarding codes) to extend Serres's extension of Shannon (regarding channels), we might also use Serres to extend Jakobson—exploring the contours of codes through the perturbations of parasites. But that move will be saved for later chapters.

That said, part of the arc of this chapter's argument is not just that circulation and interpretation have been all too often reduced to seconds (qua 'code' and 'channel') rather than thirds, except in the capable hands of Jakobson and Serres. It has also argued, more or less implicitly, that circulation and interpretation are themselves just two facets of thirdness that get separated for the sake of an analytic framing—one facet seen from the standpoint of signifying and interpreting agents, the other seen from the standpoint of significant and interpretable entities.

Such reductions are conditioned by, if not concomitant with, this separation. And, indeed, for this primary separation to occur, a framing also needs to arise—one that distinguishes between signs, objects and interpretants (qua products or actions); or between signers, objecters, and interpreters (qua producers or actors); or even between sign-event, object-event, and interpretant-event. How the hurly-burly gets framed, separated, and reduced in these ways—and then analytically recombined, for the sake of some theoretical exegesis, in the approving context of some epistemic community or disciplinary formation—is part and parcel of this process, but not our focus here.

That said, the general move from hurly-burly proper to 'circulation' and 'interpretation' (or, worse, to 'channel' and 'code') seems to suffer all the same failings as Descartes as critiqued by Heidegger (and as critiqued by Peirce, well before that). In other words, we might argue that terms like interpretation and circulation are the ontological equivalent of 'subject' and 'object'—theoretical constructs that are not adequate to any referent, but really only evince the reductive imaginary of the analyst. The real parasites would therefore be those who effect these framing, separating, and reducing perturbations. The real parasites would be us.

***

While we have been focused on Serres's understanding of the parasite, insofar as it emerged from Shannon's understanding of enemies and noise, and was eerily resonant with Peirce's understanding of thirdness, its relevance to social theory is much greater. As we saw at the end of section 2.4, for example, if we think of a path (channel or action) as a means, and a destination (addressee or purpose) as an end, then whatever prevents a traveler from arriving at their destination, or diverts a traveler onto a different path with a different destination, is a parasite. From such a vantage, the parasite involves not just diversions from intended paths, but also exploitations of design weakness, and preying on others by playing with conventional appearances—from pirates to hackers, from symbols to skate-rats, from ninjas to capitalists.

In the *Nicomachean Ethics*, for example, Aristotle (2001d) understood action in terms of means-ends chains, in that everything one does is a means for some end, which is itself a means for a further end, and so on indefinitely. For example, you set your alarm in order to wake up at 7:00 am; you woke up at 7:00 am in order to get to class on time; you got to class on time in order to get a good grade; you got a good grade in order to have a high GPA; you got a high GPA in order to get a good job; you got a good job in order to . . . and so on, and so forth. In some sense, then, almost every end is 'exploited': used as a means for some further end. We say 'almost' because there seems to be one end that exploits all the others, but is not itself exploited in turn: the final end, or *summum bonum*. Aristotle called this arch-parasite, this end that is not itself a means for further ends, 'happiness', or *eudamonia*. And he thought that inquiry into its nature and conditions was of utmost importance.

Interestingly, the word *eudamonia* has at its root, dæmon (or 'demon') which, in the guise of Maxwell's (2001 [1871]) 'finite being', or mediating creature, was the selecting and sieving entity that could upend the laws of thermodynamics by being well-positioned at a partition. Such a creature was itself the quintessential parasite in Serres's cybernetic-thermodynamic imaginary. Funnily enough, a frequent English translation of the word *eudamonia* is 'felicity', which brings us to John Austin, whose influential theory of performativity was, in some sense, a theory of *the pragmatics of parasites*.

This is for two reasons. First, in developing his account of performative utterances Austin (1962) famously introduced the notion of 'felicity conditions'. Loosely speaking, any such utterance is felicitous if it is normatively appropriate in context (that is, it conforms to certain parameters of the social world) and normatively effective on context (that is, it transforms certain parameters of the social world). For example, a wedding ceremony is only appropriate (in most countries, alas) insofar as the two people to be married have the social statuses of unmarried, adult, man and woman; and insofar as the one doing the marrying has a social status such as priest, rabbi, or captain at sea. Moreover, a wedding ceremony is only effective insofar as the two people come to occupy the statuses of husband and wife.[25] Crucially, he detailed such felicity conditions by analyzing all the ways such utterances might fail, or be 'infelicitous', by either failing to conform or failing to transform in all their conventionally recognized ways.

Second, Austin used the term 'parasite' to describe all the ways that performative utterances could be strategically and creatively used in nonconventional contexts, such that their usual felicity conditions were suspended. Such parasitic, tropic, or 'etiolated' uses not only included situations like reported speech and theater, but also irony, sarcasm, and humor, as well as lying and dissembling more generally, not to mention winks, finger-crossing, play bows, and 'keying' (Bateson 1972).[26] Ironically, while his theory implicitly dealt with parasites in the first sense (qua failure to achieve ends), he explicitly didn't deal with parasites in this second sense (qua diversion from conventional ends). Indeed, Austin said that he was precisely not interested in such parasitic usages of language, which are literally ways of preying on (and playing with) conventional appearances, or ways of suspending felicity conditions such that speech acts can *fail to fail*.

Erving Goffman (1959, 1981a, 1981b, 1983) took up both such issues at length. He focused on conventional ways of handling breakdowns in conventions. And he focused on tropic usages: the ways conventional signs are routinely and creatively used in nonconventional ways. Indeed, his theory of the performance of self in everyday life was essentially parasites all the way down.

In capitalizing on Austin's aporia, Goffman was himself heavily indebted to George Herbert Mead's (1934) understanding of the symbol (as opposed to the gesture), which foregrounded the symbol's capacity to be parasited. In particular, unlike most definitions of symbols, which treat them as signs which relate to their objects in relatively arbitrary ways, and hence through something like a social contract or convention (Peirce, Saussure, etc.), Mead understood symbols as self-reflexive signs (Kockelman 2007a). In particular, a sign is a symbol insofar as the signer can anticipate the interpreter's interpretant of it; and this is possible insofar as signers can understand how interpreters will react to the sign, insofar as they know how they themselves would react if they were similarly situated (recalling the third dimension of semiotic agency described in section 2.3: commitment to, or anticipation of, an interpretant of a sign-object relation). In this way, anytime one can seize control of one's appearance—modifying it so as to modify others' interpretants of oneself, or one's actions (through such signs)—one is engaged in 'symbolic behavior'.[27] Note, then, the 'symbolic order' in this reading is precisely the (potentially) parasitic order.

Indeed, Goffman theorized a class of individuals that he called assassins, but which might just as well be called parasites: agents who prey on conventional appearances, or shared understandings of the proper functioning of symbols (qua felicity conditions), in order to divert them to other ends. His insight was that such assassins are us: and our weapon of choice is the symbol, a sign whose object is intersubjectively agreed upon, and hence routinely depended on, and so can be surreptitiously reframed for other effects. Indeed, he even couched his theory of assassins in infrastructural terms: "Assassins must rely on and profit from conventional traffic flow and conventional understanding regarding normal appearances if they are to get into a position to attack their victim and escape from the scene of the crime" (1983, 5).

In *Civilization and Capitalism*, the economic historian Claude Braudel (1992) argued that the essence of capitalism is not the market, but rather one group of actors' ability to relate to the rest of society's relation to the market. As he saw it, "active social hierarchies were constructed on top of [the market economy]: they could manipulate exchange to their advantage and disturb the established order. In their desire to do so . . . they created anomalies, 'zones of turbulence', and conducted their affairs in a very individual way. At this exalted level, a few wealthy merchants in eighteenth-century Amsterdam or sixteenth-century Genoa could throw whole sectors of the European or even the world economy into confusion, from a distance. . . .Without this zone, capitalism is unthinkable: this is where it takes up residence and prospers" (24).

All of which brings us to affordances—which may be maximally contrasted with Aristotle's *eudamonia*: not ends which are not themselves means (qua final ends), but rather means which were not themselves ends (qua initial means). For a key way to redefine an affordance (Gibson 1986; Kockelman 2006b, 2013a) is by contrasting it with an instrument, as was done in chapter 1. In this reading, the latter are designed with specific functions in mind; whereas the former are undesigned: they don't so much serve functions as provide purchase, enabling and constraining actions by virtue of their relatively happenstance properties. The purchase provided by an affordance, then, is evinced in the actions it prohibits or constrains as much as by the actions it permits or enables. And just as culture is often imagined as a set of values (toward which all practices tend, qua 'felicity'), nature is often imagined as a set of initial, or pre-telic, properties out of which everything else is built. Thus if *eudamonia* is the highest end, affordances are the lowest means. And, in this way, both are parasiteless creatures—the first because it stands on the top of the chain and so cannot be reduced to an end; the second because it stands at the bottom of the chain and so, having no end, cannot fail to achieve that end, or be diverted from it.

Indeed, most parasites of the quotidian kind work by reducing instruments to affordances—finding unintentional purchase in entities that have been purposely designed for their functions. And crucially, a key way to do this is to find a novel purchase in an old form—often via the introduction of a new technology (or semiotic process, or social convention) which can heed, or take advantage of, the purchase provided by the affordance. For example, the appropriately named 'skate rat' does precisely this: a skateboard is a certain form of media, turning on wheels of a certain diameter and durometer, that allows a skateboarder to find a set of purchases in a built environs that was designed with a radically different set of functions in mind. But more generally, most 'exploits', hacks, or creative reappropriations of the computational kind are precisely of this variety (Erikson 2008, Graham 2004). In this reading, the creative power of parasites, qua unintended media-enabled affordances for novel actions and ideas, is foregrounded; and the stereotypic sense of a parasite, as that which takes without giving, or benefits at the expense of another, is backgrounded.[28]

Finally, somewhat orthogonal to all these ideas, we might end this section with a startling image from Samuel Butler (1872): "May not man himself become a sort of parasite upon the machines? An affectionate machine-tickling aphid?" Or, as my mother would say, An ineffectual iPhone-tickling idiot.

2.7. Enclosure, Disclosure, and Value

Let us return to the description of joint attention offered in section 2.2, and thereby relate some of the foregoing ideas to more conventional understandings of circulation and value—both in the sense of the 'highest values' (qua felicity), and in the sense of the 'lowest values' (qua affordances). In particular, the object that we jointly attend to (i.e., the pen) may itself be or become a sign. And this sign may be further interpreted in a variety of ways, each of which involves the projection of value. For example, one may wield the pen (as a sign) to write a letter (as an interpretant), and thereby construe the pen in terms of use-value. One may give the pen to someone else for something else (for example, a pencil), and thereby construe it in terms of exchange-value. And one may represent the pen with an utterance (e.g., by saying "this pen is out of ink"), and thereby construe it in terms of semantic meaning or "truth-value."[29] If we might radically update a Simmelian metaphor that otherwise obscures as much as it illuminates, value might be understood as the shadow something casts from a light-source outside of itself—where the thing is a sign, the shadow is an object, and the light-source is an interpretant (such that properties of all three entities, both causal and normative, in a particular arrangement, contribute to the highly emergent process of evaluation). And here we have characterized three common kinds of light-sources—the instrumental, the economic, and the linguistic—which cast shadows like functions, prices, and concepts.

In this context, communicative infrastructure is not just the conditions of possibility (physical contacts, social conventions, psychological connections) for actors within a semiotic event to attend to the same object; nor is it just that which relates a signer to an interpreter, such that a sign expressed by the former may be interpreted by the latter; nor is it merely something that serves our original delimiting, facilitating, and forestalling functions; nor is it simply that which relates to information as ground to figure, or the tacit to the occurrent (not to mention all the parasitic ways each of these can go awry). Infrastructure is also a condition of possibility for the relative comparability of value judgments across actors within a collectivity who are using, exchanging, and representing things during semiotic events that are relatively displaced from each other in space, time, and person.

As is often postulated by theorists of modern social-formations (Kockelman 2015), each of the three kinds of evaluative projection may be subject to intensification (through processes like quantification, abstraction, and standardization) and extension (over historical time and across geographic space). For example, just as a more originary form of use-value is remade as 'technology', a more original form of exchange-value is remade as 'economy', and a more originary form of truth-value is remade as 'science'. Moreover, these three kinds of values are co-articulated: means and ends, investments and returns, premises and conclusions become mutually implicated. That is, the three kinds of projections become part and parcel of a single project. Here infrastructure might be understood as not only a condition of possibility for the relative comparability of value-judgments across all events of wielding, exchanging, and representing (within a collectivity). It also becomes a condition of possibility for the relative commensurability of value-judgments across all collectivities (of wielders, exchangers, and representers).

In all three cases above we focused on the conditions of possibility for there to be objects (attention), understood as having different kinds of values (projection), which may be more or less commensurate with each other, across events, collectivities, and scales (intensification and extension). At some point, perhaps concomitantly with the above processes, *the conditions of possibility for such extreme forms of portability* become the object of joint attention, are subject to evaluative projection, and undergo extended intensification. That is, the ground, qua conditions of possibility for the foregoing processes, becomes figured—and thereby reflexively becomes both the means and ends of such processes. Infrastructure (channels and institutions)—as an assemblage of material, social, and psychological affordances—becomes itself the object (qua means, ends, or value) of technology, economy, and knowledge. The end result is knowledge about (science), power over (technology), and profit from (economy) the conditions of possibility for knowledge, power, and profit.

Optimists might think that by enclosing the conditions for disclosure in this way we have built a bridge to carry bridges across banks, such that we might one day cross more distal waters; whereas pessimists might worry that we are in danger of damming the river.

3

Secrecy, Poetry, and Being-Free

3.1. The Structure (and Event) of Networks

As we saw in chapter 2, with many caveats, classic treatments of channels are very similar to those of codes. Just as a sign relates to an object (or a signifier relates to a signified) by way of a code, a signer relates to an interpreter (or a speaker relates to an addressee) by way of a channel. In each case, there is something like an origin, a destination, and a path. We might therefore hypothesize that, just as there is a kind of structure underlying codes, so too is there a kind of structure underlying channels. In offering this hypothesis—or, really, exploring this metaphor—we are using the term structure in a relatively constrained way: the value of any element within a system is partially mediated by its relation to other elements within the system.[1] (Not to mention its mediation by all the parasitic agents that relate to such relations, actively engaged in the work of inference and interception.)

In particular, Saussure thought that the relation between a signifier (such as a sound pattern) and a signified (such as a concept) could not be properly understood unless one took into account the way that relation could combine with other such relations, and substitute for other such relations, within some larger system (such as a language). A similar move can be made for channels. Two channels may be said to combine with each other when the destination of one is the origin of the other. Two channels may be said to substitute for each other when they both start off from the same origin and/or end up at the same destination (while otherwise taking different paths). And so we might characterize the structural mediation of channels as follows: the relation between a signer and an interpreter (qua channel) cannot be properly understood unless one takes into account the way that relation can combine with other such relations, and substitute for other such relations, within some larger system (such as a network).[2] See Figure 3.1.[3]

For example, the particular affordances of gestural language (or written language) come to the fore when contrasted with verbal language. That is, the communicative value of the manual-visual modality, its particular forms and functions,

Paul Kockelman. *The Art of Interpretation in the Age of Computation.* © Oxford University Press 2017

Subject	Auxiliary Verb	Main Verb (Intransitive)	Illocutionary Force
I	can	go	.
you	may	come	?
he, she, it	must	hop	!
we	should	skip	
you all	would	snuggle	
they	could	etc.	
	will		

Each column is a *paradigm*, or form class; and any element in a column may be selected. The combination of paradigms is a *syntagm*, or construction. This construction can produce a large number of different utterances by selecting one element from each column: *I can go? You all will snuggle! They will hop.* And so forth.

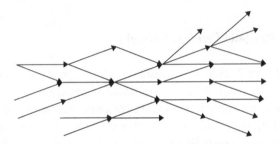

In this tiny portion of a network there are many possible routes that could be taken—many different start and end points that could be connected, and many different ways of connecting the same start and end points. At each juncture one may 'select' the next section to take. And any actual route 'combines' a set of different selections.

FIGURE 3.1 Selection and Combination in Channels and Codes

its aesthetics and pragmatics, is in part constituted through its relation to the mouth-ear modality (and vice-versa). One modality can substitute for the other (or combine with the other), under various conditions, with particular consequences. Furthermore, both kinds of communicative values may be transformed when other channels begin to combine with them, or substitute for them, in larger networks: megaphones, telephones, books, hearing aids, photographs, tape recorders, video recorders, and the like. What a particular channel (or form of media more generally) enables one to do, or constrains one from doing, can only properly be understood when compared and contrasted with other possible channels— channels that it can substitute for, or combine with (as well as displace, replace, or efface) in some environs, or era, given the actions and interests of its inhabitants.

As another example, we may return to enemies, and the channels we use to secure the secrecy of our communication. Shannon understood enemies, like noise, to be constituted by a relation to a relation. In particular, an enemy (call her Eve) relates to a channel that connects two parties (call them Alice and Bob). When Shannon described this system (1946, 661), he included an extra channel in addition to this main channel—a secure channel that would run in parallel with this potentially insecure channel. See Figure 3.2. Such a secure channel was similar to

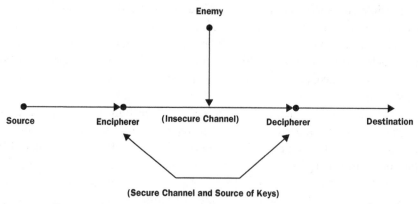

FIGURE 3.2 Shannon's Secure and Insecure Channels

the insecure channel insofar as it connected Alice and Bob, but it was different insofar as it shut out Eve. It should ideally turn on a kind of channel that involves less 'mediation' than the insecure channel, and so offers less opportunities for an intercepting enemy. For example, it might involve face-to-face contact, or physical transport through a known courier, as opposed to communication through phone calls or mailed letters. In this way, the affordances of the secure channel complement the affordances of the insecure channel: while it is more secure and immediate, it is also less efficient and convenient. And precisely because of its complementary features, the secure channel could serve a special function: with it, Alice and Bob could share a 'key', some piece of information that would allow them to encipher and decipher messages, so that they could safely share such enciphered messages through the otherwise insecure channel. That is, a small amount of information that they previously shared through the secure channel could be subsequently used to securely share a large amount of information through the otherwise insecure channel.[4] A relatively 'private' channel secures its value in relation to a relatively 'public' channel.

If codes and channels are similarly mediated (in this relatively narrow structural sense), then each system of relations between relations might be understood from two different perspectives. From the first perspective, both codes and channels may be seen in the light of necessity or constraint: here is a set of values one must conform to if one is to communicate with others, such that one's uptake and deployment of such values is regimented in particular ways. Think, for example, of conventions and protocols as stereotypically understood: the relatively arbitrary social facts we must adhere to if we wish to be understood or even heard (when we encode meanings or address others). This is akin to Saussure's vision of *langue*, or grammatical structure, but now extended from codes to include channels. From the second perspective, codes and channels may be seen in the light of possibility, or freedom: here is a finite set of constraints that can be used to create an infinite (or at least relatively large) range of configurations: the space of possible utterances, the space of possible routes. Think, for example, of train tracks sections (straight, curved, Y, X, etc.) as a small set of combining elements; and contrast this with the space of all possible configurations that can be made with such sections. This is akin to von Humboldt's vision of language, qua *energeia*, but now extended from codes to include channels, and infrastructure more generally.

Indeed, just as structure has two valences (constraint, freedom), so does practice or 'event'. In particular, any such configuration can both instantiate the constraints (constituting a relatively repeatable event, as it were) or undermine the constraints (constituting a relatively singular occurrence). That is, when we play with train tracks, just like when we play with words, we often simply do or say what is usually done or said. But sometimes, however serendipitously, we do or say something unexpected, irrevocable, unreproducible, disturbing, or new. This may involve creating a novel configuration with old constraints (as opposed to simply repeating the usual configurations—the figure 8, the how-do-you-do). Or this may involve going beyond the constraints: saying something judged ungrammatical (that catches), engineering something thought impossible (that holds).

***

We could go on making similar sorts of moves, understanding channels by way of codes, all the while tacking between all of Saussure's oppositions: from the arbitrary to the motivated, from the synchronic to the diachronic, from the internal to the external, and so forth. We could thereby offer a structuralism of channels, as well as an antistructuralism, and a poststructuralism, and a neostructuralism.[5] But these first three moves are enough for present purposes: from the structure (and practice) of codes to the structure (and practice) of channels; from structure as constraint (or demand) to structure as creativity (or invitation); from practice as conforming to structure to practice as transforming of structure. So let us instead use this minimalist refiguring of channels in terms of codes to take up Sapir on secrets and Jakobson on poetics. In particular, we might ask: What are some of the secrets of networks, of systems of interconnected channels, of infrastructure more generally? That is, what are the logics organizing them as systems of constraints; and what are the potentialities within them as spaces of configurations? And what might constitute their poetics—an aesthetic and pragmatic means of revealing their secrets?

To answer these questions—and, indeed, to even motivate why they should be posed and how they might be understood—we will need to step back a ways. The rest of this chapter will continue to examine and leverage the relation between codes and channels by delving into two topics that link them: degrees of freedom and secrets. This chapter thereby functions as a bridge between chapters 2 and 4, insofar as the topics it takes up are crucial to channels as much as codes, infrastructure as much as information, interaction as much as meaning.

Section 3.2 will introduce the notion of degrees of freedom: the number of independent dimensions needed to specify the state of a system. Section 3.3 will show how, as a function of different frames of relevance and scales of resolution, seemingly similar systems can have different degrees of freedom, and seemingly different systems can have similar degrees of freedom. These ideas will turn out to be fundamental for understanding information, and the way information systems mediate our experience, intuitions, and agency.

Section 3.4 will show that even relatively commensurate systems, that have identical degrees of freedom, can have different secrets—understood as the inherent symmetries that organize their sense-making capacities. This claim is closely related to the Sapir-Whorf hypothesis (the idea that the language you speak may affect the way you think), but generalized to include other kinds of media (channels, interfaces, algorithms, etc.), and concretized so as to have demonstrable effects.

Sections 3.5 will review different understandings of secrets, and show how channels as well as codes can have inherent secrets (in addition to their ability to keep and reveal secrets). Section 3.6 will offer an extended notion of poetics, showing how such a poetics sheds light on those secrets.

And the conclusion will return to some of the core ideas of chapter 2, and relate them to the ideas offered here. This move will allow us to bridge some otherwise distant banks: Heidegger's references and Google's rankings, banishing enemies and citing sources, *homo sacer* and HTML.

3.2. Degrees of Freedom

By *degrees of freedom*, we mean the number of independent dimensions needed to specify the state of a system. For example, if my goal is to specify where something is along a line, there is one degree of freedom. If my goal is to specify where something is in a plane, there are two degrees of freedom. If my goal is to specify where something is within a volume, there are three degrees of freedom. If my goal is to specify not only where something is in a volume, but also what direction it is moving, then there are six degrees of freedom—one for each position and velocity component of the entity in question. If my goal is to specify not only where something is and what direction it is moving, but also which direction it is facing and how it is spinning, there are 12 degrees of freedom. If my goal is to specify the position and velocity, as well as orientation and spin, of 10^{23} particles in a volume (such as a gas), then there are 12×10^{23} degrees of freedom. In short, different kinds of systems can have different degrees of freedom—and hence often wildly different dimensionalities.

Crucially, the systems in question are not confined to spatial coordinates, or physical variables. Anything whose possible states can be represented can be framed as having particular degrees of freedom. For example, just as the spatial positions and orientations of particles in a gas can constitute a system, so can the sexual positions and orientations of people in a city. And the systems do not have to involve representations per se; they can also involve interventions. For example, the interface for playing a video game like Pong has just a few degrees of freedom, whereas the interface for playing a game like Call of Duty, or piloting a surveillance drone, has very many degrees of freedom.

Moreover, the particular values a given dimension takes need not be continuously variable and potentially infinite (like positions along a line), but may instead be discretely variable and finite (like the outcome of a coin toss). For example, a word that is six characters in length can be framed as having six degrees of freedom, each with 26 (or so) possible values. Each possible character in a 140 character tweet can constitute a dimension, and each such dimension can have (at least) 256 values. A particle in a box one cubic meter in volume, whose position along each dimension can be measured with a precision up to one centimeter, has three degrees of freedom, each of which has one hundred values. Your favorite Dungeons and Dragons character has about six degrees of freedom, each of which may take one of eighteen values: wisdom, strength, dexterity, intelligence, charisma, and constitution. And you yourself, insofar as you have various offline and online profiles, may have dozens of degrees of freedom in each profile—some entered freely and manually, others calculated algorithmically and secretly. Such dimensions are known as 'fields' (your name, relationship status, address, occupation, high school, sexuality, political party, risk level, and so forth), and are designed to accommodate different ranges of 'values' (in every sense of this word).

We could go on and on and on—for almost any kind of system, any kind of experience, any kind of identity, is capable of having a particular dimensionality projected onto it. And different systems—eras, ideologies, technologies, personalities, characters, applications, interfaces, games, and governments—have their characteristic degrees of freedom. There are many different ways of being positioned, profiled, governed, recorded, represented, sampled, or 'boxed'.

Less abstractly, different kinds of action figures have different degrees of freedom in regards to the configurability of their bodies: a Lego mini-figure, for example, has about seven degrees of freedom (the angles of its head, wrists, shoulders, hips). Other dolls may be more or less 'richly articulated'. Such an expression is itself entangled in class (wealth) as much as language (articulateness). In any case, one relatively damning definition of what it means to be 'free' (having wealth, power, movement) is to have many degrees of freedom. And conversely, to bind something—either physically (with chains and manacles), or normatively (with mays and musts), is to reduce its degrees of freedom. Still other systems—language being the most famous example—require one to submit to a finite number of constraints (say, words and rules), and thereby enable one to express an infinite range of configurations (all those utterances). However, as is well known to linguistic anthropologists, depending on one's position in a language community or semiotic collectivity, one may be obliged to submit more, one may be allowed to express less.

Many channels—which are somewhere between mays and musts and chains and manacles—constitute reductions in the degrees of freedom of a system and yet are simultaneously freeings. For example, to position someone in the woods might require two degrees of freedom (their longitude and latitude, for example). However, if there is path that goes through the woods, this two-dimensional space has been reduced to a one-dimensional system: how far one is along the path, suitably paramaterized. Paths, then, usually have fewer degrees of freedom than the environments they move through: they reduce the dimensionality of a system, by constraining the space of possible positions. Such a reduction, or constraining, is not necessarily—or even usually—a bad thing. Perhaps a path through the woods constrains where you can go in the woods; but without a path, short of building one yourself, you couldn't go anywhere at all. This is an essential characteristic of infrastructure.

To offer one last example, an adult skull with a jawbone only has about one degree of freedom: how open or shut the jaw is with respect to the rest of the skull. In contrast, a human face—with all its independently movable muscles—has around two hundred degrees of freedom (estimates vary). A recent attempt to model human facial emotions using only twelve degrees of freedom has some scary results. We might hypothesize that a key factor in our sense of the virtual, as something not quite real, or even in our sense of the uncanny and eerie, is our intuition that something that usually has many degrees of freedom has been constrained (or simply not yet enabled) to exhibit fewer degrees of freedom. Another key issue is whether all those independently moving parts 'move together' in some coherent fashion, as opposed to just randomly varying their potential values. Such entities suffer from a 'lack of coordination'. And another key issue is whether the value along each dimension stays within some 'normal range'. Contrast the head of a doll, or a possessed child, when it spins all the way around. Such disparities in dimensionality are thus not only related to 'realism', and the 'real', but also to the imaginary, the uncanny, and the diabolical.

3.3. Frames of Relevance, Scales of Resolution

As the foregoing examples should illustrate, by *system* we mean nothing more than an entity or event (or ensemble of entities and events) that can show up in a particular state, typically as the outcome of a particular process, however complicated, out-of-control, or chaotic. All that really matters is that, to some *agent* who interacts with the system, the various states it can show up in are *distinguishable* (from other states, against some background) and *decisive* (for some mode of calculation, form of communication, course of action, affective unfolding, or aesthetic effect). Such states are thereby hooked into the sensory and instigatory capabilities of the agent (not to mention the interests of the agent and the features of the objects in its environment): they are qualitatively different signs that can lead to qualitatively different interpretants. In this way, anything that produces distinguishable and decisive states can constitute a system to such an agent; and thus what counts as a system is usually the projection of a particular agent—its beliefs and values, its ontologies and interests, its frames and fashions.

Because such interacting agents are crucial in determining what counts as a system, most systems are sensitive to the agent's *frame of relevance*.[6] In particular, most entities, events, or experiences could have many possible degrees of freedom projected onto them; and different agents may frame the same entity, event, or experience in different ways, such that only some of its degrees of freedom are salient. For example, you might be interested in the latitude of a city, whereas all I care about is its longitude. You might be interested in all the controls of an automobile's interface, whereas all I care about is the station its radio is tuned to. You might be interested in the configuration of a mini-figure's body parts, whereas I am interested in the position or orientation of its body, or the symbol on its chest, or the whereabouts of its owner. You might be interested in the values of all the grammatical categories in a clause, whereas all I care about is its tense inflection or emotive intonation. Indeed, even further afield, imagine an alien dice-game in which it doesn't matter what number comes up, but only where the die lands on the board, or how long it takes to come to rest.

Even if two agents have similar frames of relevance, they may have different *scales of resolution*. For example, suppose we are both interested in where a person is in a given terrain, but you are sensitive to precisions up to one square-meter, whereas I am only sensitive to (or interested in) precisions up to one square mile. More metaphorically, I may characterize the world in black and white terms, whereas you are sensitive to 256 different shades of gray. Again, the agent's ability to sense and instigate comes to the fore: all the mobility in a mini-figure's body doesn't matter, or may matter for different reasons, if you have a giant's hands (or are wearing thick gloves), or if you forgot to wear your glasses (or have antennae instead of eyes).

A key feature of our understanding of 'material' objects (in the most stereotypic sense) is that, to our experience, they have very few degrees of freedom. All the parts in a rock move as one part, so to speak—even though a physicist would tell us that this is at best a useful fiction, that matter, even the most seemingly inert matter, has many degrees of freedom (indeed, many more than 12×10^{23}).[7] Part of the trick then is not to 'vitalize' matter, it is to 'free' it in an extended sense—to liberate matter from our usual frames of relevance and scales of resolution. Note, then, that these three concepts (degrees of freedom, frames of relevance, scales of resolution) go to the heart of not just realism, but also materialism.

Conversely, we humans might seem at first to be three-dimensional spatial beings. However, seen from another scale, we are constrained to the surface of a sphere (and hence two-dimensional beings), itself hurling around an ellipse (and hence one dimensional beings), itself stuck in a particular galaxy (and hence zero dimensional beings). The original cyborg imaginary (Clynes and Kline 1960) was ostensibly a liberatory politics of the human species, however icky and eerie. It had the goal of making 'the human capacity for imagination' as portable as possible. It asked and attempted to answer: How to overcome our physical constraints? How to free the human body to move through spaces in which it is otherwise unfit to move? (For 'space' is, in great measure, the sheer absence of affordances.) What media can we add to ourselves? What channels can we use to alter our sensations and instigations, to extend or buffer our inputs and outputs; such that our bodily functions remain autonomous and unconscious, such that our minds are alert and unburdened; so that we can once again be three-dimensionalings, but now on inter-stellar scales?[8]

In short, while any experience, event or entity may have many different possible degrees of freedom, different agents may highlight particular degrees of freedom (given their frame of relevance), and be more or less sensitive to different intensi-ties along the various dimensions (given their scale of resolution). Such frames and scales are not just a function of the features of objects. They are also a function of the interests of agents and, in particular, the sensory and instigatory, cognitive and communicative, and affective and aesthetic capacities and commitments of those agents. Such capacities and commitments can be individual-specific, as well as col-lectivity dependent, subject to transformations on a wide variety of timescales, with more or less historical inertia, social conflict, and 'goodness of fit' (however imag-ined and evinced). There is thus a history and culture, as much as a politics and unconscious, not to mention an ontology and cosmology, of particular frames of relevance and scales of resolution—and thus genealogies waiting to be written of their uptake and use, their standardization and rationalization, their imposition and naturalization, their pragmatics and poetics, their switches and shifts. Different media have their characteristic frames of relevance and scales of resolution, and thereby transform (as much as conform to) the frames and scales of those agents who utilize them. *Such ideas should be key terms in social and critical theory, and not just engineering and physics.*

In his famous account of media McLuhan (1996 [1964]) focused on scales of perception in relation to selfhood: "the personal and social consequences of any medium—that is, of any extension of ourselves—result from the new scale that is introduced into our affairs by each extension of ourselves, or by any new tech-nology" (7). As should now be clear, just as action is as important as perception, and transformations in society and world are as important as changes in selfhood, frames of relevance are as important as scales of resolution. (Not to mention the secrets of sense, as will be explored in the next section.) A key function of media, then, is not so much to extend (or amputate) ourselves, as to transform our frames of relevance and scales of resolution, and hence our experience of, and interactions with, one or more worlds.

Perhaps more importantly, however, a key feature of various media is to couple (conduct or coerce) systems that otherwise have (or have had) different degrees of freedom, different frames of relevance, or different scales of resolution, such that they may interact. And this process usually involves at least a double-coupling turning on the interaction of three or more such systems: not so much the mind to the world through the sign, or the buyer to the seller through the currency (though there is that), but also the hand to the hide through the knife; the army to the enemy through the drone; the host to the guest through the gift. The issue, then, is not different cultures or languages, and how to translate them (though, to be sure, there are many interesting things to say about that intersection with this schema, as we will see in the next section). The issue, rather, is different systems of any sort (from real people to virtual profiles, from hands to tools, from children to toys, from bodies to interfaces, from eyes to images, from the analog to the digital, from organisms to environments, from skateboarders to cities) and how to conduct, and obstruct, their coupling.

And so many interesting questions arise like: What's our experience of being coupled with a system that has greater or fewer degrees of freedom than ourselves, or larger or smaller scales of resolution, or different frames of relevance? How do agents experience and manage these few-to-many or many-to-few interactions, these gross-to-fine or fine-to-gross couplings, these subdued-to-intense or intense-to-subdued scalings, these well-suited or poorly-fitted framings? What novel affordances avail themselves? What erroneous assumptions, clumsy movements, or vertigous feelings, emerge? What possibilities for action, or imagining, are opened up or closed off? What new ways arise for being, or at least seeming to be, weird or eerie, aloof or intimate, creative or dull, detached or entangled, loud or quiet, scathing or subtle, precise or crude, deft or daft, agentive or inept, political or promiscuous? And, insofar as we become more (or less) capable, conscious, and in control, more or less flexible and powerful in our imagining and channeling of causality, what happens to our accountability?

While it is thereby tempting to say that most frames of relevance and scales of resolution are relatively artificial, that is too easy. In part, this is because they are quickly naturalized, or 'second-natured' by the agents who adopt them (however often, and predictably, they will be denatured when a new technology arises). In part, it is because the frame of relevance and scale of resolution of some particular system of representation or intervention may match, in crucial ways, the frame of relevance and scale of resolution of the world being represented or intervened in. (Such systems can be highly iconic and indexical, or 'motivated'.) In part, this is because such inherent or imposed dimensionalities often count as meters—a kind of built in constraint that one may creatively work with and around (and not simply be regimented by). Particular frames and scales may thereby foster creativity as much as constrain it. In part, it is because notions like 'objective' and 'subjective' or 'natural' and 'artificial' don't easily apply to such systems—they are not so much 'in between' such distinctions, as outside of the space in which such distinctions may usefully be drawn. In part, it is because there are arguably better and worse frames and scales; sometimes our projections are more than adequate to the worlds we wish to interact with; sometimes they are less than adequate. And so it is worth highlighting various kinds of *strain* that may arise: when my framing and scaling does not adequately match its frame and scale (for a given task); or when my framing and scaling is too distinct from your framing and scaling (for a given interaction). How does one experience this inadequacy? What evidence or symptoms arise (and who is sensitive to such symptoms) such that some frame of relevance, or degree of resolution, is 'out of touch' with some other, or 'out of sync' with some world?

There are also relatively natural frames of relevance and scales of resolution, some of which are quite celebrated. For example, for physicists a key frame of relevance is phase space (say, the position and momenta of all particles of interest). Recall our example of the gas. Only when one adopts this frame are physical problems formulated in a solvable way, such that the future states, or macroscopic properties, of such systems are made relatively predictable. Relatedly, a key scale of resolution is given by Planck's constant, which may be understood as a natural limit on our resolution of phase space. In particular, Heisenberg's famous uncertainty principle is a kind of economics of nature, the sacrifice inherent in systems: if you want a finer scale of resolution along one dimension (such as position, or energy), you have to give up the fineness of scale on another dimension (such as momentum, or time).

Finally, and looking ahead to the concerns of chapter 4, many of the foregoing issues can be quantified. Indeed that is often the essence what we do with 'information'. If you project a certain frame of relevance onto a system, such that it has a certain number of degrees of freedom, each with a certain scale of resolution, you can specify precisely how many states that system can show up in. And, following Shannon (1948) if you take the logarithm (base 2) of that number, you know how many bits it would require to store a representation of the state of that system (assuming each state is equally likely). This number tells you the number of questions you would have to ask to figure out what state the system is in (given its potential states). Inversely, it is the number of decisions you would have to make to put the system into a particular state. It is simultaneously a measure of your knowledge of the system and your power over the system. Or, more pessimistically, it is a measure of your ignorance and ineffectualness in regards to that system. It is, then, a measure of your (lack of) agency. Note, then, that while these three concepts (degrees of freedom, frames of relevance, scales of resolution) go far beyond the digital (to the real, the analog, the lively, the material, the body, the uncanny, the natural), the digital itself doesn't go far beyond these three concepts.

3.4. Sense and Sensibility

In this section we will be focused on systems that have identical degrees of freedom and scales of resolution, as well as quasi-identical frames of relevance. We want to see if systems that otherwise seem to be so perfectly overlapping nonetheless exhibit key discrepancies when they are 'coupled'. In particular, we want to get at the slippage and strain in such couplings—a slippage and strain which is very much the same as a 'secret'.

Suppose we want to represent the location of something in two dimensions, such as the position of a person in a city. And suppose we want to position that person to a precision of one square-meter in a relatively flat space. In effect, our frame of relevance and scale of resolution have been set. Nonetheless, there are still an infinity of mappings, of representational systems, that could do 'equivalent' jobs (insofar as they are more or less 'commensurate'). For example, even using simple Cartesian coordinates (the familiar x- and y-axes), different coordinate systems can be 'translated' relative to each other (and thereby have different origos). They can be rotated relative to each other (around the same origo, or around different origos). And they can even be moving along more or less complex trajectories relative to the other. One has to choose a particular *frame of reference*, which is not the same as a frame of relevance. As readers no doubt already know, the situation can get even trickier, such that one has to worry about issues like non-flat spaces (e.g., locating a ship at sea) and relativistic frames of reference (e.g., moving close to the speed of light, or near a massive object).

For present purposes, even a seemingly simple issue such as what constitutes the *origo* of a coordinate system is already interesting enough. This is because such a position constitutes the unmarked value, privileged point, or center—hence the implicit origin relative to which all other positions are organized. More generally, different frames of reference offer different *vantage points*. To offer just one example (Kockelman and Bernstein 2013), even though modern calendars and clocks can be used to reckon on any scale (and thus seem to instantiate the 'empty homogeneous time' long thought by critical theorists to be indicative of 'capitalist modernity'), they have privileged points (whens) and periods (how longs) built into them: not just the birth of Christ, Monday, and midnight, but also seconds, hours, and years. And so, while we are not beholden to such points and periods, they nonetheless have a hold on us—precisely because they so readily offer themselves up as unmarked handles to hold on to while reckoning time and space. In short, systems which have identical frames of relevance and degrees of resolution may nonetheless have different frames of reference, and thereby offer different vantage points and origos, which might be likened to implicit (unmarked, easily available, default, unconscious, or normative) affordances for orienting.

***

Such issues should be familiar enough to any anthropologist interested in maps, calendars, grammatical categories, and similar reckoning technologies. So we need not dwell on them here. We should rather focus on something much more insidious—what Sapir (1949 [1924]) called *secrets,* which are akin to differences in sense with sameness in reference. For example, two different coordinate systems (such as Cartesian coordinates, turning on an x position and a y position, and polar coordinates, turning on a radius *r*, and an angle *θ*) may be equivalent in regards to the 'world of positions' they can refer to. In particular, both can be used to designate any point in a two-dimensional plane, and can be therefore used to specify the state of such a system with identical frames of relevance and scales of resolution. In particular, any expression in one may be perfectly translated into the other (via equations like $x = r \cos \theta$ and $y = r \sin \theta$, for instance). Yet they are fundamentally different in regards to their underlying organization, or 'formal method of approach': Cartesian coordinates involve linear symmetry (and an inherent sympathy for lines); polar coordinates involve circular symmetry (and an inherent sympathy for circles). See Figure 3.3. Such differences have quite real effects: physicists often transform their problems from one coordinate system to the other because the symmetry of their problem matches the symmetry of the coordinate system, and so the problem may be much more easily understood or solved in one coordinate system rather than the other (and thus 'sympathized with').

While similar points can arguably be found in Frege, Saussure, and Boas, the general issues involved were articulated most forcibly by Sapir:

> To pass from one language to another is psychologically parallel to passing from one geometrical system of reference to another. The environing world

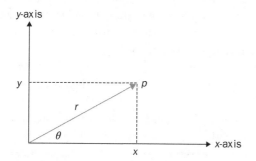

The same point *p* may be expressed in terms of either coordinate system:

$p = (x, y)$
$p = (r, \theta)$

Expressions in either system may be translated into the other:

$x = r \cos \theta$
$y = r \sin \theta$
$r = (x^2 + y^2)^{1/2}$
$\theta = \arctan y/x$

Geometric figures may be more or less simply and perspicaciously represented in either system, depending on the inherent symmetries of the figures in question:

$r = R$	*(circle in Polar coordinates)*
$y = mx + b$	*(line in Cartesian coordinates)*
$y = (R^2 - x^2)^{1/2}$	*(circle in Cartesian coordinates)*
$r = b/(\sin \theta - m \cos \theta)$	*(line in Polar coordinates)*

FIGURE 3.3 Comparison of Cartesian and Polar Coordinate Systems

which is referred to is the same for either language; the world of points is the same in either frame of reference. But *the formal method of approach* to the expressed item of experience, as to the given point of space, is so different that the resulting feeling of orientation can be the same neither in the two languages nor in the two frames of reference (1949 [1924], 153, italics added).

To paraphrase another passage from Sapir, while all languages are arguably 'formally complete' (in that they are more or less able to capture all that their speakers might like to say, and hence more or less able to refer to the same set of experiences if need, or desire, be), each has its own 'secret' (both a way of orienting to a referent and an associated feeling of orientation).[9] We might reframe all these insights as follows: while different systems may allow us to 'touch' (and 'move') the same worlds, the worlds so touched may nonetheless be 'felt' in distinctly different ways.

While Sapir was focused on natural languages, and used coordinate systems to understand them, we are interested in different 'systems' (in the expanded sense of this term, as developed in sections 3.2 and 3.3). We may nonetheless hypothesize that such claims not only hold for so-called natural languages (like Q'eqchi' and Japanese), but also for so-called artificial languages (like C and LISP); and not only for language-like entities, but also for semiotic systems and media technologies more generally (and thus anything involving mediation, from algorithms and epistemes to legal systems and logics, from mathematical notations and weapons to interface designs and architecture styles). Indeed, and quite crucially for what follows, we may hypothesize that such claims not only hold for 'codes' (or relations between signs and objects), they also hold for 'channels' (or relations between signers and interpreters).[10]

So let us return to the questions we asked in the introduction: what are the secrets of channels (as well as networks and infrastructure more generally), and what constitutes their poetics? Before answering these questions, let me note one small irony: while we are using ideas about codes to understand channels, something like a channel was originally used to understand codes. Frege, in particular, used a path metaphor when he distinguished between sense and referent: if the *referent* of an expression constitutes a kind of destination, the *sense* of an expression constitutes a kind of path that the expression takes to get to that destination (Frege 1960 [1892]; and see Dummet 1981, 96). And thus, even though expressions like *Hillary Clinton's husband* and *Chelsea Clinton's father* have the same referent, they have different senses. To get to the referent of either expression requires knowledge of a different kind of path: what's a husband versus what's a father, who is Hillary versus who is Chelsea.[11]

(Interestingly, especially in light of chapter 2, Frege also took up in this same essay all the productively puzzling categories that most interested Jakobson in his essay on duplex categories: reported speech, metalanguage, proper names, and shifters. And Frege is himself the foundational figure of the formal semantics of natural languages [Heim and Kratzner 1998], that account of linguistic meaning that is most like a computational algorithm, in that it foregrounds the mathematical sense of *function* as opposed to the pragmatic sense so dramatically highlighted by Jakobson, as we saw in the last chapter.)

Saussure made a distinction between significance and value that was similar to Frege's distinction between referent and sense, with the key issue being that value was mediated by an ensemble of relations between relations, or linguistic structure itself. And so even though two expressions (in different languages or in the same language) might point to the same place (qua referent or significance), to understand their sense or value, and hence to understand the route they took to get there, one had to understand the structure of the language being used—with all of its system-internal values—as mediated by relations of combination and selection (as was discussed in section 3.1). For example, even though Spanish *tú* and English *you* might often have the same referent or significance (for example, whomever you happen to be speaking to), they have very different senses, or values, in that *tú* contrasts with *usted* (and even with *vos* in some dialects of Spanish, not to mention plural forms like *ustedes* and *vosotros*), and may thus frame that addressee as a respected superior or an intimate friend, a drinking mate or a new acquaintance, a deity or a child, an individual or a group. Similarly, even though English *he* and Q'eqchi' *a'an* might often have the same referent (say, some topic one is speaking about), they have different senses in that in English *he* contrasts with *she*, *it*, and *they*, whereas in Q'eqchi' *a'an* can cover all four cases (recall part (b) of Figure 1.2). Seemingly equivalent forms project different ontological commitments in regards to animacy and number, gender and age, formality and intimacy. And these differences arise because of system-specific structural mediation.

In short, and somewhat ironically, Sapir, Saussure, and Frege converged on similar destinations (sense versus reference, value versus significance, formal completeness versus secret), even though the paths they took to get there were quite different. Crucially, such distinctions should hold, or at least be useful to consider, in the domain of channels (or signer-interpreter relations) as much as in the domain of codes (qua sign-object relations). See Figure 3.4. That is, while two travelers may

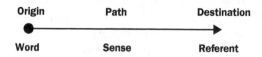

FIGURE 3.4 Sense versus Reference, Path versus Destination

arrive at the same destination, they might have taken different paths to get there. The organizational logic underlying the space of possible paths (as opposed to the set of possible destinations) in an environment, just like the overarching symmetries underlying the sense of a language (as opposed to its possible referents), are its 'secrets'.

This means that, when we translate—or, more importantly, *couple*—two systems, whether they turn on channels or codes, the issue is not simply to make sure that two expressions in different codes have the same referent, or that two channels in different networks have the same destination. Rather, assuming we don't just want to touch the same worlds, but also to feel them in the same ways, the issue is to understand the differential logics organizing the space of routes that each system takes to get to its referents and destinations. (Not to mention all the anti-logics that disorganize the space of routes, via processes like interception by enemies and interference through noise. For unruliness is as important as rules.) Like codes, different channels have different underlying symmetries, and so beget different sympathies (and antipathies). How then might we study such secrets?

3.5. Enemies and Insecurities

Before we turn to practical and aesthetic ways of making systems show their 'secrets', it is useful to review some of the stakes of secrets—as illuminated by such otherwise disparate thinkers as Hobbes, Shannon, Boas, and Schroedinger. Marx (1967 [1867]) famously introduced a treasure trove of secrets: the secret of commodity fetishism, the secret of profitmaking, the secret of primitive accumulation, and so forth. And critical theorists have had a field day ever since. For present purposes, what matters is that so many of these secrets turned on path metaphors, and thus the hiddenness of sense. This is arguably due to Marx's dependence on Hobbes, whose definition of the fetish turned on causality and propinquity: "Ignorance of remote causes disposeth men to attribute all events to the causes immediate and instrumental; for these are all the causes they perceive" (1994 [1668], 61–62; Kockelman 2015). That is, the fetish in this framing is the misconstrual of causality due to the limits of perception. In particular, a key issue in Marx's uptake of Hobbes is that, while effects, or precipitates, are open to experience, the distal causes (that lead to those effects), or the complicated processes (that give rise to those precipitates), are outside of one's experience—confined as they are, relatively speaking, to domains that are usually outside of one's ken: the factory (as opposed to the market), infrastructure (as opposed to ideology), the past (as opposed to the present), and so forth.

Understood another way, insofar as one does not have an adequate ground (in the sense of a causal understanding of the world, itself acquired through relatively direct experience of such causes), one cannot figure an effect as evidence for a cause, or frame a precipitate as the symptom of a process; and so one tends to posit forces and project connections that are not really there, or not really there in that particular way. In the idiom introduced above, insofar as one doesn't have access to, or knowledge of, certain paths (qua causal channels), one cannot correctly retrodict the probable origins of particular destinations, or predict the likely destinations of particular origins. (We will return to these issues when we theorize interpretive grounds in chapter 5.)

In this regard, the etymology of the German word for 'secret' (*das Geheimnis*) is very well-known and quite relevant, as it turns on the same root as *heimlich* (secretly), *heimelig* (cosy), *heimish* (homey), and *das Heimat* (home, homeland). Something is *unheimlich* (uncanny, eerie) if it used to be enclosed (kept private by being hidden behind the walls of a house, so to speak), but is no longer. Secrets, in this sense, are related to secretions—something should have stayed down inside, but bubbled up through the cracks. Recall our discussion of circles in chapter 1. Secrets, in such a framing, are not simply that which is enclosed insofar as it is closed off from experience—one knows the destination, but doesn't know the origin or path. They are also that which threatens to be disclosed—in particular, threatens to take unintended or insecure paths, to secrete through the surface, often through some kind of rechanneling or recoding that enables them to slip past a censor or constraint, such that they may elude such enemies and parasites, such that they can come within one's 'ken'.[12]

As we saw in chapter 2, Shannon understood information systems to be essentially secrecy systems: not only must a message get to an addressee without being garbled by noise; it must also get there without being intercepted by an enemy. It must get to the right person (without interruption), and it must not get to the wrong person (through interception). And if either condition is violated it is not a secret— for it is either *not* shared with the right person, or it *is* shared with the wrong person.[13] Phrased another way, for something to be disclosed (properly speaking) it must first be enclosed—and the enclosure must be such that the right addressee can open it at the destination, but the wrong addressee cannot open it along the way. It requires a mode of enclosure that permits it to move along certain paths, and be opened by certain addressees; and, simultaneously, a mode of enclosure that prohibits it from moving along other paths, or being opened by other addressees. In short, the task of a channel is to protect secrets from interception (*enemy*, wrong addressee gets them) and interference (*noise*, right addressee doesn't get them).[14] And so the notion of a code, like the notion of channel, will always have a double-valence: something which permits communication with one group of people (a language), and prohibits communication with another group of people (a cipher). In some sense, the parasitic function was meant to include both kinds of entities, and hence both kinds of interruptions. But nonetheless, enemies—and the secrets they strive to intercept—deserve an extended discussion, especially in regards to conventional understandings of the stakes.

Many understandings of 'culture', as well as many characterizations of 'life', make reference to the notion of patterns, and their potential to be disrupted.

Bateson (1972 [1954]) is probably the key figure in this regard. In some sense, to be alive is to constitute a figure that is distinguishable from a ground. On the one hand, we have the Boasians themselves, with their particular attention to 'patterns of culture' (themselves threatened by a globalized, capitalist homogeneity). On the other hand, we have biologists who focus on life as a kind of pattern (one which persists in the face of another enemy, the second law of thermodynamics). Schroedinger's (1944) thoughts on life are critical, and critiquable, here. That is, both forms of life (qua cultures, or shared ways of being) and life forms (qua living organisms, or particular species) exhibit distinctive patterns. And both kinds of life have enemies: that which threatens to disrupt their patterns, if not extinguish them altogether, such that their unique signals become indistinguishable from noise, such that what was once 'figure' comes to equilibrium with the 'ground'.

We will return to this issue in chapter 5 when we discuss archeology in relation to entropy and materiality. For the moment, it is enough to realize that many accounts of enemies focus on the existential nature of their threat (they are aimed at extinguishing our patterning, qua life form), or on the cultural nature of their threat (they are aimed at disrupting our patterning, qua form of life). And channels are precisely that which, by relaying one party's message to another, create patterns in the most simplistic sense: insofar as two parties have effectively communicated, what was 'over here' (some sign-object correlation on the side of the sender) now correlates with what is 'over there' (some interpretant-object correlation on the side of the receiver). Enemies (parasites and noise), then, intercept messages and interfere with messages, both so that one's communication goes to the wrong addressee and so that it doesn't go to the right addressee; such that a pattern is propagated in the wrong place and a pattern fails to propagate in the right place; and such that one overall pattern is extinguished (be it cultural or biological) while another is extended. Such agents disrupt, or displace, the communicative patterning that allows for a unique cultural or biological patterning. In short, if one sense of infrastructure is that which uses our common values as a means in order to create our common values as an end (recall the conclusion of chapter 2), one sense of an enemy is that which doesn't have values in common with us, and threatens to disrupt our commonality with each other.

All that is not to be melodramatic, paranoid, or Hobbesian; it is simply to underline two widespread rationales for why so many people will go to such great lengths to keep a secret. Of course there are other kinds of secrets, and other kinds of parasites and enemies, that may not seem so forbidding, but nonetheless—by themselves, and certainly in the aggregate—constitute good reasons for securing secrets: our love letters and diaries, our browsing and buying habits, our friendly interactions and financial transactions. And, to be sure, most will argue that simply being able to have privacy in the most conventional sense is key feature of a certain highly valuably form of governance, if not an essential characteristic of freedom in the abstract. And so the key enemy is easy enough to indicate: it is often 'us' instead of 'them', in the sense of one's very own government, internet service provider, or social network application. Facebook, Google, and the NSA, not to mention Capital and the USA, often relate to your relations much more insistently than any other perceived 'enemy'. The stakes of secure secrets, whatever the scope of their significance, or the insidiousness of their agents, are thus simple enough to state (however easy they are to mistake).

3.6. The Poetics of Channels, The Secrets of Infrastructure

We made a series of moves in section 3.1. Just as codes link signs and objects, channels link signers and interpreters. Just as the value of any sign-object relation (code) is mediated by its relation to other sign-object relations via processes of combination and substitution, the value of any signer-interpreter relation (channel) is mediated by its relation to other signer-interpreter relations via similar processes. Just as the structure of codes can be framed in terms of necessity or possibility, so may the structure of channels: we can frame structures as ensembles of conventions (qua social facts that regiment individual behavior), or as finite means with infinite ends (a small number of constraints that leads to a large number of configurations). And just as any instance of *parole* (qua discourse practice) may undermine, as much as instantiate, *langue* (qua grammatical structure), any actual configuration of channels may undermine, as much as instantiate, the constraints (rules, norms, protocols) that underlie and generate it.

In section 3.4, we saw that both codes and channels, or 'languages' and 'networks', could be understood in terms of a path metaphor: just as many paths can lead to the same destination, many codes can refer to the same object, and many channels can relate to the same interpreter. We saw that one important way to understand the 'secret' of a channel or code is in terms of the underlying sense, or path, that governs its movements, that organizes its modes of reference and relation. And we saw that this path is not only linked to issues like structure and practice (in an expanded sense, as reviewed above), but also to sensibility and symmetry and sympathy. So now the question is this: How do we reveal this underlying organizational structure through actual events, through concrete practices, through particular configurations? Phrased another way: How might there be a poetry of channels, just as there is a poetry of codes? And how might such forms of poetry be ways of disclosing, or making intuitively known, the secrets of channels and codes?

Crucially, such secrets are inherently Sapirian (or Fregean, or Saussurian), having to do with the underlying structure of a network or language (as per section 3.4); they complement, but should not be confused with, the more stereotypic kinds of secrets that codes and channels help us to keep (as was the focus of section 3.5).

Such questions, and the conundrums they generate, can be framed in a slightly different way. In another tradition, Wittgenstein (1958 [1953]) famously remarked that a portrait has something in common with a person, but this [commonality] one cannot paint. We might say, rather, that a system of signs has an underlying sense, such as the organizational logic of its structure (e.g., circular symmetry); and it is only through such sense that such signs may touch a world of objects (e.g., points in the plane); but this sense is, perhaps paradoxically, not part of the world so touched (Kockelman 1999). That is to say, even though sense organizes our approach toward, and thus our sympathies for, possible objects, it is not itself a possible object. Interestingly, followers of Deleuze often characterize the 'virtual' in ways that are similar to sense: that which cannot be actual, and yet is nonetheless real insofar as it organizes the range of what is actually possible.

We will return to the virtual in chapter 5. For present purposes, the key question is this: How to make a system show its sense (even if it cannot state its sense)? To try to answer this question, let us first review and expand Jakobson's classic claims regarding the poetic function of language. Jakobson (1990a) initially defined the poetic function as a focus on the message and, in particular, a focus on the sensual qualities of the signs that make up the message. (Recall our initial discussion of his categories in section 2.2.). In other words, whereas the referential function highlights the referent (object, or signified), the poetic function highlights the words (signs, or signifiers). Very loosely speaking, that which is usually just a window on the referent is itself brought into view. More carefully, and with a nod to the parasitic function introduced in chapter 2, that which is usually just a path becomes a destination.[15]

In an aesthetic tradition that goes back thousands of years, Jakobson argued that this focusing is primarily done through the repetition of tokens of common types—a kind of generalized poetic meter. He framed this repetitive process in terms of the two properties of linguistic structure that were reviewed above: combination and selection. In particular, the poetic function could be understood as "the projection of the axis of selection onto the axis of combination," such that possible selections (e.g., alternative members of a paradigm, form class, or category) are made to show up in actual combinations (e.g., as parts of the same construction, utterance, or text). For example, *veni, vidi, vici* (same person-number-tense and initial consonant); *today, tomorrow, Toyota* (alliteration and temporal adverbs); *The winter evening settles down/With smell of steaks in passageways* (iambic feet and tetrametric lines); and so forth. Such texts draw attention to the underlying structure (and practice) of language: its syntactic rules, its semantic features, its phonological patterns, its grammatical categories, its discourse genres, its interpretive grounds, its pragmatic functions. They make such properties sensually present and perchance affectively palpable, if not cognitively perspicacious.

In short, if the metalinguistic function explicitly states the structure, or underlying sense, of a code, the poetic function implicitly shows it. And while both functions use practice (*parole*, event) to get at structure (*langue*, grammar), poetry does this in real-time and text-internally, through the succession and unfolding of signs, whereas metalanguage—at least stereotypically—does this text-externally, with one or more complicated signs (a dictionary, a definition, a grammatical treatise, a gloss). Loosely speaking, the former functions as a kind of transcendent reflectivity; whereas the latter functions as a kind of immanent reflexivity. This means that poetry ends up doing far more than focusing our attention on the sensual properties of signs per se (though it still does that). It brings into view, through a kind of situated intuition, *the underlying organization of the sense-making system itself,* as an ensemble of values mediated by relations between relations.[16]

So what would a poetry of channels look like? In particular, how to trace out the sense underlying an ensemble of channels, themselves constitutive of the sensory and instigatory capacities of signers and interpreters, through something like poetic meter—that repetition of tokens of a common type, that projection of the axes of selection onto the axes of combination?

There are at least two perspective one might take on this question, depending on the system at issue. On the one hand, we might suppose there is already something like a network out there (some ensemble of nodes and relations, some particular train track or highway system, some particular economic or communicative infrastructure), and we are interested in learning the various 'routes' one might take through it. On the other hand, we might suppose we have a relatively finite number of constraints (for example, types of train tracks, and ways they may be connected; or kinds of electronic components, and ways they may be assembled), and we are interested in understanding the relatively large number of configurations that could be built from them. In both cases, ultimately, we get at something like the 'secret' or 'potentiality' of a system. But in the first case we are focused on potential paths through a configuration that is already in place. And in the second case we are focused on possible configurations that may be assembled through a given set of constraints.

We will have a lot to say about the relation between finite constraints and infinite configurations in chapter 5, when we take up virtuality at length and, in particular, when we discuss strategies for intuiting and tapping the potentiality of such generative systems. For the moment, then, we will focus on the first kind of issue, and hence on the being of a network (and being-within-a-network), as opposed to its becoming.

Suppose we have some kind of network (e.g., an ensemble of interconnected paths) and are interested in learning its secrets. If poetry turns on the repetition of tokens of a common type, then iteratively taking alternative routes through such a network is the simplest way of foregrounding its sense-making capacities. We might, for example, successively explore the possible paths that link an origin and a destination, the possible destinations that follow from the same origin, or the possible origins that lead to the same destination.[17] In this way, we iteratively explore the space of combination and selection. Every such iteration thereby implicitly compares and contrasts possible paths within that space, making the traveler reflexively aware, however partially, of the relative affordances of those paths.[18]

For example, what are different paths better or worse at doing—if only by degrees, and along certain dimensions? Is one such channel faster or slower, more or less secure, more or less costly. Is one mode of infrastructure, or route through a particular infrastructure, more or less arduous (clean, steep, safe, colorful, peaceful, predictable, well-mapped, maintained, scenic, and so forth). Is one path more or less subject to trolls and tolls, enemies and parasites, brigands and tourists, pot holes and billboards?[19]

One can walk the streets of a city (or the paths through a forest) in such a way; or experience a subway system (or a solar system) in such a way; or move through a website (or a virtual world) in such a way; or move through a neural network (or a social network) in such a way. Indeed, even in the most flatfooted sense, just as there are different symmetries underlying different coordinate systems (linear versus circular, say), so too are there different symmetries underlying networks. For example, modern network analysis offers a range of possible structures: bus, star, ring, mesh, tree, and far beyond. And each option has different technical characteristics: its relative reliability, efficiency, secrecy, transparency, and so forth. And just as there are metalanguages for representing such geometries (diagrams, mathematical analysis, graph theory, etc.), there are poetic ways of residing in such geometries (sensing and instigating through them, communicating and communing by means of them). To be sure, as intimated by Hobbes, for most of us this infrastructure remains out of view for much of the time. Nonetheless, at certain moments, through certain movements, we can feel the contours of the channels we use to touch.

To return to some of the concerns of section 3.5, economies are spatial and temporal as much as personal and transactional—the Kula ring being a classic example (Malinowski 1922; Munn 1992). Even substantivist economics (Polanyi 1957; Sahlins 1972), building on Aristotle's classic account of different modes of justice (2001a), gave us three overarching geometries, each with different symmetries and sensibilities: redistribution (tribute economies, taxes); reciprocation (from commodity to gift); and autarchy (the relatively self-sufficient household, or domestic mode of production). For any such economy, with its underlying geometry, one can ask similar kinds of questions: given any particular good (qua origin), what are all the other goods it can get to (qua destinations), and via what kinds of transactions and with what kinds of actors (qua paths)? What can it be exchanged for, and what can it be produced or consumed with? Indeed Marx's revealing of secrets was, in part, precisely a careful figuring of the path taken by commodities—'historically' (primitive accumulation, historical materialism) as much as 'biographically' (the fetish, surplus value). And, apropos of Marx, to reveal the secret of a code or channel, an infrastructure or institution, is in part to show the origins, limits, and iniquities of value.

To be sure, Marx focused on economic value, as opposed to linguistic value (in the sense of Saussure); and neither of these is equivalent to the kinds of values we have been elucidating here. Nonetheless, all such values are amenable to metalanguage (or transcendent modes of stating and explaining their forms and functions, their properties and processes) and poetry (or immanent modes of showing and intuiting their inherent values, and the symmetries underlying their sense). And so similar kinds of issues arise, however askance: how to disclose such paths such that the origins (limits and iniquities) of value, as well as the systematic misrecognition of those origins, are no longer secret? How to make the (infra)structural logic of sense sensible?

In some sense (!), the goal is to highlight the underlying potentia of the constraints through the unfolding patterning of the configurations; to sense underlying grounds, and their potential to shift, through the shimmering of alternating figures.

To conclude, it is worth highlighting some of the stakes of the foregoing claims. If, returning to Jakobson, the poetic function of code focuses attention on the "sensual properties of signs," we might say that the poetic function of channels focuses attention on the "sensory (and instigatory) properties of signers (and interpreters)." That is, it highlights their capacities to sense and instigate, and thus the media through which they sense and instigate (as well as the media through which they think and feel, communicate and cogitate). It draws attention to the qualities (entities and events) that can count as signs and interpretants to such semiotic agents; and hence it foregrounds the possible signs and possible interpretants of different collectivities of semiotic agents, as well as their possible objects and possible interests.[20] For example, what could be distinguishable and decisive to them, and thus what could fall within (or outside) their frames of relevance and scales of resolution, what counts as a presupposed origin or a problematic coupling. And insofar as all this is also a way of tracing out whom one can communicate with (in addition to tracing out what one can communicate), it has ramifications for who counts as a member of a collectivity (an audience, a public, a network, a community), and what counts as a collective value for members of such a *phatic commons* (including the very infrastructure of sense itself). It thereby figures some of the most important grounds of politics.

3.7. Residence without Representation

In chapter 2 we invoked a metaphor that was introduced by Heidegger (1971 [1954]): the bridge that gathers the banks of a river around it. And we noted that representations—a key object of critique for Heidegger—were the prototypic bridge, in that they seem to bring together what otherwise seems ontologically unbridgeable: mind and world, experience and event, subject and object. For this reason, it is useful to reframe channels, institutions, and infrastructure in terms of 'references' (*die Verweisungen*), which were Heidegger's (1996 [1927]) way of displacing the centrality of representations. As will be seen, this is a way of getting at a kind of 'sense' and 'reference' that is very different from Frege's (1960 [1892]) famous distinction between *Sinn* and *Bedeutung*.

To understand references, as the relations things have to each other by virtue of being caught up in practical concerns, we may focus on instruments. An instrument 'refers' to the actions it may be used to undertake. For example, a doorbell *makes reference to* the action of ringing it. An instrument refers to the other instruments (and roles) that complement it. For example, a doorbell makes reference to houses and doors, visitors and occupants, fingers and ears. And an instrument refers to the work it will realize, or result in—itself often another instrument. For example, doorbells makes reference to visitors that may arrive, as well as to packages that may be delivered, or bad news that may be conveyed. Such works, in turn, refer to whoever will make use of them, or be involved in them, as actors. For example, inside a package may be a basketball, which makes reference to the person it is a purchase of, or a gift for; as well as to the actions such a person may ultimately use the ball for (dribbling and shooting, not to mention selling or losing); as well as to all the other instruments the ball is used in conjunction with (hoops and backboards, gymnasiums and schoolyards). And this work, like the initial doorbell, and every other instrument out there, also makes reference to whatever materials it incorporates, and whatever actors and instruments helped create it (and, in turn, to their references). For example, the basketball makes reference to rubber and paint, chemicals and dyes, factories and workers, even machines and money.[21]

In short, when Heidegger says one entity or event 'refers to' another, he means that it only 'makes sense' in relation to the other (where the 'entities' and 'events' in question can be affordances as much as actions, identities as much as instruments). And so, as shown in this example, one entity can only be given a coherent interpretation (in regards to its salient form or function, its use or placement, its repercussions or conditions, its meaning or significance) in the context of the other entities that it incorporates, complements, or creates in some collective world—given the organization, activities, and values of that world's inhabitants. References, then, are essential for understanding residence in the world, a mode of being that, for Heidegger, is the key infrastructure underlying our representations of the world (Kockelman 2013a, 2015).[22]

It must emphasized, then, that Heidegger does *not* mean through the referential function of language, in Jakobson's (1991a) sense. Rather, references were much more closely aligned with the phrase 'in reference to', as it was used by Jakobson (1991b) in his discussion of duplex categories. Recall our distinction, in chapter 2, between the slash (/) and the double slash (//) insofar as categories like M/M and C//C were sensitive to it. This is where, in the domain of linguistic representations proper, reference in Heidegger's sense (*Verweisung*) undergirds reference in Frege's sense (*Bedeutung*).

References, then, constitute the grounds from which we figure (through more stereotypic representational processes, such as speech acts and mental states). And yet they are themselves difficult to figure, or all too easy to disfigure, insofar as they usually come to the fore only in the midst of disturbances of reference (the package does not arrive, or is stolen; the doorbell fails to ring, or produces a ghastly buzz; the basketball is punctured or lost), and only in ways that obscure the original texture of connections.

However, as we saw in chapter 2, in contrast to thinkers like Serres and Marx, and theorists of infrastructure like Susan Leigh Star, failure does not actually illuminate what is usually obscured. According to Heidegger, the 'true' or 'real' nature of infrastructure and institutions doesn't really come into view when they break down. This is because we usually switch to representational understandings of the world in the context of such disturbances of reference; and so we fail to see the more originary ways of residing in the world that were in place before the disturbance. This is not to say that we don't 'see', or 'refer to', a piece of equipment when it breaks down. We certainly do: "look, the basketball has gone flat; it must have a hole in it; did it land on a nail?" Indeed we may see it, and state it, in stereotypic ways—such that it shows up as a material substance with various qualities, in the light of representations that may be true or false. It is, rather, that we no longer 'grasp it' through a more originary, 'referential' understanding—as an entity and event with multiple references, and dense referentiality, as 'shown' through our dribbling and shooting practices.

We may now move way past Heidegger, for what constitutes a reference should depend on the scale and frame of concern. References do not just organize the way a hammer relates to a nail and desk, as a kind of sense-making; they also organize the way a heart relates to ventricles and an aorta, a server relates to a webpage and a client, a bit-string relates to an algorithmic process and a data structure, a virus relates to a host and a cure, an equation relates to a derivative and a desire, a sentence relates to a word and a genre, a sign relates to an object and an interpretant, a disaster relates to a weather anomaly and a form of infrastructure, a facial expression relates to situation and an audience, and *the way each of these relates to the others*. Such connections do not just 'make sense' against the ground of some historically specific assemblage of human concerns (technological function, cultural values, social role, shared purposes, embodied habits, and so forth); they may also make sense against the ground of natural selection, biological function, underlying program, mode of governance, aesthetic canon, legal system, or unconscious drive. Wherever there is a telos, however nomic or gnomic, Darwinian or (Samuel) Butlerian, or a causal imaginary, however normative or unbeknown, Aristotelean or Humean, there are references. Whenever we must 'make reference' to one thing, however tacitly or implicitly, in order to understand, wield, or imagine another, we are in the domain of references. References thereby organize the inner workings of 'people' and 'things' (a body, an engine, a mind) as much as the relations between 'people' and 'things' (a context, a network, an ecosystem). Phrased another way, references scale: not just 'upwards' to being-a-component-in-the-net, but also 'downwards' to being-composed-of-neurons.

Heidegger borrowed his relatively specialized term (*die Verweisungen*) from the German word for reference which has, as one of its primary meanings, citation. For example, the way one work cites a prior work and may be cited by a subsequent work.[23] Such citations also hold for epistemic claims more generally: the way one truth claim is justified by prior truth claims (and experiences), and may be used to justify subsequent truth claims (and actions). We have seen the quantification of this principle organize our entire field of information in the most stereotypic sense. For example, one of Google's key criteria for ranking webpages, for assigning them value, is back links. As Google puts it, "a link from page A to page B [is interpreted] as a vote, by page A, for page B." From such a standpoint, however unseemly or scary, the essence, or at least importance, of any thing—as a kind of living being— is its roots and fruits: what refers to it and, in turn, what it refers to. Never have a society's values been so seemingly portable; never have they been so deeply rooted; never have they been so easily 'defruited'.

Perhaps most tellingly is a second meaning of this German word: to exile, to outcast, to throw off the field. To refer, in some sense, is to banish to the far banks by drawing up a bridge. Indeed, a key sense of banishment is captured by another German word, used by both Nietzsche and Marx: *Vogelfrei*, or 'free as a bird'. To be free as a bird was a bittersweet sort of freedom: while one can do what one wants (for one is not under the compulsion of a state), one can be killed without ramification (for one is not under the care of a state). To return to the concerns of chapter 1, Marx used this expression to characterize the mass of men kicked off of communal property through the enclosure movement: they were free from their old masters (no longer related as serf to lord), but also 'freed' of every possession except their labor power (and so related as proletariat to capitalist). Strangely, Agamben (1998) 'cites' neither Nietzsche nor Marx in his influential account of *homo sacer*; moreover, he does not cite *citation* itself.[24]

Recall that one early sense of enclosure was the ancient city, as characterized by Fustel de Coulanges: a wall, metaphorical as much as physical, that surrounds a group that is (thereby) constituted by a commons: a shared language, collective laws, standardized weights and measures, recognized conventions and currencies, culture, or common ground per se. Banishment, for both Nietzsche and Marx, was to be kicked out of such an enclosure, made to leave the comforts of the city walls, and so forced away from such a (semiotic or phatic) commons—itself just as easily framed as an external imposition as a shared resource. To cross the drawbridge, *to or fro*, and then have the bridge drawn, the references severed.

4

Meaning, Information, and Enclosure

4.1. From Tracing to Effacing

Speaking in a very provisional way, to say that one event provides information about another event is to say that the two events are correlated. That is, by knowing something about one event, one may learn something about another event.[1] The conditions of possibility for the correlation may be widely varied. For example, the two events may be correlated as cause and effect via something like 'natural processes' (e.g., fire and smoke); or they may be correlated as circumstance and behavior via something like 'cultural practices' (e.g., state of affairs and assertion); or they may be correlated through a longer chain that involves both natural processes and cultural practices (e.g., my assertion that the enemy is or is not coming is relayed by the intentional presence or absence of a smoke signal). In any case, if an interpreting agent is aware of the correlation, then the two events can relate to each other as sign and object—that is, the agent can use one to learn something about the other.[2]

Crucially, the effects (qua signs) of any cause (qua object) may be relatively localized as to their timing (when they occur), position (where they occur), and impact (what they do when and where they occur, such that they might have an effect on other entities and events). For example, a stone falling in water leaves a trace in ripples propagating across the water's surface; in sounds propagating through the air; and so forth. Such traces are not universally sensible: not only must an interpreting agent be well positioned in space-time, but its faculties of sensation must be amenable to the impact. That is, for one event to be a sign of another event to an interpreting agent requires that the first event be sensible to the agent given not only its placement in space and time, but also its capacity to sense per se. To be aware of the first event, then, an interpreting agent must not only be aware of the correlation between the first and the second events, it must also be aware of the second event. We may thereby amend Bateson (1972): a trace (or sign) is a difference

Paul Kockelman. *The Art of Interpretation in the Age of Computation.* © Oxford University Press 2017

that makes a difference (to an interpreting organism) because it is taken to correlate with a difference (in a significant environment).

A key function of media, as stereotypically understood, is to enclose such traces (storing them, transmitting them, or processing them) such that they may be disclosed at another time, in another place, with another impact. In this sense, then, media constitute traces of traces: the original event (qua cause) gives rise to the second event (qua effect, or primary trace), and this second event (qua cause) gives rise to a third event (qua effect, or secondary trace). The crucial issue is this: while both the secondary and primary trace correlate with the initial event (and thus provide information about it), the secondary trace may be better positioned in time, space, and impact from the standpoint of an interpreting agent; see Figure 4.1. For example, writing constitutes a secondary trace of speech (which itself is a primary trace of thought, or so some people like to think); and, in comparison to speech, writing may be better stored in time and transported across space (as well as be better sensed by certain kinds of interpreting agents—for example, those who can see but not hear).

The relation between the secondary trace and the primary trace may be as simple or as complicated as the relation between the primary trace and the original event. And it may involve a relatively long or short, complex or simple, intertwining of normative practices and material processes. For example, to create a written trace of a spoken word involves an entire circuit, chain of operations, or mode of (re)production: someone has to hear the word, interpret it as a string of phonemes, translate these phonemes into letters, write these letters onto paper using a pen with ink, and so forth. Broadly speaking, there need to be people with the appropriate habits and tools, or techniques and technologies; and there need to be things with the appropriate causes and effects, or inputs and outputs. Moreover, there need to be institutions that reproduce such people (and such things), as well as workshops and factories that produce such things (and such people). And there needs to be an infrastructure (however artificial or natural, embodied or embedded) that can carry such traces. And so on, and so forth. From this perspective, which we are not necessarily endorsing, media might be initially understood as everything that mediates between a secondary trace and a primary trace, thereby transforming scales of significance (where, when, with what impact, what-have-you). When McLuhan

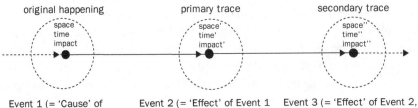

FIGURE 4.1 Media as Enclosing and Disclosing Traces

([1964] 1996) says that the medium is the message, we might understand this to mean that the importance of a medium is not the information it provides about the original event it is correlated with, but rather the ramifications that enclosing and disclosing traces has on such an ensemble of social relations, cognitive processes, affective modalities, moral compulsions, and material practices—and hence the way it affects a collectivity's institutions, imaginaries, interactions, and infrastructures (and vice-versa).

A key consequence of media, however, is not simply to link causes and effects, relate circumstances and behaviors, or connect causal processes and cultural practices; nor is it simply to mediate between primary traces and secondary traces, or secondary traces and tertiary traces (and so on, for the issues embed and enchain indefinitely). It is, rather, to constitute such distinctions for the collectivity that uses such media—to condition, stabilize, or transform what counts as a primary or secondary trace, what is understood to be a causal process versus a cultural practice, where to draw a line between cause and effect or a circumstance and behavior (and so forth). (Recall our discussion of the bridge, which enables a correlation between the activities on its banks, and which delimits a landscape as much as facilitates a passage and forestalls a loss.) Media do not just foreground and assist correlations, they also create and project, as well as alter and resist, correlations (and the correlata so correlated).

Crucially, we have been focusing on media from the standpoint of the interpreting agent, or sensation per se. This is a common bias among media theorists, stretching from Bergson (1988) to Stiegler (1998); and it is closely related to the fact that media are often understood retentively (with a focus on memories and perception) as opposed to protentively (with a focus on intentions and actions). We should also focus on media from the standpoint of the signifying agent, or instigation per se. In particular, just as one may sense events that are the effects of distal causes, one may instigate events that are the causes of distal effects. Media, in this extended sense, may be understood as everything that mediates between relatively primary and secondary traces—whether these traces are flowing into an agent's sensory faculties or flowing out of an agent's instigatory faculties. In the first case, then, we have media like telescopes and microscopes and diaries; in the second case, we have media like pulleys and tweezers and diagrams. Indeed, as Gibson (1986) so carefully showed, in acting and instigating with any tool, including that tool of tools, the body and its parts, one perceives and feels. Moreover, it is not just the case that, in acting, one perceives and feels; in many cases, one must act or instigate in order to perceive and feel.

Finally, it should be stressed that we have so far been focused on media which store, transmit, or process traces. This is truly a widespread, and erroneous, way of understanding media. At the very least, we should also focus on media that destroy, prohibit, or degrade traces. Sunglasses, for example, stop certain wavelengths (intensities and polarities) from entering one's eyes. Boxing gloves cushion the blows of fists. Bumpers cushion the blows of cars and curbs. Soft-soled shoes, and camouflaged clothing, minimize the tracks one leaves in an environment. A jetty may be used to redirect the wake of a passing ship. A white noise machine may be used to mask the sound of traffic. A foreign language may be used to hide the meaning of a message. Erasers remove the trace of previous equations on a blackboard. Sieves and filters and borders stop and capture as much as transmit and sort. Just as we may want to minimize the impact of events on our sensations, we may want to minimize the impact of our instigations on events. And, more generally, we may want to disrupt another's ability to communicate or cogitate, to feel or intuit, to sense or move. Finally, as per the concerns of the last two chapters, we may want to interfere with or intercept the traces that others sense and instigate—for parasites employ media as much as hosts, enemies as much as friends, censors as much as senders. In any case, by destroying, prohibiting, or degrading traces, we destroy, prohibit, or degrade correlations—and hence the channels that propagate information, the codes that represent meaning, and the constraints that generate patterning. Media function to efface as much as trace (Kockelman 2011a).[3]

***

At the most general level, this chapter explores the idea that *information is the enclosure of meaning*. That is, information is a species of meaning, and hence just a small piece of a much larger, and much less well-understood domain, that has been radically regimented as to its 'use-value' (the functions it may serve, the utilities it consists of, the quantities and units it comes in); its 'truth-value' (the ways it is imagined, understood, and known through scientific principles, engineering practices, and user habits); and its 'exchange-value' (not just its price, but also the ways its costs and benefits, its transactions and translations, are rendered and calculated more generally). Phrased another way, information is a species of meaning that has been deeply transformed by particular modalities of science, technology, and economy (as per the conclusion of chapter 2), such that the values in question seem to have become radically portable: not so much independent of context, as dependent on contexts which have been engineered so as to be relatively ubiquitous, and hence ostensibly and erroneously 'context-free'; not so much able to accommodate all contents, as able to assimilate all contents to its contours, and hence ostensibly and erroneously 'open content'. Such is the nature of our *universal media machines* (a claim that will be vastly extended and massively critiqued in chapter 6).

Such a relatively abstract idea is necessarily grounded in many concrete details. And so, in drawing out the ramifications of such claims, several alternative approaches for understanding information will be carefully reviewed and reworked.

Section 4.2 reviews the ideas of Donald MacKay, in relation to those of Claude Shannon, foregrounding the relation between three relatively technical and quantitative kinds of information-content: selectional (Shannon's original definition, which turns on the relative improbability of a message given an ensemble of messages); structural (which turns on the frame of relevance that is used to construct a mapping between messages and referents); and metrical (which turns on the scale of resolution such a mapping is capable of capturing). It also discusses the relation between information per se and 'meaning', as this term was understood by MacKay: the effect a message has on an interpreting agent.

Section 4.3 contrasts structural and metrical information with frames of relevance and scales of resolution, as they were defined and developed in chapter 3. It also highlights the relation between Shannon's quantification of information and Marx's understanding of modes of production, Whorf's understanding of ontological projection, and McLuhan's account of media in relation to scale. In some sense, it explores the relation between the 'surprise value' of a message, and its use-value, exchange value, deontic value, epistemic value, and semantic value.

Section 4.4 further develops Peirce's notion of the interpretant, showing its relation to MacKay's understanding of 'meaning'. As will be seen, much of what (post-) humanist scholars and critical theorists want from a theory of meaning (in relation to information), and a theory of interpretation (in relation to embodiment and affect), may be found in Peirce's work (and much more besides).[4]

Section 4.5 carefully develops two other ways of understanding information that are particularly important for understanding the relation between information as it is localized in an utterance (topic, focus, reason) and information as it is shared by a collectivity (denotation, connotation, information). In this way, it offers two ways of framing information that are relatively interaction-centered and institution-based. Such frames are particularly important in that they function as a kind of steppingstone, or bridge, between information-content in the relatively technical and quantitative sense (as developed by Shannon and MacKay), and meaning in a relatively open and relational sense.

Section 4.6 exemplifies Peirce's ideas, in relation to those of Shannon and MacKay, by showing how they apply to databases, user accounts, and social network websites.

And the conclusion returns to the notion of enclosure. It discusses various senses of this term that are particularly important in the context of information. It argues that Deleuze's famous claim that we have moved from a society of discipline to a society of control misses the mark because his notion of enclosure is far too narrow, in that it only takes into account Foucault's disciplinary formations. And it shows how many stereotypic understandings of enclosure are closely related to classic understandings of 'the beautiful'; and so should really be reframed in order to make reference to the *sublime* (and far beyond).

4.2. MacKay's Account of Information and Meaning

Donald MacKay (1922–1987) was a British physicist, and a participant in both the London Symposia on Information Theory and the American Conferences on Cybernetics (sponsored by the Josiah Macy Jr. Foundation). His essays spanned some twenty years, and ranged from popular radio broadcasts, through technical papers, to RAND memos. With the encouragement of his friend, the linguist and literary theorist Roman Jakobson (whom we met in chapter 2), many of these were collected into a book, entitled *Information, Mechanism, and Meaning* (1969a).

Throughout these essays, MacKay consistently distinguished between the everyday sense of information (i.e., when one learns something one didn't know before) and *information-content*, or the amount of information a message contains when measured through some technical means (1969b, 18). In a broad sense, then, MacKay's theory of information is concerned with the "processes by which representations come into being, together with the theory of those abstract features which are common to a representation and that which it represents" (1969f, 80). Whereas in a narrow, more technical sense, his theory is concerned with the "problem of measuring changes in knowledge" (1969h, 156).

As for information-content, MacKay thought there were three basic types: selectional, structural, and metrical (1969b). *Selectional information-content* was just Shannon's original measure (1948), and turned on the relative improbability, or surprise value, of an actual message (given an ensemble of possible messages). Loosely speaking, the less likely a message, the more informative it is. Such a measure could be used to understand the replication of representations (which MacKay took to be the central function of communication, following Shannon). Structural and metrical information-content, in contrast, were used to understand the production of representations (which MacKay took to be the central function of science). In particular, *structural information-content* turned on the degrees of freedom, or number of independently specifiable dimensions, underlying a system of representations (so far as such representations have these in common with the states of affairs they represent). And *metrical information-content* turned on the precision, or reliability, of a given measurement along any such dimension. MacKay sometimes grouped structural and metrical information-content together as "descriptive information-content" (1969b, 12) and information "by construction" (1969h, 160).

Given our extended discussion of related ideas in chapter 3, one example should suffice to give the reader a sense of how these three kinds of information-content relate to each other, as well as the details of their actual measurement. Suppose we are trying to design a representational system for describing the location of an object. The structural information-content of such a system turns on the number of dimensions we are trying to locate the object in: for example, along a line (one dimension), in a plane (two dimensions), or within a volume (three dimensions). The metrical information-content of such a system turns on the precision with which we can locate the object along any of its dimensions: say, to within a millimeter (along a line), to within a square centimeter (in a plane), or to within a cubic meter (within a volume). All things being equal, if we increase the number of dimensions in which we measure (say, from two dimensions to three dimensions), or the precision of measurement along a dimension (say, from centimeters to millimeters), we increase the structural and metrical information-content, respectively.

Suppose we have constructed a system of representations in this way, such that we can now specify where an object is located in a square meter of space to within a square centimeter. This means our system has the ability to represent 10,000 possible positions (or one message for each square centimeter in the square meter). If we now want to communicate the position of an object to another (using this system of representation), we can send one of 10,000 possible messages to them. Assuming each message is equally likely (because the object is equally likely to be located at any position), the selectional information-content of any actual message is $-\log_2(1/10,000)$, which is about 13 bits. Phrased another way, it would take them about 13 yes/no questions to figure out the position; and so receiving such a message from us would save them this effort by being so informative.[5] That is, the selectional information-content of a given message is $-\log_2(p)$, where p is the probability of that message given an ensemble of possible messages. This is just Shannon's (1948) original measure.[6]

Notice how this selectional information-content is directly related to the structural and metrical information-content: together structural and metrical information-content determine the number of possible messages, and hence the 'size' of the ensemble of messages. In this example, increasing the precision (say, to a square millimeter), or adding a dimension (say, height) would increase the number of possible messages that could be communicated. This would thereby decrease the probability that any one of them is sent, which would increase the 'surprise-value', or selectional information-content, of the actual message that is sent.

Even though he was at pains to distinguish the three kinds of information-content, MacKay also stressed their interrelatedness. In one metaphor, for example, he likened them to volume (selectional), area (structural), and width (metrical). This suggests that he understood structural and metrical information-content to be presupposed by selectional information-content (1969b). Indeed, Brillouin (1962 [1956], 291) would later argue that MacKay's usage of structural and metrical information-content was already built into selectional information-content, and so that only a single theory of information was needed—in particular, Shannon's original measure. And while this is true, in some sense, MacKay's ideas were important because they stressed the highly motivated, or relatively iconic and indexical, relation between the system of representations per se (qua signs) and the states of affairs it could represent (qua objects).[7] Such issues, then, were directly related to Wittgenstein's (1961 [1921]) famous notions of logical form and mathematical multiplicity, as well as to Peirce's much earlier notion of diagrammatic iconicity (Kockelman 1999).

***

In addition to his account of information, MacKay also offered an account of meaning—by which he meant the effect a representation has on a receiver (1969c, 1969f, 1969g). In particular, MacKay understood the meaning of a representation in terms of its selective function on the ensemble of possible states of conditional readiness of the receiver. His metaphor for this process involved keys, switch boxes, and railroad tracks. Just as a key, when placed in a switch box, changes the possible configuration of railway tracks (such that any train that subsequently arrives will have its movement *channeled* in a particular way), a representation, when interpreted by a mind, affects the interpreter's subsequent readiness to behave in a variety of circumstances—making some behaviors more likely, and other behaviors less likely; see Figure 4.2. Out of all possible states of conditional readiness (or out of all possible configurations of tracks), the representation (or key) selects only a subset. And it is this selective function—of an actual state of conditional readiness, from an ensemble of possible states of conditional readiness—that MacKay took to be the operationalizable essence of meaning. As he phrased it, the meaning of a message is

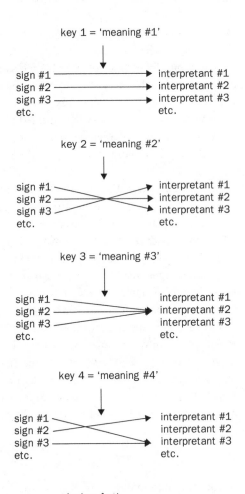

And so forth.

FIGURE 4.2 MacKay's Account of Meaning

"its selective function on the range of the recipient's states of conditional readiness for goal-directed action" (1969c, 24).

Note, then, that just as selective information-content (or Shannon information) turns on the relation between a message and an ensemble of possible messages (given structural and metrical information-content), meaning for MacKay turns on the relationship between a state of conditional readiness and an ensemble of possible states of conditional readiness. This is crucial: while meaning was, in some sense, 'in the head' (and body and world) of the receiver (and thus difficult to measure, even though its repercussions might be eminently observable), if it could be measured it would have the same metric (mathematically speaking) as selective information-content, just applied to a different ensemble (1969e, 71).

In short, MacKay's theory of information focused on three interrelated processes: the production of representations, the replication of representations, and the interpretation of representations. Producing (systems of) representations was the work of scientific research; and structural and metrical information-content were its most appropriate measures. The replication of representations was the work of communication engineers, who designed systems which would reproduce a given signal (from an ensemble of possible signals) at a different point, all the while fighting against enemies and noise. Shannon's measure of information, or selectional information-content, was designed with such transmissions in mind. And MacKay worked hard to show how it presupposed structural and metrical information-content—for together they determined the size of the ensemble of possible representations that could be sent. Moreover, they were the key means by which the representation made contact, or had features in common, with the state of affairs so represented. Finally, the interpretation of a representation involved the effect a message had on the ensemble of states of conditional readiness of the receiver— how it altered their propensity to act.

4.3. The 'Value' of Information

To return to the concerns of chapter 3, structural information-content turns on a particular *frame of relevance*, and metrical information-content turns on a particular *scale of resolution* (Kockelman 2009). The exact same entity or event may be represented using different frames of relevance with different scales of resolution, depending on the semiotic system (language, construction, theory, instrument, picture, worldview, interface, ontology, episteme, etc.) of those doing the representing. And as a function of which frame of relevance is used, with what scale of resolution, the ensemble of possible representations may vary (as well as the probability of any representation within this ensemble), and with this the selectional information-content (or Shannon measure) of any particular representation (or message).

As we also saw in chapter 3, while many physical systems *seem* to have a 'natural' frame of relevance (e.g., phase space, or the positions and momenta of all the particles in the system) and a 'natural' scale of resolution (e.g., Planck's constant, or 6.62×10^{-34} m^2kg/s), most systems have their frame of relevance and scale of resolution, or structural and metrical information-content, projected onto them by the observer or actor—and hence their selectional information-content as well.

Indeed, a key sense of portability is the capacity of a semiotic technology, such as a digital computer, to handle any frame of relevance or scale of resolution—for example, to render one and the same data set, or to record one and the same experience, in an infinity of different ways, often with just the touch of a button.

While the distinction between frame of relevance and scale of resolution maps onto the distinction between structural and metrical information, such ideas are complementary, rather than equivalent. In particular, MacKay's notions of structural and metrical information are meant to get at the commonalities between representations and states of affairs: the key dimensions and degrees. In contrast, as developed in chapter 3, a key issue for critical theory and media studies is to also understand the conditions for, and consequences of, the frames of relevance and scales of resolution that are projected onto particular domains (experiences, individuals, activities, events, etc.), such that their information-content can be reckoned in particular ways. Such a stance seeks to understand, for example, the way different scales of resolution and frames of relevance relate to different kinds of social relations, conceptual categories, and moral values. (For even though our modern media machines seem to be frame- and scale-free, most users defer to their applications' default settings, and hence to a much narrower range of possibility.) And such a stance seeks to understand the history, or genealogy, of such framing and scaling practices, as well as their political, economic, and ontological repercussions.

This is another way to reconfigure what McLuhan meant when he spoke about "the new scale that is introduced into our affairs by each extension of ourselves, or by any new technology [qua medium]" (1994 [1964], 7). Different forms of media, and not just different kinds of digital media per se, presume and produce not just different scales of resolution, *but also different frames of relevance*, and hence different kinds of selves who can sense and instigate, as well as communicate and cogitate, with such media on such scales through such frames.

From this perspective, no small part of *our experience with the digitization of our experience* involves finding ever more elaborate frames of relevance, and ever more fine-grained scales of resolution. From Flatland to Textureville, so to speak (or, at least, so it seems). Just as we can have nostalgia (or snobbery) for past frames of relevance and scales of resolution (by fetishizing vinyl records, 8 mm film, or cave paintings, for example), so too can we have hopes, and hypes, for future possibilities (say, authentic or 'real' virtual reality, as opposed to all the fake or 'virtual' virtual reality we've been offered so far). Indeed, to its detractors, just as every experience, entity, and event is threatened by commoditization, so too is it threatened by digitalization—often as part and parcel of the same process. Ironically, it often seems that we really can capture all of experience with just a single (very long) number. (For nothing scales, or frames, quite like the digital.) It just happens not to be price; and only God, or perhaps Goggle, is privy to the format it is stored in.

***

Returning to some of the concerns of chapter 1, perhaps the simplest, and yet most pervasive, mode of enclosure is evident in a seemingly innocent expression like *three bits of information* (as well as related expressions like *100 gigabytes of data*, and so forth). Such an expression presumes that we can quantify (via a number like *three* and a unit like the *bit*) a particular quality or complex of qualities (such as *information*, itself understood as a 'utility', and hence as a relatively desirable and potentially useful substance). And so just as we can speak about three bushels of wheat, two bolts of cloth, six hours of time, and 10,000 dollars of value, we can speak (and think) about three bits of information. This is one important way that *use-value*, in Marx's original sense, gets projected onto meaning (1967; Kockelman 2006a).

Such use-values are both a condition for, and a consequence of, *economic value*. For example, a USB flash drive that stores four gigabytes of data might cost you $6.99 to buy; just as the building of flash drives, and computational devices more generally, may have cost millions of workers a large chunk of their lives. Use-values, then, are caught up in labor as much as price, as well as all the reciprocities and iniquities that lay at the interface of labor and price. And just as a flash drive 'encloses' data (making it relatively portable, such that it can be carried across time, space, and persons), a factory that makes flash drives 'encloses' persons (attempting to make them relatively disciplined and calculatable, if not more and more 'programmable').

But it is not just the case that information is one essential modality of the commoditization of meaning. Information is directly related to labor, or work, in what are perhaps more subtle and far-reaching ways. When we do work on the world, we do not so much give form to matter for sake of function, which was Marx's understanding of concrete labor, itself grounded in Aristotle's account of causality (Kockelman 2015). Rather, we organize (or 'constrain') complexity for the sake of predictability (Kockelman 2009). That is, in doing detective work, scientific work or physical work, insofar as we organize matter (by giving form to materials, qualities to substances, existence to individuals, space-time to events, and so forth) it becomes more patterned, and hence more predictable. And this patterning of matter does not just occur 'internally' (by knowing a part of a thing, one learns something about the whole; by knowing a stanza, one predicts something about the sonnet); it also occurs 'externally' (in knowing the individual, one learns something about the environs; by learning something about the text, one predicts something about the context). In effect, work allows us to reduce our uncertainty as to the state of the world (or at least as to the state of some tiny slice of it).

As we saw in the last section, we can do this in part through the labor of questioning—slowly but surely reducing our uncertainty as to the state of a system.

And we can do this in part because, by producing such a state, through our labors, we already have the answers to such questions. In essence, we increase our knowledge by exercising our power. One stereotype of such a 'power' is moving a piston, or applying a pressure to decrease a volume, such that the position of gas particles are constrained to a smaller and smaller space, such that we become more and more certain, or knowledgeable, as to their position. However, as we will see in chapter 7, such powers also include extracting and identifying, shaping and sorting, separating and transporting, and much else beside. Indeed, just as computers are essentially sieves, sieving is an essential mode of production. In short, in a tradition that connects Bacon, Foucault, Marx, and Boltzmann, there is a key movement between knowledge and power, on the one hand, and information and work/labor, on the other.

Though the findings of computer science, such use-values and exchange values are mediated by a wide range of *epistemic values*, or modes of possibility and necessity, as evinced in various technological limits and opportunities: constraints on channel capacities, compression ratios, decryption strategies, transistor densities, and algorithmic solvability, *inter alia*. Indeed, computer science is essentially the science of such epistemic values. Moreover, and more important for present concerns, such use-values and exchange values are also subject to *deontic values*, such as permission and obligation. That is, just as there are 'laws' governing the speed at which one can transmit data across a channel (Shannon 1948), there are laws, norms, and conventions that govern the production, consumption, and circulation of information products. Phrased another way, and invoking Goffman (1981b), we need to understand the relation between technical constraints (or 'protocols') and ritual constraints, and not just for face-to-face communication, but for any modality of mediated interaction.

Focusing on the relation between deontic value, use-value and economic value, we are not just interested in how much a certain amount of storage (channel capacity, or processing speed) costs; or how much effort it requires to build and deliver; or how much space, time and effort it saves, or requires, once delivered. We are just as interested in issues like: how much space (capacity or speed) is one legally permitted to have or obligated to provide, and how much information (about some particular domain) is one permitted or obligated to download, share, or know? What data should states, or citizens, or service providers, be entitled to know, or prohibited from knowing? Who can own 'information goods', like intellectual property, and cultural resources more generally; who should be able to own these, for how long, under what conditions? Who can encrypt data, using what methods? When should private files be decrypted, and by whom? Given that most transactions are, nowadays, really 'tracked actions', what should be the limits of sovereignty in relation to the secrets, sharing, security and sales of their subjects? More generally, what is the relation between being free in the sense of freedom of will, being free in the sense of costing nothing, and being free in the sense of having many degrees of freedom (not to mention freedom in the sense of free speech [Moody 2001; and see Coleman 2013 and Kelty 2008, *inter alia*]). From the 'second enclosure movement' described by James Boyle, to the recent disclosures of Edward Snowden, such issues are well-known and incredibly important, justly constituting bread-and-butter topics at the intersection of law, information, politics, and technology (Boyle 1997, 2003; Litman 2000; Lessig 2006; Stallman 2010; Zimmerman 1995; *inter alia*).

Crucially, such expressions are also caught up in *semantic value*, taking their place alongside analogous morphosyntactic constructions like *three bushels of wheat, four bricks of gold,* and *two hours of time.* Extending Whorf's original formulation (1956 [1939]; and see Lucy 1992a), information seems to be a formless substance (qua mass noun) in need of a substanceless form (qua unit) if it is to be subject to precise calculations as to its quantity or number (Kockelman 2006a; Kockelman and Bernstein 2013). That is, just as words like 'mud' and 'butter' are different from words like 'cat' and 'chair'—in that only the latter can show up with an indefinite article (compare the relative grammaticality of 'a cat' with 'a mud') and be easily pluralized (compare the relative grammaticality of 'chairs' with 'muds')—the word 'information' is more like 'mud' and 'butter' than 'cat' and 'chair'. And if one wants to quantify information, or butter and mud, one must first find an appropriate unit (a mud pie, a pat of butter, a bit of information). Other languages, and linguistic practices, may have other ontological presumptions (Lucy 1992b; Quine 1969).

Moreover, with its placement in such a covert word class, in such a paradigm, features posited of the referents of the other members of this word class became easily projected onto the referent of the word 'information'—for example, not just that it is a formless substance, but also that it is a limited resource, if not a valuable commodity; as well as a relatively tangible, divisible, sharable, and even smearable, thing. Note, then, that morphosyntactic classes, and the semantic properties they are sensitive to, undergird ontological projections of the most wily and easily naturalized kind.

In short, Shannon's (1948) original formulation of information-content was particularly important not only because it defined the quality (information qua utility) so carefully, and clarified what was to be meant by the basic unit (a bit), but also because it provided a relatively precise and general way to calculate the number of such units—of the quality in question—for a given symbolic system. Through his seminal essay, and a wide range of related developments, a key modality of meaning was thereby transformed into a valuable resource—'subject' to reckoning and regimentation, quantification and qualification, limits and labor, science and technology, politics and economy. Meaning was radically refashioned in terms of 'surprise value', or calculable information-content, along with its use-value, exchange-value, epistemic value, deontic value, and semantic value.

***

Marx famously posited a relation between a society's mode of production and its political, legal, and moral principles. McLuhan replaced mode of production with means of communication, but otherwise made similar claims. In essence, and with no end of exceptions and counterclaims, they understood economic and communicative infrastructures to strongly condition the interactions, institutions, and imaginaries of the collectivities that depended on those infrastructures. While we don't need to enter into these debates per se, it is worthwhile highlighting the double sense of mediation that is operative in their arguments. First, returning to the concerns of section 4.1, to say one domain (such as an infrastructure) conditions another (such as an institution or imaginary) is to say that there is a correlation between the two domains. For example, events in one domain, qua 'causes', are *channeled* into events in the other domain, qua 'effects' (and vice-versa, depending on how sophisticated a reading one offers). And so details in one domain relate to details in the other domain as signs to objects (to an interpretive agent aware of such a correlation, qua causal patterning). Phrased in terms of section 4.2, relations found in one domain provide information about, or lessen the surprise value of, relations in the other domain. If the infrastructure is organized like 'this', so to speak, then the related institutions and imaginaries will be organized like 'that'.[8]

In short, both Marx and McLuhan were information scientists, and media theorists, not just because they studied 'media' and 'representations' in their more stereotypic, and highly reified senses (the contents, forms, and functions of beliefs, ideologies, laws, and literature, as well as CDs, cameras, printing presses, and scripts), but because they postulated relatively universal, transhistorical, and 'long-distance' modes of mediation, which thereby bridged otherwise disparate ontological domains, and which thereby mediated otherwise unrelated values. (At least to the minds of those interpreting agents committed to their frames of relevance, scales of resolution, and modes of evaluation—for critical theorists are no less subject to such concerns than the worlded media and mediated worlds they theorize and critique.[9])

4.4. Peirce's Theory of Meaning

This section and the next will focus on two aspects of Peirce's thought: first, his understanding of interpretants of signs (which are loosely akin to MacKay's responses to messages, or 'meaning'); and second, his understanding of information, or the production of new knowledge, within his broader theory of semiosis. They are meant to further highlight some of the core commitments of a semiotic stance, as it was introduced in chapter 1, and developed in the preceding chapters. Recall Table 1.1.

As inspired by Peirce, there are three basic types of interpretants (1955c, 276–277; Kockelman 2005). An *affective interpretant* is a change in one's bodily state. It can range from an increase in heart rate to a blush, from a feeling of pleasure to a loss of balance, from quickened breathing to vertigo. This change in bodily state is itself a sign that is potentially perceptible to the body's owner, or others who can perceive the owner's body. And, as signs themselves (in an incipient semiotic process), these interpretants may lead to subsequent, and perhaps more developed, interpretants.

Energetic interpretants involve effort and individual causality; they do not necessarily involve purpose, intention, or planning. For example, recoiling at the sight of blood is an energetic interpretant; as is covering one's tracks to avoid being followed; as is wielding an instrument (say, typing on a keyboard); as is heeding an affordance (say, clinging to a branch); as is performing a role (say, bowing to one's *sensei*).

And *representational interpretants* are signs with propositional content, such as an assertion (or explicit speech act more generally). Thus to describe someone's movement as 'he tried to help' is to offer an interpretant of such a controlled behavior (qua sign) so far as it has a purpose (qua object). And hence while such representations are signs (that may be subsequently interpreted), they are also interpretants (of prior signs).

It should be emphasized that the same sign can lead to different kinds of interpretants—sometimes simultaneously and sometimes sequentially. For example, upon being exposed to a bawdy (violent, or racist) meme, one may turn pink, become incensed, or feel horny (affective interpretant); one may shield one's eyes, erase one's browsing history, or lock the door (energetic interpretant); one may say 'that shocks me', respond in the comments section, or recount what one found to one's shrink (representational interpretant).

Each of these three types of interpretants may be paired with a slightly more abstract double, known as an ultimate interpretant (compare Peirce 1955c, 277). In particular, an *ultimate affective interpretant* is not a change in bodily state per se, but rather a disposition to have one's bodily state change—and hence is a disposition to express affective interpretants (of a particular type), somewhat akin to a mood. Such an interpretant, then, is not itself a sign, but is only evinced in a pattern of, or propensity for, affecting (as the exercise of that disposition, or the inhabiting of that mood).

Analogously, an *ultimate energetic interpretant* is a disposition to express energetic interpretants (of a particular type). In short, it is a disposition to behave in certain ways—as evinced in purposeful and nonpurposeful behaviors.

And finally, an *ultimate representational interpretant* is the propositional content of a representational interpretant, plus all the propositions that may be inferred from it, when all of these propositions are embodied in a change of habit, as evinced in behaviors that conform to these propositional contents. For example, a *belief* is the quintessential ultimate representational interpretant: in being committed to a proposition (i.e., 'holding a belief'), one is also normatively committed to any propositions that may be inferred from it; and one's commitment to this inferentially entangled and indexically grounded set of propositions is evinced in one's behavior: what one is likely or unlikely to do or say, or think or feel, insofar as it confirms or contradicts these propositional contents. Notice that these ultimate interpretants are not signs in themselves: while they dispose one toward certain behaviors (affectual, energetic, representational), they are not the behaviors per se—but rather dispositions, or propensities, to behave in certain ways.

Depending on the ontological commitments and disciplinary prejudices of the analyst, such ultimate interpretants can be framed, operationalized, and materialized in various ways. For example, not just as mental states, but also as cognitive representations, neuronal configurations, functional organizations, structures of feelings, mental modules, an individual's habits or *habitus*, a collectivity's mentality, and so forth.

Recall, in particular, MacKay's definition of meaning, as explicated through his metaphor of a railroad switching yard: the meaning of a message is "its selective function on the range of the recipient's states of conditional readiness for goal-directed action." This should be compared with Peirce's famous characterization of pragmatism in terms of Bain's maxim: a belief is "that upon which one is prepared to act" (1955c, 270). From the perspective of their roots, as we just saw, beliefs are ultimate representational interpretants of prior signs. From the perspective of their fruits, as should now be clear, different beliefs may be framed as different dispositions, or 'conditional readinesses', to act. More carefully, a key interpretant of many signs, their 'meaning' so to speak, is the change they make in the interpreting agent's ensuing potential to signify, objectify, and interpret in particular ways, as will be evinced in their future actions and affects, utterances and moods, inferences and interactions.[10]

Indeed, from an 'intentional stance' (itself just a minor corollary of the semiotic stance), such beliefs (and so called 'mental states' more generally) are a key form of media: not only do they represent the world (just as speech acts represent the world), they also mediate our relation to that world (Kockelman 2013a). That is, depending on one's beliefs (desires, plans, intentions, memories, etc.), one and the same entity or event (qua sign, or stimulus) can give rise to multiple and manifold interpretants or 'responses'; and radically different entities or events can give rise to one and the same response. And just as speech acts can be *infelicitous* (recall our discussion of this idea in section 4.6 of chapter 2), mental stakes can be *incoherent*—and thus semantically relate to each other, and causally relate to the world, in decidedly non-normative and unruly ways. Parasites affect mind as much as body, individuality as much as collectivity, the channeling of thoughts as much as the channeling of messages, interiority as much as infrastructure. Chapter 6 will take up such issues at length.

***

While such a sixfold typology of interpretants may seem complicated at first, it should accord with one's experience. Indeed, most *emotions* really involve a complicated bundling together of all these types of interpretants. For example, upon hearing a wrenching scream or a ferocious growl while walking through the woods (as a sign), one may be suffused with adrenaline (affective interpretant); one might make a frightened or angry facial expression (relatively non-purposeful energetic interpretant); one may take cover or draw a weapon (relatively purposeful energetic interpretant); and one might yell 'I'm calling the police' or whisper 'I mean no harm' (representational interpretant). Moreover, one might subsequently sweat or tremble when walking alone in wooded areas (ultimate affective interpretant); one might avoid that part of the forest ever after (ultimate energetic interpretant); and one might forever believe that the woods are filled with dangerous creatures (ultimate representational interpretant). In this way, most so-called emotions, or cognitive responses and affective unfoldings more generally, may be decomposed into a bouquet of more basic and varied interpretants. And, in this way, the seemingly most subjective forms of experience are easily reframed in terms of their intersubjectively available and ethnographically tractable effects (Kockelman 2011a).

Later chapters will radically complement these ideas, treating interpretants in terms of transformations in both worlded ontologies and ontologized worlds, seeing them as radically dependent on interpretive grounds, and opening up the domain of interpreting agents to include so called mechanized beings (such as algorithms and machines) as much as stereotypically lively creatures (such as cats and human beings).

4.5. Peirce's Theory of Information

From one perspective, meaning and information are closely related, corresponding more or less to Peirce's object: whatever could be stood for, or represented by, a sign. In this framing, which we pursued at length in section 4.1, information (or meaning) is simply the object of a sign, such that knowing something about the sign (including its mere existence) allows one to know something about the object. And a sign is said to encode information, or be informative, depending on the novelty and relevance of its object to an interpreting agent. Peirce had a beautiful definition of the object-as-information in this sense: "that which a sign, so far as it fulfills the function of a sign, enables one who knows that sign, and knows it as a sign, to know" (quoted in Parmentier 1994, 4). But Peirce also offered two relatively narrow and complementary definitions of information. Like MacKay's nontechnical definition of information, both of these definitions were characterized in terms of changes in knowledge. In particular, one involved the information contained in a term (like 'dog' or 'electron'), and the other involved the information contained in an assertion (like 'dogs are mammals' or 'electrons are charged particles'). In the rest of this section, we will walk through both definitions in detail. In the next section, we will see how such definitions apply to terms like, 'John Smith' and 'Janet Welby' and to assertions like, 'John Smith has the following buying habits' and 'Janet Welby has the following browser history'.

***

For Peirce, working in a logical tradition, the *denotation* of a term like 'dog' is the set of entities it refers to (within a given semiotic collectivity, or commons). It might include all the members of all the different breeds known to this collectivity. In contrast, the *connotation* of a term like 'dog' is the set of features such entities have in common. It might include predicates like 'has fur', 'is loyal friend', 'chases cats', 'descended from wolves', and so forth. Both of these are, of course, well-known ideas which loosely correspond to modern understandings of the extension and intension, or reference and sense, of a term. Recall, for example, our discussion of Frege's ideas in chapter 3. Finally, in a metaphor that hearkens back to MacKay, and goes beyond traditional understandings, Peirce defined the *information* of a term like 'dog' as the product of its denotation (or 'logical breadth') and connotation (or 'logical depth'). As he put it:

> The totality of the predicates of a sign, and also the totality of the characters it signifies, are indifferently each called its logical *depth*. This is the oldest and most convenient term. ... The totality of the subjects, and also, indifferently, the totality of the real objects of a sign, is called the logical *breadth*. ... Besides the logical depth and breadth, I have proposed (in 1867) the terms information and area to denote the total of fact (true or false) that in a given state of knowledge a sign embodies (1998 [1904], 305; and see Peirce 1992 [1867],10).[11]

While this definition may sound odd at first, it may be reworked to capture our understanding of what it means to gain new information. Suppose, for example, that members of some semiotic collectivity, or phatic commons, do not know where to place chihuahuas taxonomically. If they subsequent learn (through experiment, testimony, etc.) that chihuahuas are a breed of dogs, they have increased the denotation of the term 'dog', and hence the term's information. Similarly, suppose that members of some semiotic collectivity, who have long known that dogs are furry and bark, subsequently learn that dogs are also territorial. They have thereby increased the connotation of the term, and hence its information. In short, knowledge practices—which seek to find new members for old classes (expand denotation) or new features for old members (expand connotation)—are aimed at increasing the information of a term. In this sense, information is a product of the semantic depth and breadth of a term, as it is used by a semiotic collectivity. (We will perturb these ideas in light of Putnam's notion of the linguistic division of labor when we discuss Peirce's definition of virtuality in chapter 5.)

Note, then, the following similarities between this kind of information and MacKay's characterization. First, there is the spatial metaphor: for Peirce, information is the product of breadth (denotation) times depth (connotation); whereas MacKay likened selective information to volume, structural information to area, and metrical information to width. Next, while Peirce offered no absolute way to measure the information of a term, he did offer a relative measure which could be used to track graded increases or decreases in the extension and intension of a term: not how much information a term has per se, but whether it has more or less (in relation to some other term, or in relation to the same term at some other time, or in relation to the same term at the same time for some other collectivity, and so forth).[12] Finally, in one early essay (1969d), MacKay attempted to define information in terms of something like connotation. That is, rather than counting over the possible places an entity could be in a physical environment (recall our example from section 4.2), one could count over the possible attributes an entity could have in a semantic environment. For example, if we count over all possible attributes any entity could have, along with the relative probability it has any of these (given our current knowledge), we may thereby obtain a measure of our surprise value (that it has a particular set of such attributes).

***

Peirce also made a distinction between signs (or components of composite signs) that point to objects, and signs that provide information about such objects.[13] A weathercock, for example, simultaneously points to the wind (in the sense that its position is caused by the wind) and provides information about the wind (in the sense that knowing its position, one knows the direction of the wind). And a photograph simultaneously directs the interpreter's attention to the person so portrayed (say, Benjamin Franklin), and provides information about this person (say, what they were wearing, or how old they were). Indeed, Peirce also described propositions as consisting of two composite parts: one to "express its information" and the other to "indicate the *subject* of that information" (117; emphasis added). This division is so important for linguistics, and the study of discourse and media more generally, that it is worth taking up at length.

Many current linguists, like Lambrecht (1996; and see Van Valin and LaPolla 1997), distinguish between the *topic* and *focus* of an utterance (or of a 'message' more generally). For example, when I say, 'my dog died', *my dog* is the topic and *died* is the focus. In particular, the topic is that part of an utterance that constitutes relatively 'old information': the speaker presumes that its referent is already known (or at least readily identifiable) to the addressee. The focus is that part of an utterance that constitutes relatively 'new information': the speaker presumes that the addressee is not yet aware of its applicability to the topic.[14] While most utterances have both a topic and a focus, some utterances have only a focus. For example, existential constructions such as 'there was an old woman' are designed to topicalize referents, such that subsequent utterances can predicate features of those topics via their own foci: 'and she lived in a shoe'. Indeed, just as an interpretant in one semiotic process may become a sign in a subsequent semiotic process, this example shows that the focus of one utterance ('an old woman') can become the topic of a subsequent utterance ('she'). That is, what is being proposed as new information in an earlier utterance (its focus) can be presupposed as old information in a later utterance (its topic).

For present purposes, what is important is that such utterances usually involve some relatively indexical sign (that points to some referent, qua topic) and some relatively iconic sign (that predicates features of such referents, qua focus). While both kinds of signs constitute 'information' in the general sense, foci are that part of composite signs that constitute 'new information', or information proper (in the nontechnical sense of providing 'new knowledge' about their topics, or 'subjects').

Crucially, not only can we think of every 'utterance' (or message more generally) as pointing backward and forward in regards to its information structure (topic-focus), we may also think of every utterance as pointing forward and backward as to its argumentation or reasoning. That is, one and the same utterance may be *grounded in* some previous utterance or event (for example, what inference or experience led to it) and *grounding of* a subsequent utterance or action (for example, what can be inferred from it, or undertaken in light of it). Recall the way that Heidegger's references were related to citations, and epistemic chains more generally, in chapter 3. Such modes of argumentation or reasoning may be relatively logical (inferential) or relatively empirical (indexical), relatively public (as a conversational thread) or relatively private (as a stream of thoughts), relatively local and idiosyncratic (in terms of their sources of evidence and logics of argumentation) or relatively global and standardized.[15] What is crucial about this modality of information, then, is not just the proposition per se (composed as it is of a topic and focus), but also what it both rests on and gives rise to, as regimented by the logical and empirical norms of the interacting agents in question—not just their *epistemes*, but also their 'epistemologies of the everyday' (Kockelman 1999).[16]

Phrased another way, the relation between old and new information contained in a proposition (that is, the topic-focus relation) should be both *justified* (by past beliefs and utterances, experiences and events) and *relevant* (to future beliefs and utterances, actions and events). This means that such chains are inherently distributed across space, time, and agent. Interestingly, theorists of modern forms of digitally encoded and network-distributed information, such as Benkler (2006, 68), stress very similar dimensions (such as 'accreditation' and 'relevance') when they try to account for the importance of peer-produced modes of information. Information in this second sense is thus directly tied to ultimate interpretants, as discussed in the last section: for the interpretant of such an informative sign is often precisely a justified and relevant belief, or a disposition on which one is strongly inclined (or encouraged) to act. As should be clear from Peirce's highly prescient framing, however, information has always been produced by 'peers' (as much as by politburos, books, parents, classrooms, newspapers, laboratories, parasites, and other powers-that-be).

***

We may now bring Peirce's two accounts of information together. In particular, notice how the relation between denotation and connotation relates to the relation between topic and focus. The first two foreground the information contained in a word or term (as recognized by members of a semiotic collectivity); the latter two foreground the information contained in an utterance or proposition (as unfolding in the discursive interaction or informational exchange of two semiotic agents). In this way, one can keep separate what counts as new or old information to a semiotic collectivity on a historical timescale, and what counts as new or old information to a semiotic agent (or to a relation between such agents) on an interactional timescale. Relatively speaking, if the first kind of information binds a signer to a semiotic collectivity, the second kind of information binds a signer to an interpreter. And both kinds of information can be condition and consequence, or root and fruit, of the other. For example, the information contained in a term provides a kind of background knowledge, ontology, or semantic commons, that members of a collectivity share, and so may never need to make explicit in an actual proposition. An actual utterance or 'message' may thus implicitly show, yet never explicitly state, such knowledge. Concomitantly, the members of a semiotic collectivity come to a large part of their shared knowledge precisely through a huge number of individual communicative events, whereby one agent informs another agent (or many other agents) of something.

In short, if one attends to Peirce's first definition (qua denotation, connotation, and information), one attends to information as it is structured in the knowledge base, lexicon, or semantics of a semiotic collectivity (community, culture, or commons). If one attends to Peirce's second definition (qua topics, foci, and reasons), one attends to information as it unfolds in actual interactions, as pragmatic relations, between speakers and addressees (or signers and interpreters more generally). The former relates to information qua institution and history; the latter relates to information qua practice and interaction. Both frames are, to be sure, needed: if the second is often the precipitate (or figure) of the first, the first is often the well (or ground) of the second. Such frames are particularly important in that they function as a kind of stepping stone, or bridge, between information-content in the relatively specific and quantitative sense (section 4.2) and meaning in the relatively general and qualitative sense (section 4.4).[17] See Table 4.1.

TABLE 4.1
Various Senses of Meaning and Information

Peirce	*sign*: whatever stands for something else	*object*: whatever is stood for by a sign (for some, 'information' proper)	*interpretant*: whatever a sign creates insofar as it stands for an object (for some, 'meaning' proper)	Components of Semiotic Processes
Weaver/ Shannon	*technical level*: how representation encoded ('syntax')	*semantic level*: what representation refers to ('semantics')	*effectiveness level*: what effect representation has ('pragmatics')	Levels of Communication
Peirce/Mill/ etc.	*denotation*: set of entities a sign refers to ('logical depth')	*connotation*: set of features such entities have in common ('logical breadth')	*information*: the product of denotation and connotation ('logical area')	Information Institutionalized, or Embodied in Semantics
Peirce/ Lambrecht/ etc.	*focus*: whatever a representation predicates (for some, 'new information')	*topic*: whatever a representation presupposes (for some, 'old information')	*reason*: whatever justifies a representation, or is justified by a representation (either logically or empirically)	Information Interactionalized, or Embodied in Pragmatics
Kittler/von Neumann	*store data*: some number represents a value	*transmit data*: some number represents an address	*process data*: some number represents a command	Information Mechanized, or Embodied in Particular Media Technology
MacKay/ Shannon	*structural information*: number of independent dimensions underlying system of representations ('area')	*metrical information*: precision or reliability of values along such dimensions ('width')	*selectional information*: relative improbability of representation given ensemble of possible representations ('volume')	Information Quantified, Embodied in Mathematical Equations and Scientific Principles

4.6. The Matrix

From the vantage of Peirce's first definition of information (connotation, denotation, information), perhaps the key set of terms for social networking sites are the names (and referents) of all the users of that application (John Smith, Janet Welby, etc.). Of interest is not just who does the name, or user ID really refer to (qua denotation), or at least point to, but also what are the key attributes of that user (qua connotation): their likes and dislikes, their zip code and age, their friends and family, their buying habits and voting records, their musical tastes and sexual proclivities, their mental states and physical characteristics, their identities and values, their beliefs and desires, their dreams and fears, their occupations and *résumé*, what they've posted and how they've commented, their signs and interpretants more generally.

Indeed the attributes, or connotations, that come to be associated with a user ID are often more than enough to find the referent, or denotation, of that user ID. They provide the path, so to speak, for identification. This sense of connotation or 'sense' is, it might seem, a long way off from Frege's sense (*Sinn*) as discussed in chapter 3; and so it is. But, as is well known, such services (platforms, websites, applications) are designed to attract users and gain information about the attributes of those users, and thus expand the application's 'denotation' and 'connotation', and thus increase the service's 'information'—a mode of capital that is as iconic and indexical as it is 'symbolic', and very often—at least to the many critics of such services—precisely what should have best been kept a 'secret'.

Table 4.2 shows the ways all this may be easily *enclosed* in a simple database.[18] Down the leftmost column are all the denotata: each and every user of an application, with the dots at the bottom simply indicating the ease with which this user base easily scales to infinity. Across the topmost row are all the connotations: each and every attribute, or important characteristic, of all those users (including their relations to other users), with the dots at the right indicating the ease with which such attributes scale to infinity. Returning to the issues raised in section 4.2, such an embedding ensemble of rows and columns constitutes a frame of relevance, and provides a scale of resolution, both of which are easily transformed—simply add and delete, expand and collapse, or alter and adjust, all those rows and columns, and hence all those users with all their attributes. Moreover, the entries in any box, the embedded 'values' themselves, are also formatted to satisfy particular frames of relevance and scales of resolution, and hence contain both structural information and metrical information, with all the ontological commitments thereby entailed. For example, what range of values can constitute a valid entry for attributes like gender, religion, sexuality, political party, and so forth. Moreover, as a function of such frames and scales, each and every entry may have a characteristic number of bits assigned to them; and so the selectional information contained in such a format has a relatively precise numerical value as well (however much of it may end up being predictable bit-padding). This issue, then, is not how many questions would you have to ask to pinpoint an object's position in physical space, but rather how many questions would you have to ask to locate an individual's positioning in 'social space' or 'database space'.

Returning to the issues in section 4.1, the values in different parts of this table are very often correlated, or patterned. For example, by learning something about John Smith's zip code (say, row 1, column 11), we may learn something about his political party (row 1, column 3). Or by learning something about his friends (row 1, column 6), and by knowing something about his buying habits (row 1, column 10), we may learn something about their buying habits (rows 2–6, column 10). And so forth. Such databases constitute particularly relevant 'environments', and interpreting agents—or 'organisms'—both seek and wield correlations when sensing and moving in such environments. A large part of 'data mining' is precisely finding

TABLE 4.2
Information as Enclosed in a Database

	Age	Gender	Party	Religion	Dreams	Family	Friends	Enemies	Sexuality	Purchases	Zip Code	And so on...
John Smith	value	value	value	value	value	value	value	value	value	value	value	...
Sally Hanks	value	value	value	value	value	value	value	value	value	value	value	...
Jeffry Catzen	value	value	value	value	value	value	value	value	value	value	value	...
Sarah Fariah	value	value	value	value	value	value	value	value	value	value	value	...
Fritz Eggleby	value	value	value	value	value	value	value	value	value	value	value	...
Janet Welby	value	value	value	value	value	value	value	value	value	value	value	...
Brett Gookey	value	value	value	value	value	value	value	value	value	value	value	...
Tanya Booker	value	value	value	value	value	value	value	value	value	value	value	...
And so on...	...	...	...	...	...	...	...	...	...	...	...	...

the correlations that allow one to make connections (and thereby channel transactions) in such environments; it is precisely a form of work. In some sense, then, such an ensemble of rows and columns is the real matrix. And all these correlations are 'patterns of culture', be they genuine or spurious.

***

From the vantage of Peirce's second framing of information (topic, focus, reason), a user-profile, or row in a matrix, simultaneously directs an interpreting agent's attention to the person indexed (say, Joe Smith) and provides information about this person (where they live and how they live, what they like, and what they're like). This means that whenever one creates an account in a social network one is essentially topicalizing oneself. (Recall the first part of our example: 'There was an old woman'.) More pointedly, and to use a metaphor that goes back to John Stuart Mill (2002 [1843]), one is just setting oneself up as a hook (or topic) on which an ensemble of coats (or foci) may hang. And every time you check a box, fill in a bubble, enter features into a field, link to another user, read a post, or update your profile, you are 'uttering' more and more messages, each of which constitutes a more or less true 'proposition', where the topic is your self (now 'old information' to that application), and the foci are such attributes (qua 'new information'). (Recall the second part of our example: 'And she lived in a shoe'.) In other words, now that you have an account, the topic may be presumed while the foci are predicated. And once a focus is predicated of a topic, that focus can go on to become a topic in its own right: having learned that John went to a concert, we can inquire into what band was playing at that concert, where and when it occurred, and who else was there.

Moreover, each such proposition (qua topic-focus relation), and so each such possible 'belief' an application may thereby come to hold about you, may be treated as more or less justified and more or less true. This means that one can inquire into the evidence an interpreting agent is trained or programmed to look for. For example, what logics or algorithms does it use to determine how 'certain' it is that the propositions you offer, or the inferences it makes, are 'true'. And this means that one can inquire into the strategies such seemingly true propositions are put to. For example, what inferences do they license that agent to make, however 'programmatically', such that it may arrive at other seemingly true propositions about you, and those you relate to (recall how we used the matrix to infer Smith's buying habits from his zip code). Relatedly, since propositions license actions as much as inferences, what behaviors should it should take 'on your behalf'—what reminders should it send you, advertisements should it show you, advice should it give you, directions should it nudge you toward, authorities should it mention you to. In short, just as such 'assertions' have a topic-focus structure, they are also both grounded in and grounding of other assertions—in long, tangled, indexical and inferential chains, mediated by machines and algorithms as much as by humans.

These, then, are some of the key messages that must be sent across one channel (from you to the service, so to speak) such that you can connect to others through the channels provided by that service. Such services, then, are signers and interpreters (agents you send messages to and receive messages from). They are channels (or infrastructure you use to send messages to others, and receive messages from others). And they are parasites (agents that intercept all those sent and received messages in order to become more informed about you and your values, in order to increase the 'wealth of their service' [precisely through the use-value and exchange-value of this information]). To return to Mill, in signing up for such a 'service', which most of humanity is probably soon to do, you literally hang your 'self'.

4.7. From the Beautiful to the Sublime

One way to interrelate all the foregoing accounts of information is as follows. As introduced in chapter 1, and further discussed in section 4.4, start with Peirce and his general theory of meaningful processes, which turn on embedding and enchaining relations between signs, objects, and interpretants. Such semiotic processes may be used to understand human and nonhuman communication systems, communicative and noncommunicative signs, and meaning that is as embodied and embedded as it is enminded and encoded, across an enormous range of historical eras and cultural milieus (Kockelman 2011a). Next, as also introduced in chapter 1, and discussed at length in chapter 2, note the various ways such meaningful processes can be relatively abstracted, reduced, quantified, objectified, or captured. More generally, note the ways they can be *enclosed*—by various theorists in their attempts to understand informational technologies, and by various actors in their attempts to design, produce, and wield such technologies. For example, as per section 4.2, we have scholars like Shannon and MacKay who want to understand meaning in terms of mathematical expressions and scientific formulations. As per section 4.5, we have scholars like Peirce (in some of his writings), and linguists like Lambrecht, who want to understand meaning in terms of logical propositions and linguistic utterances. And, as discussed in section 4.3, we have economies more generally, and all the ways economic actors put a price on the storage size, channel capacity, and processing speed of various devices (as well as the contents stored, transmitted, and processed by such devices). That is, each of these moves attempts to render some aspect of meaning, and often a theory of meaning more generally, in terms that are relatively formal, quantitative, content-free, and context-independent. To return to the concerns raised at the end of chapter 2, if we think about meaning as disclosure—in the sense of bringing something to the attention of another—each of these understandings of information may be understood as an attempt to enclose disclosure.

None of this, it should be emphasized, is a bad thing or a good thing per se. In enclosing a phenomenon (like 'meaning'), in acquiring knowledge about it or power over it, one acquires (and requires) a huge amount of agency. Many forms of enclosure, then, are simultaneously risks we run and benefits we reap. As we saw in chapter 1, they are inherently bittersweet.

To be sure, some modes of enclosure are far more bitter than sweet, especially as understood within the broad tradition of critical theory. From this vantage, for example, the most relevant senses of enclosure belong to Foucault (qua disciplinary enclosure, such as the prison, factory, or asylum) and Marx (qua enclosure of the commons, whereby the collective resources of many became the private property of a few). As should be apparent from the examples offered in this chapter, especially in sections 4.2 and 4.6, both of these more notorious kinds of enclosure are also operating with respect to information, and so intersect with the foregoing concepts and commitments.

In the first sense, we are confronted by informational enclosures from all sides: not just interfaces, algorithms, data structures, and protocols, but also the so-called walled gardens of our applications, platforms, and providers. With subtly shiftable frames of relevance and ever-increasing scales of resolution, individuals have become the key topics (and denotations), and their likes and dislikes, friends and families, memories and plans, feelings and dreams, pictures and poems, interactions and transactions, cravings and crimes, have become the foci (and connotations). And, in the second sense, as intersecting with the first, we have willfully—indeed, happily—handed over all this information about ourselves—and about our kith, kin and acquaintances, and much else beside—to a handful of third parties (whom Shannon would have called enemies, and Serres would have called parasites).

Taking into account these facts, it should be clear that Deleuze's (1991) famous claim that we were moving from a society of discipline to a society of control, such that "we are in a generalized crisis in relation to all the environments of enclosure" (3-4), is only correct if one understands enclosure in an extremely narrow sense. As he saw it, such "enclosures are *molds*, distinct castings, but controls are a *modulation*, like a self-deforming cast that will continuously change from one moment to the other, or like a sieve whose mesh will transmit from point to point" (4). In particular, Deleuze's understanding of enclosure was confined (!) to Foucault's disciplinary institution, in the most stereotypic sense: the school, the factory, the asylum. As should be clear from all the examples marshaled in chapter 1, and further enumerated in Kockelman (2016), techniques of enclosure are much broader than this, much more transmitting and transmuting than this, much earlier and more extensive than this, and radically modulating. (Indeed, as will be shown in chapter 6, perhaps the least interesting thing about sieves is that they 'transmit from point to point'; a short section of pipe, or a thrown rock's wake in a pond, will do that.) Not only have we undergone a 'second enclosure movement', in the terms of James Boyle (2003), invoking the tradition of critical historiography, but even the Marxist and Foucauldian understanding of such processes, and their logics, are but a tiny section of a much larger terrain.

But that said, all those more extended senses of enclosure are still grounded in an imaginary that is tightly coupled to classic understandings of the beautiful (themselves closely linked to notions of form and boundedness and objectivity). For example, in his *Critique of Judgment*, Kant (2000 [1790]) argued that "beauty discovers to us a Technic of nature, which represents it as a system in accordance with laws", which in turn "leads to profound investigations as to the possibility of such a form". Yet, if Kant argued that "Beauty is connected to the form of an object, which consists in having boundaries", he also argued that "the sublime is felt in formless objects, so far as in it or by occasion of it boundlessness is represented, and yet its totality is also present to thought". We began to investigate these forms through our reading of Sapir in chapter 3; and we will go on to investigate these forms through Peirce (and Deleuze) in chapter 5.

Phrased another way, Deleuze's (Kantian and Peircean) interpretation of Francis Bacon's paintings (the artist himself probably a descendant of that other Francis Bacon, a key originator of the concept of enclosure as it was introduced in chapter 1), seen partially in the light of John Berger's (2015) more 'damning' interpretations, is a far more interesting analysis, however unintended, of the effects of novel techniques of governance (or media) than his account of 'societies of control' (itself a kind of Foucault 2.0).

There may be a way out of enclosures yet by rethinking their contours, and re-relating to their contents, via categories and practices more closely linked to the sublime (and far beyond). And hence to categories which are themselves much more difficult to subjectively experience, rationally conceive, discursively articulate, mathematically formulate, technologically produce, economically value, experimentally reproduce, legally enforce, culturally authenticate, or parasitically intercept.

5

Materiality, Virtuality, and Temporality

5.1. How to Buy Yourself a Night in Minecraft

Let's begin with five observations: 1) what is particularly important about mirrors is not that you can see yourself in them, but that you cannot see behind them;[1] 2) the exemplary medium, the 'queen' of all media, is therefore the thermos, understood as an internally mirrored container; 3) thermoses preserve differences across distances by ensuring that their contents stave off thermal equilibrium for short periods of time; 4) but they only do so at the expense of not just binding the contents to the container, but also blinding the contents to whatever surrounds the container; 5) if you want to survive your first night in Minecraft, and not get eaten by some creep, the simplest strategy is to dig down your own height (plus one) in distance, and then put a block above you; see Figure 5.1. In some sense, you trade your ability to sense and move in exchange for about ten minutes of time. Like the contents of a thermos, you buy yourself a 'night' by allowing yourself to be blinded and bound.

With these observations in mind, we may define archeology in a relatively broad way. But to do that, we need a workable notion of death—say, coming to equilibrium with one's environment (which is precisely what a thermos, or a manhole in Minecraft, allows one to avoid).[2] From such a vantage, not just anyone, but also anything, can die insofar as it becomes indistinguishable from its surroundings (disappearing, as it were, without a trace).[3] Understood as such, archeology is interested in anything that didn't die insofar as it tells a tale about something that did. That is, something must not have come to equilibrium with its environment, such that it can be distinguished as figure to ground (or signal in noise). And this same something, by reference to a ground, figures as evidence of something else (itself otherwise lost in the noise). Phrased another way, archeology is interested in whatever 'stands out' insofar as it 'stands for' that which is no longer 'standing'.[4]

Notice, then, that this definition turns on two kinds of *grounds*. The first kind of ground is relatively sensorial (figure to ground, signal in noise). And the second

Paul Kockelman. *The Art of Interpretation in the Age of Computation.* © Oxford University Press 2017

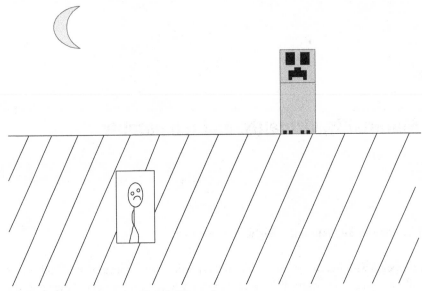

FIGURE 5.1 Surviving Your First Night in Minecraft

kind of ground is relatively semiotic (figurable as sign of something else in reference to an interpretive ground). Phrased another way, one and the same agent, however distributed or collective, needs to both signify and interpret. They must sense something as a sign and, concomitantly, actually create the sign—if only by bringing it into view as such. And they must interpret this sign, by treating it as a sign of something else and, concomitantly, relating to that something else—whatever the degree of remove.

We will take up these and many other senses of ground below. For the moment, though, it is enough to focus on two overarching points. First, archeology, like any other art or science, is a semiotic endeavor: a sign gives rise to an interpretant in reference to the features of an object and the interests of an agent. That hardly needs to be argued. And second, a key thing that differentiates archeology (in a narrow sense) from other semiotic endeavors (such that the discipline itself 'stands out', so to speak, and doesn't die) is that both of these grounds—sensorial and semiotic—are tightly coupled to, if not coterminous with, 'the ground'. That is, the sensorial ground is the semiotic ground is the ground you're standing on (and often buried in).

***

This chapter is, in part, about the relation between preservation and presumption. Returning to some of the issues raised at the beginning of chapter 4, it focuses on the relation between that which is lost and that which is preserved, where the latter is understood as a trace of the former. And it focuses on the nature of the assumptions that ground such understandings: what must an interpreting agent assume about a given environment, and the organisms that inhabit it, in order to notice, connect, and leverage such traces. This chapter is also, in part, about the relation between meaning and materiality. It focuses on various kinds of durability that allow particular materials to last, and thereby preserve meaning, by leaving relatively enduring traces. And it focuses on various ways both durability and ephemerality are produced and incorporated by particular media, and imagined and critiqued by various theorists of media. Finally, this chapter is also, in part, about reality and virtuality. It focuses on various ways this distinction has been understood and leveraged by media theorists. And it focuses on the relation between virtuality per se, and other species of modality, such as the possible, quali-, and potential, as well as the actual, necessary and obligatory. As will be seen, a central concern of this chapter, one which underlies all these crisscrossing connections, is *time*.

Section 5.2 explores such connections by asking, why is archeology so 'hard'. It introduces six key grounds that, while necessarily presumed, are rarely proposed, when figuring past life-worlds through their material remains. And it compares and contrasts the grounds of archeology with the grounds of other kinds of historical semiotic endeavors, such as astrophysics, geology and cosmology. It incorporates, and goes beyond, the relatively Peircean account of meaning offered in chapter 4, as well as the more conventional approaches to media and mediation that were described and critiqued there.

Section 5.3 develops Peirce's understanding of semiotic grounds, focusing not on iconic, indexical, and symbolic relations between signs and objects (itself a relatively tired topic), but rather on the assumptions and abilities semiotic agents must have in order to perceive, understand, and wield such relations. And it pushes past Peirce by focusing on situations in which there are two overlapping grounds, such as in Grice's understanding of nonconventional communication, and Freud's interpretation of dreams.

The next three sections return to the account of sense and secrets offered in chapter 3, leveraging this understanding of grounds to develop an account of the virtual. Section 5.4 reviews Peirce's notion of token and type, and introduces the notion of singularities to contrast with his notion of replicas. It uses these concepts to reinterpret classic ideas from von Humboldt (on generativity) and Benjamin (on aura). Section 5.5 reviews and critiques Deleuze's influential understanding of the virtual. It focuses on how we develop intuitions for the (otherwise secret) sense-making capabilities of highly complex systems. Section 5.6 offers an alternative vision of the virtual, using some key concepts from Peirce. And the conclusion focuses on the ways different grounds license different understandings of the virtual, and the way these grounds are ontology-specific and frame-dependent, and thereby differ across collectivities, and change over time.

5.2. Why Archeology Is So Hard

Let us return to our thermos, our manhole, our mirror. Two entities, call them 'big L' and 'little l', had to interact, such that each could leave an impression on the other. (And if you don't like the Hegelian story [there were two entities, who came to interact], you can have the Heideggerian story [there was interaction, until the interactants got distracted].) How they interact (hit, shake, pound, etc.) is not of concern for the moment. At some point, they go their separate ways in a very peculiar way. Little l says, *bind me and blind me, for I want to live.* And big L says, *unbind me and unblind me, for I would rather die.* If you want big L, you want to live it up, you've got to give up little l. Conversely, if you want little l, you want to live a long time, you've got to give up big L. This is as much a thermodynamic parable as it is a moral law—where the physicist Boltzmann and the fabulist Aesop meet. And it is a basic insight that allows archeology to work—we can learn about big L (the hand) from little l (the handle), given that they once danced, got distracted, and opted for different deals. To return to Minecraft, one half of the interaction (little l) remained in the manhole; and the other half (big L) went up to confront the creep. And the creep is creepy. Its name is *entropy* (information's daemonic twin).

With this parable/law in mind, and setting aside that odd overlapping of grounds for the moment, notice that this definition of archeology is otherwise radically portable, in the sense of 'broad in scope' or 'independent of scale'. To see how, note the following three points. First, it is not that one thing is completely alive, and the other thing is completely dead. All that matters is that one thing resists coming to equilibrium for a little longer than the other thing. And this should make sense—it's not usually the living that speaks most articulately about the dead, but more often the dying. Second, the duration that the living has to go the distance (in comparison to the dead), doesn't have to be historical in magnitude. If it lasts a picosecond longer that is enough (think of the trace of collisions in a particle detector, and the tale this tells of whatever just collided). Indeed, the scales can be wider as well: if it lasts fourteen billion years that is also enough (think of microwave background radiation, and the tale this tells of the origins of the universe). And third, the 'duration' does not even have to be temporal per se (though it is usually, and perhaps necessarily, if not definitionally, coupled to time). All that is required—to return to some of the concerns of chapter 2—is that something bridges a distance, any distance: *here* and *there, this* and *that, I* and *you, us* and *them, here* and the *hereafter.*[5] Indeed, if archaeologists (in the narrow sense) often focus on the *there*-after, linguistic anthropologists often focus on a kind of *hear*-after. In short, all we need to be doing archeology (in the wide sense) is a difference in liveliness (big L, little l), however slight, and a distance between the differentiated (above ground, below ground), however small.

That is all we can ever mean by 'materiality'. And so there are as many 'materialities', and thus potential archeologies, as there are modes of differentiation and distance.[6] But archeology, in a narrow sense, has nonetheless focused on materiality in a very conventional sense—that which is both hard and handy. And so one overarching question is, *why*? Well, if all you need is for one medium to live (little l) and another medium to die (big L), the discipline relies on some stereotypic forms of media, both to establish and to extend itself. As for establishment, verbal language and embodied habit (big L) had to die in order that 'materiality' (little l) could live. (We needn't be sad for their sacrifice; they really got to live it up while they lasted.) As for extension, when archaeologists do take archeology to another scale, they usually depend on the relative liveliness (little l) of some particular medium: into the archive (written language), onto the internet (HTML), back to the genome (DNA). That should be obvious enough; materiality is defined by contrast to other media and, in particular, stereotypes about other media.

But conventional understandings of materiality do not just turn on relative durability. Bones and stones, if you can forgive this vulgar formulation, are both holdable and beholdable. They are suitably scaled to the size, strength, shape, senses, and even sapience of people. They are *whats* that can be sensed and moved by *whos*.[7] And it is not without reason that similar kinds of objects constitute our stereotype of material culture. As we said above, before big L and little l got distracted and went their separate ways, they had to have danced, precisely so that each could leave its impression (or expression) on the other, such that little l can subsequently shed light on big L, not only illuminating it as a life-form but also as a form of life. Finally, if archaeologists insist on a certain scale, it is really a question of their own survival: they necessarily bind themselves to certain scales, while blinding themselves from other scales, in order to both stand out, and stay standing, as a discipline.[8]

So now we may return to our initial question: Why is archeology so 'hard'? And the answer offered so far is fourfold. First, archaeologists are hardened: theirs is a discipline that deals with death on a daily basis. They don't just have one foot in the grave, they've got one hand and one eye as well. (It's no wonder they run in packs and drink like fish.) Second, their media is necessarily durable in relation to a variety of other media. Third, archaeologists are obdurate: they insist on a certain scale—not just the hard but also the handy, not just the holdable but also the beholdable—and not without reason. And finally, as we will now see, archeology as a discipline is quite difficult to do.

Figure 5.2 shows a distinction which is relatively untenable (or perhaps simply upsetting) for the following reasons. As we will discuss at length in chapter 6, where we draw line between causality and semiosis is itself grounded in semiosis (or is it causality?).[9] Causality can be framed as semiosis ('fetishization') and semiosis can be framed as causality ('reification'), with more or less *semiotic strain* (understood as symptoms of improper framings, themselves only available as 'symptoms' in a particular frame). And most actually occurring semiotic processes depend on long chains of causal processes; and many actually occurring causal processes turn on long chains of semiotic processes (where both such facts are key attributes of 'infrastructure' in an expanded sense). Such caveats aside, this will prove to be a useful distinction in what follows.

Figure 5.3 foregrounds the key components of semiotic processes, as introduced above. If we take S to mean 'sign' and I to mean 'interpretant', the upper ellipse may be framed as an *environment*. If we take S to mean 'sensation' and I to

FIGURE 5.2 Causality and Semiosis Compared

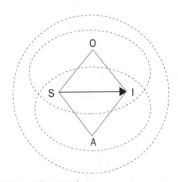

FIGURE 5.3 Environment, Organism, Envorganism

mean 'instigation', the lower ellipse may be framed as an *organism.* Putting both together as inseparably coupled, as per the encompassing circle, we have an *envorganism.* This entity is suitably simplified such that it may usefully scale to describe distributed and collective entities of various temporal, spatial, and social sizes (Kockelman 2011a, 2013). Recall Figure 1.1 and, in particular, our discussion of the actor-environment interface.

So much for semiotic processes, and their components (S, O, I, A), as figures. Let us now return to grounds—the otherwise empty boxes behind the figures. Going from top to bottom, and from left to right, in Figure 5.4, we have the following kinds of grounds. First, pushing past Bateson (1972), the sign (S) must be able to stand out in an environment (be a difference) and, concomitantly, be sensible to an organism. Reciprocally, the interpretant (I) must be able to stand up in an environment (make a difference) and, concomitantly, be instigatable by an organism.

Note, then, that the gestalt intuition is true for action as much as perception. And thus to simply figure something as a sign or interpretant requires an enormous set of relatively backgrounded assumptions about the various propensities of, and interrelations between, organisms and environments.

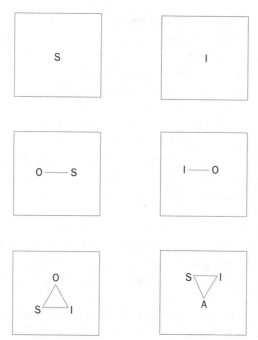

FIGURE 5.4 Figures and Grounds

Second, following the usual Peircean formulation (1955a; Parmentier 1994; Kockelman 2015), the object must (seem to) have qualities in common with the sign, be causally related to the sign, or be conventionally associated with the sign. Crucially, this O-S relation only holds in a particular environment (qua ontologized world) and to a particular organism (qua worlded ontology). Reciprocally, the exact same issues arise in intervention (I-O) as in representation. Just as an organism cannot infer fire from smoke without 'reference to' such a ground, an organism cannot act to extinguish fire by throwing water on it without 'reference to' such a ground.[10]

Such assumptions (about qualities, causes, and conventions) are as likely to be embodied in an organism and embedded in an environment as they are encoded and enminded; and they are as likely to be distributed across organisms as they are evinced in the actions of a single organism. Such assumptions, then, may be relatively narrow or wide, shifting or stable, individual or collective, instinctive or instituted, taken for granted or called into question.

Third, a key question here is not, what is the object of this sign (given such a Peircean ground), but rather what is an appropriate and effective interpretant of this sign-object relation (S-O-I) given the 'selfhood' of the interpreting organism, with its distinctly reflexive modes of desire, affect, and accountability (Kockelman 2011b, 2016). For example, it's not just that one can infer fire from smoke (O-S), or even use water to extinguish fire (I-O), but that one can flee or fight, weep or rejoice, depending on what or who is burning. Reciprocally, a key question here is why does the agent instigate how it does in the context of sensing what it does (S-A-I) given the 'otherhood' of the sensed environment, with its distinctly complementary qualia, affordances, and properties.

To understand semiotic processes (qua figures) we need to have access to these grounds. And to know such grounds and, in particular, to know about transformations in such grounds over time is, in no small part, to know much of what there is to be known about a given form of life (or life form). Needless to say, and following our discussion of Heidegger in chapter 3 and Jakobson in chapter 2, human-specific modes of semiosis are especially powerful precisely because they can so readily be used to figure their own grounds, not just by implicitly showing them (via something akin to the poetic function) but also by explicitly stating them (via something akin to the metalinguistic function).

(Phrased another way, such grounds are another another way of thinking about sense [or value or secrets], as it was characterized in chapter 3. And just as we have techniques for stating and showing the sense of a system through the system itself, so we have techniques for explicitly or implicitly figuring the grounds from which we figure.)

Figure 5.5 rotates the envorganism, blows up the O-S ground (thereby highlighting some of its fine structure), and shows characteristic differences in that ground as a function of whether the semiotic agent is an archaeologist or an astrophysicist.[11] As may be seen, part of what makes archeology so difficult is that, to get to big O, they need to go through a long line of not just cause-effect relations, but also sign-interpretant relations. Recall Figure 5.2 and note the relation to Figure 4.1. And to get through such sign-interpretant relations (themselves interrelated with various other objects and agents), they need to already know quite a lot about the six grounds just described. But here's the rub: it's often precisely those grounds that constitute big O—that is, precisely what they're trying to find out about. In some sense, they need to have already gotten where they're going in order to get there.[12] And if one thinks semiotic processes, such as verbal language and gesture, qua big L, are soft in comparison to bones and stones, qua little l, these grounds are usually far softer than such stereotypic figures.

So what do archaeologists do in the face of such difficulties? Well, one possibility is to find the archaeological equivalent of 'reflexive language' (Jakobson 1990a)—a modality of material culture in which its own grounds get figured. And the intentional grave, qua burial ground, is probably as close as can be. Another possibility is this: if you can't find something that lives forever (or even ever really shows its face in the first place), find something that is perpetually born again. And what is born again? Common ground or, in this case, common grounds. And, indeed, what is perhaps most interesting about archeology is not their findings per se, nor even the history of their findings, but rather the genealogy of the common grounds that they had to presume in order to find anything in the first place. We might call the discipline that studies this genealogy *arch-aeology*. And we might say

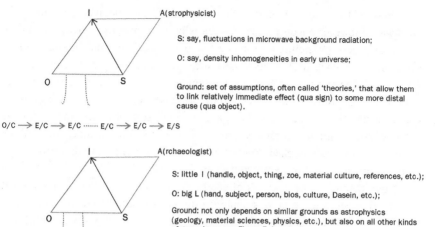

FIGURE 5.5 Archeology and Astrophysics Compared

that one reason archeology as a discipline has proven to be particularly enduring—and thus 'hard' in a fifth and final sense—is that many of its members are arch-aeologists as much as archaeologists.

5.3. Figure and Ground, Grice and Freud

In a narrow sense, then, the ground is the set of sensibilities to, and assumptions about, qualities, causes, and conventions that an interpreter must have in order to move from a sign to an object (or a signer must have to move from an object to a sign), and hence whatever makes a sign-object relation more or less iconic, indexical, or symbolic. For example, just as the word 'apple' can only stand for a particular kind of fruit to an agent who has a particular linguistic convention, a fever can only stand for the flu to an agent who has a particular causal understanding of illnesses, and red can only stand for blood to an agent that can attend to such a shared quality across otherwise different experiences (Kockelman 2013a, 2015). In a broad sense, the ground is this relation plus every other kind of relation in Figure 5.4, and so constitutes everything an analyst must investigate when trying to understand how and why an interpreter attended to a particular sign, arrived at a particular object, and expressed a particular interpretant.

That is, far more important than attending to the iconic, indexical or symbolic nature of a sign per se is to, first, attend to the sensibilities and assumptions semiotic agents must have (and the qualia, affordances, and properties their environments must have) if they are to connect signs and objects in iconic, indexical, and sym-bolic ways (however unconsciously, ill-advisedly, or erroneously). Second, analyze the conditions of possibility for such agents to have such sensibilities and assump-tions (and for such environments to have such qualia, affordances, and properties). Third, given the fact that such agents have many such grounds, some of which are quite shaky and idiosyncratic, attend to the strategies they have for shifting among them, shoring them up, sharing them, keeping their secrets secure, and outing (as well as overlooking) their ostensible errors. Finally, attend to the other five kinds of grounds just as carefully, each of which involves similar issues and undergoes simi-lar dynamics, in highly entangled and emergent ways.

Note, then, that the contents of the books you read and the images you see and the theories your equations demonstrate and the ideas your diagrams illus-trate have radically important effects on your assumptions about, and abilities to attend to, possible qualities, causes, and conventions; and, hence, have radically important effects on your semiotic processes insofar as such processes proceed in reference to such assumptions and abilities (Kockelman 2016). Contra McLuhan's (1996) famous dictum, *the message—and much else besides—is just as important as the medium* (for mediation).

Note, then, that to understand how agents come to figure (and figurate) objects (selves, and others) by reference to such grounds, we must simultaneously understand their figuring of such grounds (as a kind of semiotic object), and their grounding of such grounds (through processes and practices that often seem to be minimally semiotic).

Chapter 7 will return to these issues at length, focusing on the temporality of (ontological) grounds: for not only are grounds a condition for interpretation, they are also a consequence of interpretation, and so transform on various timescales (while transforming various timescales), by means of various processes, with more or less inertia (as well as with more or less strife, strategy, strain, and serendipity). In the rest of this section, we turn to a particularly important class of semiotic pro-cesses that turn on the intersection of two different grounds, by reinterpreting and radically generalizing some ideas of Paul Grice (1989) and Sigmund Freud (1999).

To do this, we first need to introduce a distinction made by Peirce (1998 [1903]) between dynamic and immediate objects. For present purposes, a *dynamic object* relates to a sign as cause to effect. It is whatever brings the sign into being as such—for example, the signer's intention to communicate, itself a cause of the sign they use to communicate. An *immediate object* relates to a sign as effect to cause. It is whatever the sign brings into being—(e.g., whatever the sign points to, or provides information about, and thereby brings to another's attention).[13] For example, when I say, 'the train is arriving at 6:00', the dynamic object is my intention to commu-nicate (a desire to tell you something, itself functioning to affiliate as much as to inform); and the immediate object is the content so communicated (some fact about the scheduling of infrastructure). Similarly, symptoms, as classically understood, have immediate objects which are dynamic objects: the symptom (say, some kind of rash) brings to the doctor's attention that which causes the symptom (say, a particular illness, or past contact with a particular plant or parasite).

Many forms of communication seem to turn on two interlocking semiotic processes, one relatively indexical (or 'concrete'), and the other relatively inferential (or 'abstract'); see Figure 5.6. Let me use this framework to retheorize an example that was offered by Tomasello (2008, 3–5). Suppose we are college-age friends, and are walking toward the library to study. With a simple gesture you direct my attention to a bicycle that is locked outside the entrance. Such a sign may be framed as having a relatively dynamic object (your intention to communicate), and a relatively immediate object (the bicycle, which is what you are ostensibly pointing at). That is, not only do you directly point out the bicycle (through your gesture), you also indirectly point out that you are pointing it out ('on purpose'). And so, as an interpreter, I not only attend to the bicycle, I also attend to your intention to draw my attention to it. This is the first semiotic process, the relatively concrete one, grounded as it is in indexical contiguities, such that its immediate object is relatively available in the current context.

Crucially, my interpretant is not just to look at, or attend to, the bicycle (immediate object), and attend to your attention to it (dynamic object), it is to then take the bicycle as a sign that points to something else in a less immediate, or more abstract, inferential context. In particular, knowing what you pointed out, and knowing that you pointed it out on purpose, may lead me to a hypothesis (itself a kind of interpretant): my friend wants me to see that the bicycle belongs to my ex-boyfriend, someone he knows I want to avoid, and so is probably indicating that we should go somewhere else to study. That is, in the first semiotic process, the immediate object was the bicycle and the sign was my friend's gesture; in the second semiotic processes, the bicycle has become a sign whose immediate object is my friend's desire to study somewhere else so as to avoid an awkward situation. Crucially, to

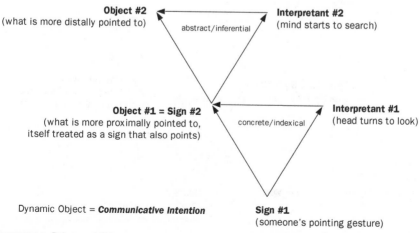

FIGURE 5.6 Peirce and Grice

get to this immediate object, I had to attend to its dynamic object, which is, in some sense, the proceeding semiotic process: my friend purposely pointed to the bicycle and so probably wants me to draw an inference from it. This interpretation, then, is relatively abstract or inferential: a hypothesis, or abduction, grounded in my assumptions about minds as much as worlds, grounded in me and my friend's common ground (what we both know we each know), itself grounded in the ongoing dynamics of our current interaction (and past interactions), as well as in our shared culture (that ultimate interpretive ground, which harbors notions like 'awkward situation', 'ex-boyfriend', and 'university library').[14]

Such a formulation of complex, doubly grounded semiotic processes is meant to capture not only classic Gricean processes (sometimes called 'ostensive-inferential' communication, or conversational implicature[15]), but also much else besides. In particular, Freudian processes arguably turn on a similar logic (with, to be sure, radically different grounds, qua assumptions about minds, signs, and worlds). As this story goes, my dreams have a manifest content (what they point to concretely, or conventionally) and a latent content (what they point to abstractly, or elliptically). And to recover the latent content (that is, the immediate object of the second semiotic process) from the manifest content (that is, the immediate object of the first semiotic process), an analyst has to make reference to the dynamic objects of these semiotic processes. See Figure 5.7. Crucially, from the standpoint of such a hermeneutic, *such dynamic objects are not communicative intentions, but rather repressed wishes*. It is only by knowing (or positing) that a dream was the product (qua effect) of a censored desire, itself due to the superego's parasitic interference of the id's wishfulness, that an analyst can figure out what the latent content of the dream actually is.[16] See Figure 5.8.

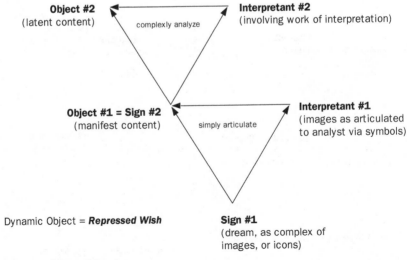

FIGURE 5.7 Grice and Freud

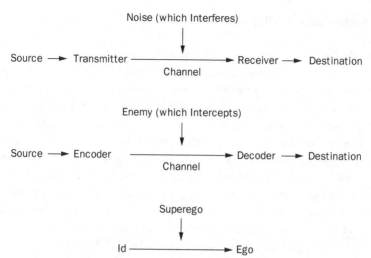

FIGURE 5.8 Shannon and Freud

Freud was indeed a kind of archaeologist—not just digging down into the sediments of the soul, but also teaching us to interpret what there is to be found, by hypothesizing a variety of causal processes that lay below. And Foucault, perhaps more importantly, was a kind of arch-aeologist—offering a genealogy of such hermeneutic grounds, describing the conditions and consequences of a variety of disciplinary enclosures, and the kinds of concrete and abstract objects (or rather 'subjects') that are their effects. (Recall Figure 5.5, but now replace A with 'psycho-Analyst', and add such complexly cascading 'double grounds' along all the paths between the S's and O's, as well as all the historical grounds, as revealed through a genealogical stance, that lead to such shared hermeneutics.)

To tie in with our previous discussion, note how we now have to take into account at least two grounds (and potentially four) in figuring out the ultimate object of a sign: how to get to the first immediate object (and what was the first dynamic object); and how to get to the second immediate object (by way of the first immediate and dynamic objects, themselves a key component of the second dynamic object). To return to chapter 4, note how simplistic stereotypic understandings of sense can be—as a conventionally encoded path between a word and a referent. We now have two paths to trace out, each moving along a different kind of ground, neither of which, *pace* Saussure and Frege, is particularly semantic (deductive) or symbolic, but rather highly abductive (hypothetical) and indexical.

Ironically, poetry is precisely that semiotic phenomenon which is closest to dreams in terms of Freudian processes like condensation, displacement, and allusion. And it is precisely poetic processes, in the sense of repetition, that are so useful for recovering sense. And, perhaps more ironic still, repetition was precisely a key symptom of repressed desires, or those experiences that 'we just cannot quit', for which we cannot secure (en)closure.

5.4. Singularities and Replicas, Qualia and Aura

Before entering into Peirce's discussion of the virtual, let us take up his notion of replicas, and derive a notion of singularities. Peirce (1955a; and see Parmentier 1994) framed the sign component of a semiotic process in terms of three modalities: *quali-signs* (that is, qualities that could constitute signs if actually embodied); *sin-signs* (that is, actual occurring signs, also known as 'tokens', themselves made up of one or more quali-signs); and *legi-signs* (that is, relatively shared and collectively regimented signs, also known as 'types'). For example, all the words in the English language, understood as distinctive sound patterns (as normatively established by some semiotic collectivity), are legi-signs, or types. And any actual instance of usage, in which someone says such a word at a particular moment in space-time through some eventive sounding, is a sin-sign, or token. (We will return to the more elusive notion of quali-signs below.) Recall Table 1.1.

From this perspective, Saussure's signifiers are legi-signs: a type of sign whose identity, or essential characteristic, is its difference from the other signs that it may combine with, or substitute for, in some larger, socially governed and historically given system. And if a signifier seen through the lens of *langue* is a legi-sign, a signifier seen through the lens of *parole* is a sign-token: some actually occurring instance of a word. Most actually occurring words are tokens of preestablished types, and so count as *replicas* for Peirce. Note, then, that a replica is not, by definition, a copy of an original (though it may be). A replica is a concrete token of an abstract type. And, to introduce a new term, while staying within Peirce's system, we might use the word *singularity* to mean an unprecedented or unreplicatable token (Kockelman 2005). Singularities are actually occurring signs that have never occurred before, and may never occur again.

Just as there are tokens and types at the level of words, so there are tokens and types at smaller scales of linguistic structure (e.g., affixes and roots) and tokens and types at larger scales of linguistic structure (e.g., sentences and speech genres). In light of these facts, we might reinterpret von Humboldt's (1999) famous insight, itself thoroughly rechanneled through Chomsky (1965), as to the inherent generativity of language: we are each given a finite set of types (say, a lexicon and a grammar, or an ensemble of words and rules); with these types, we can construct an infinite number of tokens (say, all the possible sentences that may be built with such resources, as uttered in particular contexts) where, crucially, such tokens may be singularities (in the sense of sentences never said before) as much as replicas (sentences said over and over again).

Just as we can ask, what is a possible language (or quali-language), given the particular cognitive and social capacities of humans, so we can ask what is a possible sentence, given the grammar of a particular language. And if each of us really is given a finite number of constraints (qua lexical and grammatical types) with which we can produce an infinite number of configurations (qua utterance tokens), how do we develop an intuition for such an infinity of quali-signs? What are some of the ways we have of figuring such grounds, of coming to an understanding—however partial—of our own creative capacities?

All this is another way of talking about infinite ends with finite means, as was first introduced in chapter 3, and as will be further developed in sections 5.5 and 5.6. As will be developed in chapter 6, such an important insight undergirds our understanding of symbolic systems—not just natural languages, but also computer languages, and automata more generally. That said, the Gricean claim is arguably more astounding, and certainly much less celebrated: with a single sign (such as the pointing gesture) we can point out an infinity of different objects (insofar as the meaning of such a gesture is context-dependent, and so shifts accordingly); moreover, any one of these relatively immediate objects can itself be understood as a sign of a relatively abstract object, itself inferred 'by reference to' a communicative intention, common ground, and culture more generally (recall our discussion of Heidegger and Jakobson). The indexical-inferential is potentially far more creative than the symbolic-grammatical.

Perhaps nothing is so productive, or poignant, as a *pointer*—at least when understood *not* simply as a shifter, or indexical symbol (the finger, 'the digital', and so forth); but when understood as an indexical-inferential process, productively and parasitically channeled through both concrete and abstract grounds, referring to immediate objects 'in reference to' dynamic objects (and thereby able to 'refer to' everything else under the sun).

***

Sin-signs and legi-signs, as well as replicas and singularities, are relatively easy to understand. But quali-signs are a bit tricky. In some sense, any conceivable quality is a potential sign to a creature that can sense that quality (when actually embodied in some event or entity), and so the category is too large and nebulous as such. For present purposes, what makes quali-signs so interesting is the way we understand possible limitations on such possibilities. We might do this by focusing on the sensory and instigatory capacities of the agents that express and interpret them. For example, what kinds of words are possible (given the phonology of a particular language, or the habits of a particular language community)? What kinds of facial expressions are possible (given the physiology of the human face, or culture specific ways of regimenting and registering facial expressions)? What kinds of paintings are possible (given the affordances of a particular medium, or the norms of a particular aesthetic tradition)? What kinds of sounds are possible (given the physiology of the human ear and tongue, and the channeling of these abilities, by institutions and infrastructure as much as instincts)? More generally, what can make a difference to a ship's radar, an insect's antenna, a dog's nose, or a tongue's taste buds? Such issues are key for understanding life-forms as much as forms of life. To return to the concerns of sections 5.1 and 5.2, in outlining possible signs one is simultaneously outlining key properties of organisms and environments, of collectivities and histories, of poetics and politics, of agents and worlds.

Crucially, if we define *quali-signs* as whatever could be sensed by a semiotic agent (and thus possibly stand for an object to that agent, when embodied), we may define *quali-interpretants* as whatever could be instigated by a semiotic agent (and, hence, be created by a sign insofar as it stands for an object), and *quali-objects* as whatever could organize the quali-signs (or sensations) and quali-interpretants (or instigations) of some agent. That is, a quali-object is whatever could be a significant feature in some environment given the agent's selective interests. From this standpoint, to return to the concerns of section 4.1, one function of media is precisely to extend (as well as augment, intensify, buffer, mollify, and mitigate) the sensory and instigatory capabilities of semiotic agents (as well as their communicative and cognitive abilities more generally). In this way, gloves, camouflage, drones, erasers, ice-picks, and sunglasses are media, as much as gramophones, film, and typewriters. Such entities not only transform the quali-signs and quali-interpretants of semiotic agents (and, concomitantly, their quali-objects); they also transform the semiotic agents per se, as *quali-agents*, insofar as the features of such objects are so tightly coupled to the interests of such agents (Kockelman 2013a, 53).

***

These concepts, along with those developed in the last two sections, can be used to reinterpret Benjamin's (1968a) somewhat elusive notion of 'aura', as well as several supplementary notions it depends on.

An individual work of art (some singularity), in contrast to any of its copies (qua replicas), has *presence*: its actual trajectory through space-time, from the context in which it was created, through all the contexts in which it was carried, to the context in which it confronts us.

Such a trajectory left a causal (indexical) and conventional (symbolic) trace, both in the world and on the work of art, via the material transformations it went through and the social transactions it passed through. Such a trace is what secures the *authenticity* of the original in confrontation with any copy, insofar as any copy necessarily lacks these features in comparison.

For these reasons, the original work has *authority*. In part, this means that the work can, with a little help, speak on its own behalf (proving itself authentic in comparison to any copy via its trace). And, in part, this means that the traditions (which not only created the work, but also carried it, such that it may subsequently confront us) have a hold on us, in the sense that their values continue to make a claim on us.

Copies, in contrast, have two competing values: they can highlight features of the original that might otherwise go unnoticed (new perspectives, or quali-signs); and they can be brought to audiences that might otherwise be unawares (expanded publics, or quali-agents). And so while the copies don't have the virtues of authenticity and authority, they nevertheless have the values of adjustable perspective and increased portability—and thus enable radical changes in social and sensory scales.

In effect, it becomes easier and easier to attend to the copies, and more and more difficult to attend to the original. And this fact is enough to lessen the authority that the original holds over us, to make the tradition that it attests to less important, and thus to make our experience of its presence diminish. *Aura* is precisely this experience of the work's presence; and precisely that which 'whithers' in the age of reproduction (if you believe Benjamin).

Crucially, this lessening of authority constitutes a vicious circle in two intimately related ways. First, the tradition is at once a *dynamic and immediate object* of the work: it brought the work into being as such; and yet, its being is mainly known through the work. And, secondly, the tradition is at once a *dynamic and immediate interpretant* of the work: only through it, as a kind of ground, can we understand the relevance of the work; and yet, only by having interpreted the work, can we see the relevance of the tradition. Recall *the rub* of archaeological hermeneutics, and source-dependent channels more generally.

To reframe some of these claims in terms of earlier categories: the parasites kill their host, the effects destroy their cause, the interpretants destroy their object. A plethora of replicas replaces an original singularity. In repetitively tracing we efface what is traced.

5.5. Deleuze's Understanding of the Virtual

In his *Critique of Pure Reason*, Kant introduced the Table of Categories: quality, quantity, relation, and modality. He characterized these categories as, "[a] list of all original pure concepts of synthesis that the understanding contains within itself a priori" (1965 [1781], 114). And he argued that such seemingly universal conceptions, while a condition of possibility for experience, are not themselves able to be experienced. In some sense, they are human-specific forms of mediation, or 'universal media': a condition of possibility for our minds to meet the world, but not able to be met like the world itself. As is well known, early anthropologists (Durkheim and Mauss, especially) were interested in the collective conditions of possibility for such categories (as well as similar categories from other philosophers, such as Aristotle's notion of animacy and causality). In particular, they were interested in studying the ways different collectivities, from 'primitive communities' to 'modern societies', conceived of such categories, and thus the inherently social and historical origins of such conceptions. And just as Mauss and Durkheim were interested in the social and historical mediation of such categories, anthropologists and linguists, such as Boas and Sapir, were interested in the cultural and grammatical mediation of such categories.

For present purposes, Kant's category of modality is the most relevant. In *The Critique of Pure Reason*, Kant described three kinds of modality: possibility, existence, necessity. And he noted that, "The categories of modality have the peculiarity that, in determining an object, they do not in the least enlarge the concept to which they are attached as predicates. They only express the *relation* of the concept to the faculty of knowledge" (1965 [1781], 239; italics added). In the *Critique of Practical Reason*, Kant also described three kinds of modality: permission, action, and obligation. Modern linguists usually call the first kinds of modality *epistemic* (having to do with degrees of certainty, or grounds for inference); and the latter kinds of modality *deontic* (having to do with degrees of obligation, or grounds for action). Interestingly, certain grammatical categories in English, known as modal auxiliary verbs, serve both kinds of functions. Compare, for example *he may/must be rich* (indicating epistemic possibility/necessity, turning on a kind of inference in relation to knowledge) and *you may/must go to the store* (indicating deontic permission/obligation, turning on a kind of normativity in relation to power). Finally, notice how such grammatical categories evince that particular 'peculiarity' that Kant noticed: they don't just relate subject (he/you) and predicate (is rich, go to store), they relate that relation back to the knowing (or speaking) subject.

Following our discussion of semiotic processes in chapter 1, readers will note that both kinds of modality, in a radically generalized sense, map onto Peirce's distinctions between firstness, secondness, and thirdness (1955b). Recall Table 1.1. Compare, for example, quali-signs, sin-signs, and legi-signs. And following our discussion of duplex categories in chapter 2, and in line with Kant's definition of modality, readers will note that both kinds of categories are shifters, indicating the speaker's *relation* to what she is saying, qua epistemic or deontic stance, as opposed to what she is saying per se (Jakobson 1990b; Kockelman 2010a).

Current scholarly interest in virtuality—itself a seemingly novel kind of modality—has many origins. Let us focus on Giles Deleuze's (1966, 1994 [1968]) conception of this category, insofar as it underlies two often cited understandings of the virtual: those by Brian Massumi (2002) and Manuel Delanda (2011). Deleuze was heavily influenced by Poincaré's understanding of mathematical singularities underlying the phase space of physical systems. He understood the virtual to be real, but not actual (or existent). It was real insofar as it organized the possibility space of actual trajectories taken by physical systems through phase space; but it was not actual insofar as it could never show up as a sensible event, located at some point in space and time. Note, then, that the virtual, in this conception, is effectively a new kind of epistemic modality (in particular, a novel species of possibility). While not given in Kant's formulation, it is part of the same paradigm, and thus partakes of similar presumptions. All this needs to be unpacked.

As was shown in chapter 3, one prominent function of coordinate systems is to represent the trajectory, or path, of a physical system over time: from a mass oscillating on a spring to a solar system, and far beyond. For classic systems of interest, such representations involve the following sorts of assumptions. There is a set of laws that applies to some phenomenon (say, Newton's laws, as applying to relatively massive objects moving at low speeds). There is some system of interest whose behavior can be modeled by such laws (say, a pendulum swinging under the effect of gravity). There is the phase space of possible states such a system could be in (say, all possible combinations of the pendulum's angular position and momentum, as generalized coordinates). Recall our discussion of frames of relevance in chapter 3. There are the equations of motion themselves (derived by applying the physical laws to the system of interest in terms of the coordinates of phase space). There are the initial conditions (where, in phase space, the system begins: say, its angular position and momentum at time t = 0). And there is the actual trajectory, through phase space, of the system (from its initial conditions on, as determined by the equations of motion)—the planets' orbits, the pendulum's swing.

Finally, and perhaps most interestingly, there is the set of fixed points. These are special positions in phase space, determined by extrema of the equations of motion, whose values provide key information about the general characteristics of all possible trajectories of such systems. (While such fixed points are sometimes called 'singularities', they should not be confused with the semiotic notion of singularities, as contrasted with replicas, that was introduced in section 5.4.) For example, a simple pendulum has two fixed points: that place in phase space where both its angular position and angular momentum are zero (i.e., the pendulum is at its lowest point and stationary, or 'fixed'); and that place in phase space where its angle is 180 degrees and its angular momentum is zero (i.e., the pendulum is at its highest point and stationary). The first position constitutes a stable equilibrium (a pendulum put there will stay there, even if perturbed), and the second position constitutes an unstable equilibrium (a pendulum put there will move away from there when perturbed).

(Note, by the way, that one sense of the parasite for Serres is precisely such a perturbation. Note as well that, another key sense of the parasite is friction—in particular, that which causes all such simple harmonic oscillators, no matter where they start out from, to eventually end up in the first sort of fixed point. Recall our discussion of entropy, that ultimate enemy of all that is lively, that key agent giving a directionality to temporality.)

Deleuze (1994), building on Lautman's interpretation of Poincaré's ideas (DeLanda 2011), was presciently interested in these fixed points, using them to ground a theory of the virtual. In particular, if points in phase space could be understood as the possible, and trajectories through phase space could be understood as the actual (or existent), then fixed points in phase space could be understood as the virtual. Such points were 'real', even though the system might never actually pass through them, insofar as their values organized the actual trajectories of a system, such that knowing their values shed light on the essential dynamics of such systems. As Deleuze famously put it:

> The virtual is not opposed to the real but to the actual. The virtual is fully real in so far as it is virtual. [. . .] Indeed, the virtual must be defined as strictly a part of the real object [qua physical system, or ensemble of such

systems]—as though the object had one part of itself in the virtual into which it is plunged as though into an objective dimension. [. . .] [T]he reality of the virtual consists of the differential elements and relations [qua equations of motion] along with the singular points [qua fixed points] which correspond to them. The reality of the virtual is a structure. We must avoid giving the elements and relations that form a structure an actuality which they do not have, and withdrawing from them a reality which they have (ibid., 260; bracketed material added).

So what to make of such captivating claims? First, notice that Deleuze is, in part, simply taking issues well-known to physicists and mathematicians (differential equations and their extrema) and reworking them in philosophical terms ('let us not confuse the actual with the real'). Translation is fine, and often incredibly useful—but in this case the result is so watered down and elliptical that most of the original insights (from Newton to Poincaré, and everyone since) are lost. Indeed, the final claim is also misleading, if not incorrect. As seen in our example of the pendulum, many systems actualize their fixed points (e.g., any time a playground swing comes to a stop). Such extrema are experienced everyday.

Second, in reaching out to mathematical physics, whose equations have long constituted our stereotype of laws that represents the truly 'real', we end up focusing on epistemic modality (pure reason) at the expense of deontic modality (practical reason), not to mention *dynamic modality* and *gnomic modality*. Recall our discussion of Kant's categories, and the division of labor between his two great works. If we are to understand human reality, surely norms, 'second nature', social facts, thirdness, and various modes of permission and obligation are just as important as causes, 'first nature', facts per se, secondness, and various forms of possibility and necessity. Is it not strange that an understanding of the virtual that has been so influential among social scientists is grounded in pure reason as opposed to practical reason, in 'objectivity' as opposed to 'intersubjectivity'? Indeed, pushing past both practical and pure reason, is it not strange that a theory of the virtual that has been celebrated by theorists of affect and embodiment is so squarely centered in the most rationalist, human specific, ego-centered, and mind-centric of traditions?

And finally, as closely related to these last two points, while it is often very interesting to look for 'transcendental forms', or the universal a prioris of all experience, it is also pretty fruitful to study, with anthropologists like Durkheim and Boas, the cultural particularities and historical trajectories of beliefs in such universal conceptions—the particular ontologies, and ontological transformations, that both license and undercut such claims. That so many theorists of the virtual take up Deleuze's commitments without even recognizing such issues seems particularly problematic. As we'll see in the next section, the virtual is best understood not as some kind of 'transcendental form', but rather as a multiplicity of shifting historical formulations.

***

But these critiques aside, Massumi (2002, 134) makes a compelling distinction between the virtual as such, the possible ("the differences in content and form considered as organizable alternatives"), and the potential ("the tension between materially superposed possibilities and the advent of the new"). Let's rework these ideas from a semiotic stance in order to avoid some of the issues just mentioned, connect back to our ongoing discussion of secrets and singularities, and bypass otherwise problematic notions like 'content' and 'form'.

There is the *possible*: tokens that would conform to types, and so constitute replicas, given the constraints of a system (such as the grammar of a language). There is the *potential*: tokens that would constitute singularities (in the sense of section 5.4); they are possible, given the constraints of a system, but so infrequent, or improbable, that to sense them is to sense their novelty as much as their fit, and hence their changing of what fits, and even their contribution to changing sensibilities as to fittedness. Sometimes this strain is felt as a barrier (shoring up structure); other times as an invitation (to perturb structure). And then there is the *virtual*: some kind of self-movement that shows both the possible and the potential; not a single event that actualizes it, but a movement across such actualizations, qua continuous deformation, *qua poetic function*.

Massumi was particularly interested in how we develop an intuition of the virtual—even though we can never really form an image of it (insofar as it is not sensible, insofar as it will never be actual). And theorizing this development, as well as its limits, is certainly a goal that is worth pursuing—with a few caveats. First, recall the criticism we made above in regards to physical systems: we have very precise intuitions for, and images of, the fixed points (and typical trajectories) of many widespread systems. Indeed, as is well known to physicists and mathematicians, even if one cannot solve the differential equations governing some system of interest (and one usually cannot, for most systems are highly nonlinear, chaotic, perturbation-sensitive, non-deterministic, emergent, and so forth), one can develop an intuition for, or qualitative sense of, the space of typical trajectories by finding and categorizing the fixed points of that system according to well known principles (Strogatz 1994). To return to our last section: one doesn't have to figure out the infinity of possible trajectories; one only has to develop a qualitative intuition for their generalized behavior, or 'tendencies' (DeLanda 2011). Poincaré led the way in this respect, and there have been many techniques developed since his pioneering work.

Second, as shown in chapter 3, sense (Frege), value (Saussure) and secrets (Sapir) have most of the key features of Deleuze's understanding of virtuality, though vastly generalized and concretized: they organize the range of possible referents (and, in particular, the path taken to get to those referents), but are not themselves (usually) referents. Metalanguage can attempt to make them referents, by stating claims about them. But poetry can make them aesthetically intuitable, by showing features of them. In some ways, the poetic function of language was precisely a means of making intuitable that which cannot be sensed (Kockelman 1999), allowing us to touch (and feel) the channels through which we feel (and touch). And so, as was shown in the last section, we may investigate ways of developing such intuitions through seemingly 'aesthetic' means.

Interestingly, Massumi too uses the metaphor of language, but in a different way. For him, signs disappear, and become at best windows for seeing referents. As he puts it, "When we read, we do not see the individual letters and words. That is what learning to read is all about: learning to stop seeing the letters so you can see through them" (2002, 138). This is precisely not what we mean. Rather, focusing on signs, in their interrelationality, we make sense—as the path to referents—intuitable. Recall Jakobson's alternative definition of the poetic function: to highlight the 'sensual' (*Sinnhaft* or *Sinnlich*) features of signs. Such a move was meant to capture deontic systems (language, generalized from code to channel, and so much else besides) as much as epistemic systems (say, Cartesian versus polar coordinates, and far beyond).

Finally, do not confuse the 'poetic function' (or, really, *the poetic strategy*) with poetry as it is stereotypically understood: say, relatively solitary agents folding their own texts back in on themselves. Rather, even the simplest kind of interaction between two people evinces a repetitive organization, a poetic structure (Du Bois 2014; Sacks et al. 1974; Silverstein 1984; Tannen 1987). The repetition of tokens of common types—and their various modalities of possibility, potentiality, and virtuality—is interactionally distributed and 'dialogically emergent' (Tedlock and Mannheim 1995), which means that most 'poetry' is produced not by you or by me, but by *us* (which includes you, me, it, them, and everything else). Indeed, building on Malinowski's ethnography of Trobriand Islanders, and the language and magic of their gardening practices, Tambiah (1968) long ago showed that there is a dialogical emergence of garden and gardener alike, as mediated through magic, by means of the poetic texture of spells (not just repetition, but also metaphor and metonym, or selection and combination), and the ways this texture diagrams both the gardener's actions and the garden itself, where such a diagrammatic process is fundamental to the performative efficacy of words and actions alike, be they sacred or profane.

In short, contra notions like 'intuition', this showing of sense is not so much a giving intuition to, insofar as this is imagined in Cartesian or Kantian terms: me and my intuition (here in this empty room, confronted by a system I am determined to understand). In particular, the key agents making 'poetry' in this expanded sense are not individuals, but distributed agents, like participants (in a conversation), individuals (in an interaction), or organisms (in an environment). And so such sense-making strategies should be understood not in terms of their products, but as processes—indeed as open, never-ending, transformative, context-rich, interactions between various kinds of distributed agencies; the systems (networks, infrastructures, etc.) they work with; and the worlds they both represent and reside in. Such sense-making strategies are inherently collective and historical, distributed and contingent, performative and poetic.

The best way to 'intuit' the virtual is to inhabit it.

5.6. Peirce's Understanding of the Virtual

Let's briefly return to the discussion of affordances and instruments that was offered in chapter 1. As such examples should intimate, the object of a sign may often be usefully understood as a *correspondence-preserving projection* from all interpretants of that sign. See Figure 5.9. For example, to say that the object of an instrument is a 'function' means that a function may be understood as a correspondence-preserving projection from the ensemble of behaviors (*qua* interpretants) that one is entitled or committed to doing, within some semiotic collectivity, while wielding the instrument. That is, it consists of (normatively) appropriate and effective actions, as well as (causally) feasible and efficacious actions, that one might use the instrument to undertake. Loosely speaking, this means what the world around you, and others watching you, both 'enable' and 'constrain' you to do with that instrument.

For example, while you *should* use a hammer to hit nails (insofar as that was why it was designed), it *can* also be used to bang pipes or threaten neighbors; while you *may* use a teaspoon to dig a ditch (insofar as no one will arrest you), you probably *couldn't* dig that ditch very fast or deep. Note how deeply we are embedded in 'modality' here (*can, may, should, couldn't*). Insofar as such interpretant-sign relations are just as mediated by 'causes' and infrastructure as they are mediated by 'norms' and institutions (not to mention interactions and imaginaries), so too are such objects. This means that objects are relatively abstract or virtual entities

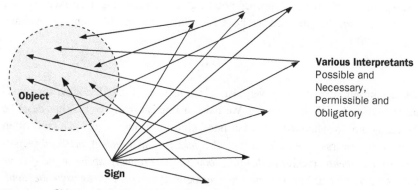

FIGURE 5.9 Object as Projection and Objection

by definition. They should not be confused with 'objects' in the Cartesian sense of *res extensa*. Nor should they be confused with the 'things' that words seem to stand for—be they entities like Saussure's ox, Descartes's wax, or even Thor's hammer.

But they certainly can be such things. Indeed it is sometimes best to think of a sign's object as an 'objection', and thus as that which the sign's interpretant (and hence the semiotic agent per se) is imaginatively, infrastructurally, and institutionally forced to contend. And just as the interpretant relates to the sign through the object, the object relates to the sign through the interpretant—so there always is, in some sense, a double contention. Objects are objections (to our interpretants, through our signs) as much as projections (from our interpretants, through our signs). As we will show now, they are as real as they are virtual, even if not always actual(ized).[17]

***

As we just saw, Peirce's understanding of objects, and of semiotic processes more generally, took virtuality to be a matter of course: many objects were, as correspondence-preserving projections, virtual by definition. They were absolutely 'real' though not actual in their realization. Peirce also offered a more narrow and explicit definition of the virtual: "A virtual X (where X is a common noun) is something, not an X, which has the efficiency (virtus) of an X" (Peirce 1902; Skagestad 1998).[18] From this perspective, every sign is a virtual object (and every interpretant is a virtual sign). That is, any sign of an object, while not the object itself, has (to some degree) the virtus of the object—insofar as one can come to understand the object, or intervene in the object, through the sign (within limits). In these ways, semiotics has always been the study of virtuality. And so it should be no surprise that a semiotic stance could so easily account for the Deleuzian move, as well as undermine the Deleuzean move; and do so much else besides. The rest of this section will perturb Peirce's more technical definition of the virtual, using it to understand not only virtual versions of the referents of common nouns, qua relatively replicated tokens (dog, cat, person, chair, world, etc.), but also virtual versions of the referents of proper nouns, qua relatively singular tokens (Dave, The *Mona Lisa*, the gun used to shoot Lincoln, 110th and Morningside Avenue, and so forth).

***

Before continuing, a few relatively pernicious aspects of the discourse surrounding virtuality should be taken up. We have in English many words that describe seemingly 'non-original' or 'less than pure' kinds: not only *virtual* (which is often erroneously contrasted with *real*), but also *fake* (versus *genuine*), *artificial* (versus *natural*), *inauthentic* (versus *authentic*), *copy* (versus *original*), *disingenuous* (versus *honest*), *spam* (versus *ham*); as well as *prosthetic, synthetic, pseudo, wannabe, adulterated, ersatz,* and many other words besides. In almost all such cases, there is a value-judgment regarding which side is good (the authentic, the natural, the original) and which side is bad (the inauthentic, the artificial, the derived). Such judgments are all too easily projected onto our understanding of the virtual as opposed to the non-virtual, especially when this distinction is itself conflated with other distinctions, such as the digital versus the analog, the imaginary versus the real, or the mediated versus the immediate. Counter to such discourses, it must be emphasized that one should not be disappointed (angry, critical, etc.) that the virtual is not the non-virtual, any more than one is disappointed that a sign is not its object, or the mediate is not the immediate. And, in this regard, the words of Santayana are particularly fitting:

> Masks are arrested expressions and admirable echoes of feeling, at once faithful, discrete, and superlative. Living things in contact with the air must acquire a cuticle, and it is not urged against cuticles that they are not hearts; yet some philosophers seem to be angry with images for not being things, and with words for not being feelings. Words and images are like shells, no less integral parts of nature than are the substances they cover, but better addressed to the eye and more open to observation. I would not say that substance exists for the sake of appearance, or faces for the sake of masks, or the passions for the sake of poetry. No thing arises in nature for the sake of anything else; all these phrases and products are involved equally in the round of existence (quoted in Goffman 1959).

To return to some of the concerns of chapter 1, there will always be a (relatively mediated) difference between the relatively immediate and the relatively mediated. And there will always be a bind that, while we can only get to the immediate through the mediate, the mediate is not the immediate, and so feels easy to forsake. Indeed, as we saw in section 2, the advent of any new medium usually inaugurates such a difference: what counts as 'close' and 'far', or 'raw' and 'cooked', is really the effect of a particular form of media, or mode of mediation (usually through a contrastive relation to other, often older, media). And so attempts to privilege the 'closer' are rarely grounded in a natural stance, reasoned judgment, or phenomenological a priori per se. Arguably, one of the greatest virtues (!) of *homo sapiens* is our relative independence of scale and frame: we have no natural medium, even if we always feel more 'at home' in our (projected) penultimate medium. In the face of such issues, our advice, following Santayana, is this: put aside your misgivings and learn to love the mediate. To return to the concerns of section 5.2, don't despise big L and celebrate little l; rather, treat them with equal compassion. The sign may not have all the affordances (qualia, properties, functions) of the object, but it has so many additional affordances of its own that, for many purposes, it is just as good if not better than the object. The non-virtual—be it construed as actual, real, or immediate—is not that which is 'closer' or 'better' than the virtual. Indeed, it usually works the other way: signs and interpretants are often much more amenable to our senses and instigations than objects; they are precisely where we grab hold of the world (if only to steady ourselves); and so often where we touch, feel, and *feel for* the world most intimately. The will to get 'closer' (in the sense of returning to some imaginary premediated past) is so often simply a desire to turn back, and thereby turn one's back. *The world never was what it used to be (and nevermore the less so than 'now').*

Erving Goffman used Santayana's statement as the preface to his classic work, *The Performance of Self in Everyday Life* (1959). Building on the ideas of George Herbert Mead, who built on the ideas of Peirce, this book brilliantly showed the ways that face to face interaction—that stereotype of naked inter-relating, that alleged Eden of premediated being—is radically and essentially mediated. Each of us is a parasite on our self when we host an other. Indeed, as we will see in chapter 7, many of the key dynamics of spam filtering—and infiltration—can be applied to his descriptions of selfhood. And ironically, a key 'reference' for Goffman, one of his early footnotes in this text, was von Neumann and Morgenstern's (1944) *Theory of Games and Economic Behavior*. From language games versus game theory to 'language game theory'. In some sense, then, the ostensibly primordial and pre-mediated interactional order is itself the most 'cybernetic' and media-centric of ideas.

***

Peirce's definition of virtuality rests, in large measure, on the notion of 'virtus' (originally a kind of manly virtue, closely related to words like *virile*, and so an easy target for critical theory), and this word can be reinterpreted in many ways. For example, if we pair this term with Aristotle's (2001a) typology of four causes (substantive, material, effective, and telic), as potential modes of 'virtus', we get the prototype of virtuality: a virtual X may have the same form (appearance) or function (utility) of X, and yet be composed of a different substance (material) or made by a different artificer (origin).[19] At one extreme, then, we might have a prosthetic arm (functioning, but not appearing, like a real arm). At another extreme, we might have a gadget that functions like a camera but looks like a cigarette. And somewhere at the intersection of these is the poster-child of virtuality: a digitally rendered experience (linking sensory-motor interaction) that looks and feels like a 'real' experience, but is rendered with bits and pixels, and regimented with algorithms and interfaces. However, through our pairing of Aristotle and Peirce, we also get some more far-flung possibilities. For example, two entities might be composed of the same materials and created by the same artificer, yet have different forms and serve different functions (for example, the range of products produced by a silversmith). A knife would be a virtual fork. Or, less prototypic still, entities might have the same artificer (say, sieving and serendipity, or parasites and noise), but be composed of different materials, exist in different forms, and have radically different functions (for example, the world of living kinds as generated by natural selection). A spider would be a virtual fly.

(Note, by the way, how short-sighted it is to claim that two things that function the same [whatever their inner-workings] are 'essentially' the same. See, for example, the key conceits of many members of the artificial life community that Helmreich [1998] described. If two things are different in regards to their form and substance, not to mention their artificer, they will necessarily fail in different ways— and failure, as we saw in chapter 2, is arguably the essence of functioning. Anyone can make a copy that functions like the original; what is hard to do is make a copy that fails like the original. This is because the space of possible failures is usually so much richer than the space of actual functions.)

5.7. Ontology and Virtuality

Aristotle's causes, however, are just one particular way of understanding 'virtus'. Depending on how such a term is defined, other kinds of virtualities (and hence realities) are possible. For example, let's use the term *index* in a relatively narrow way to mean any quality (or relation between qualities, or sensation-instigation relation) that is relatively perceivable to some agent. (Other terms would work just as well: trace, evidence, quality, sign, interaction, difference, text, etc.) Let's use the term *kind* to mean any (agent-projected) propensity to exhibit particular indices. (Other terms would work just as well: type, sort, substance, identity, status, etc.) Let's use the term *individual* to mean any entity or event, process or phenomenon, that can exhibit indices (to an agent) and therefore be a site to project kindedness (by that agent). (Do not then confuse such individuals with 'individuals', like Dave or Sue; a lake, era, nation, collectivity, part, collection, network, or ontology can be an individual.) Let's use the term *agent* to mean any entity that can perceive indices and project kinds. (Agents themselves are usually complexly kinded individuals, or collectivities of such individuals.) And let's use the term *ontology* to mean the set of assumptions an agent has as to the indices, individuals, and kinds that constitute a particular world, as well as the assumptions an agent has as to the kinds (!) of worlds that could be constituted.

From this perspective, agents, insofar as they have a particular ontology, perceive the indices of particular individuals, project kinds onto them, and thereby come to expect other indices from those individuals that would be in keeping with those kinds. Crucially, an agent's kinding of an individual is as much a way of interacting with it, or being affected by it, as it is a way of thinking about it, or referring to it. That is, in kinding an individual, an agent offers an interpretant of an individual—and, as we saw in chapter 4, interpretants can be affective and energetic, as much as representational or habitual. An ontology is a set of assumptions (be these embodied or embedded, encoded or enminded, distributed or concentrated) about the patterning of possible worlds. Ontologies, then, are closely related to grounds. And, from this perspective a 'thing' is an individual, kinded by an agent, through its indices, in light of an ontology (and thus a particular kind of figure in relation to a particular kind of ground).

This framework will be justified, refined, hedged, and extended in chapter 7. For the moment, we want to focus on situations in which there exist two closely overlapping, but nonidentical kinds: a virtual kind and a non-virtual kind. (Recall Peirce's definition: a virtual kind (not X) is no less 'real' than a non-virtual kind (X); it is simply that which has some, but not all, of the virtues of the non-virtual kind. Moreover, even the kind one designates as non-virtual, relative to which one judges something else as virtual, is grounded in frame-specific and ontology-dependent commitments. And so the relative positioning of the two kinds is potentially quite unstable; and so is often able to be inverted, or obviated, in a different context.) To distinguish between individuals of the virtual kind and individuals of the non-virtual kind requires that there be two sets of indices experientially, or experimentally, available to some agent. In particular, there is the set of indices that the virtual kind shares with the non-virtual kind (qua 'virtus'). And there is the set of indices which only the non-virtual kind has (or doesn't have), whose presence (or absence) thereby allows it to be distinguished from the virtual kind.[20] To return to Peirce's definition, such indices, in their presence or absence, are precisely what make 'not X' *not* 'X', so to speak. Stereotypically, the distinguishing indices (which secure the non-virtual) count as necessary and sufficient conditions for identification (and thus function as definitional criteria for the kind). However, as indices, they are not so easily perceived by an agent or not so ever-present in an environment. This means they are relatively difficult to disclose, such that to distinguish between the non-virtual and the virtual is not always easy. We might say that such distinguishing indices, while often ontologically criterial of the kind in question, are not always readily available. They are simultaneously important and elusive.

Such a characterization of the virtual has some interesting entailments. First, some agents, or agentive collectivities, may be more easily able to sense such indices than others, as a function of their tools, training, techniques, and so forth. And so particular kinds of social relations are constituted between those agents who can more easily sense such indices (and thereby secure the non-virtual, or 'real', through some kind of assay) and those who cannot. For example, the existence of any assayer (jeweler, chemist, etc.) allows the rest of us (who depend on their judgments) to live in a world in which the boundary between non-virtual and virtual things, or genuine and fake things, can be maintained (even though we cannot maintain it ourselves). And their ability to do this may be grounded in any number of reasons: more advanced coursework, more familiarity with the kind in question, easier access to archival material, better funding, more sensitive eyes, better assaying instruments, and *different media more generally*. That is to say, there are two classes of agents, united by a shared ontology, and divided by a difference in indexical sensitivity—a division that is closely correlated with differential access to resources, and hence differential relations to knowledge and power.

(Think, for example, of Putnam's [1975] classic account of the social division of linguistic labor, as an important factor in distinguishing between water (on Earth) and 'water' (on Twin Earth), where the latter is phenomenally similar to, but physically different from, the former. And recall our discussion, and extension, of proper names in chapter 2 and 4. Here we are, in part, offering an account of *the social division of ontological labor*, or *the social division of interpretive grounds*.)

Next, suppose that we exist in an environment where trials designed to determine the presence of such criterial indices are no longer feasible. For example, while a well-trained chemist with a well-equipped lab could tell the difference between 'real' gold (i.e., X) and 'fake' gold (i.e., not X), the only chemists nowadays (or in this town) are poorly trained or shoddily equipped. The dualist ontology that was available in a richer environment (in which non-virtual things could be distinguished from virtual things) can no longer be sustained. And so the local ontology might collapse to include only one kind of thing (say, mere reality, or perhaps some unsatisfying and forever suspicious mixture of the two). One can even imagine a lingering nostalgia for the indexical richness of the prior, or neighboring, environment, where such distinguishing judgments could actually be made (even if only imagined or projected rather than remembered or known). This might lead to not only an entrenched suspicion of things, but also to a host of alchemy-like trials for justifying differences, however ultimately ineffective. Or it might lead to attempts to restore the original environs, or travel to the neighboring environs, so that such criterial indices could once again be assayed, and such differences in kinds could be once again justified. In short, just as indices may be differentially accessible to agents, ontologies can easily be out of step with worlds. More canonically, the virtual and the non-virtual may come to coincide not by the greater perfection of the virtual, but also through the degradation of the 'real', with a variety of consequences. Such issues are some of the staple goods of science fiction. Our interest here is simply to highlight some of the affectual and indexical dynamics of such ontological transformations.

A related process could also occur, in which a group of people envision a future, be it hopeful or fearful, in which some new index, or some new assay, will be discovered that will allow them to distinguish between what are two currently indistinguishable entities—real money and fake money; cyborgs and citizens; GMOs and NGMOs; those susceptible to, or safe from, some disease; good and bad stocks; digital currency with and without a viable future; and so forth. While this issue may seem far-fetched, or relevant only to science fiction, Max Weber's (1976) description of the Protestant ethic in relation to capitalism offers a compelling example. In particular, success in worldly affairs (as evidence of self-confidence in one's salvation) could become a relatively criterial index of one's elected status. And thus, in an environment in which one's status was in question, people found a trial (worldly affairs) that would reveal (or not) the indices (wealth and activity) that would imply the status (divine election). Note then that persons are ontologized as kinded individuals (with particular ethnicities, genders, sexualities, etc.) as much as things. The issues developed here, then, are not just relevant to future technologies, 'virtual worlds', or speculative fiction, they go to the heart of classic concerns in the study of economy and society, interaction and selfhood, culture and environment.

Finally, we may return to Aristotle's four causes (substance, form, function, artificer) and relate them to indices, individuals, and kinds. First note that if two substances have exactly the same form and material, then we might think that they are essentially the same thing—as they should have the same indices, and so no distinction between the virtual and the non-virtual should be possible. Furthermore, it would be unlikely that their functions differed for the simple reason that, by having the same form and material, they should afford the same possibilities for action. Recall our discussion of affordances and instruments in chapter 1. This brings us to Aristotle's fourth cause, the artificer. In particular, we might want to make sure that not only do two things have the same properties (or forms, materials, and functions), but also the same artificer. Indeed, what is perhaps most interesting about this dimension is that implies that what makes one individual non-virtual (and hence seem more 'real', 'authentic' or 'original') is not determinable by that individual's indices alone, but rather by all the indices of its interactions with all the other individuals with which it has interacted—insofar as these individuals caused it to become what it is (qua artificer), or were caused by its becoming what it is. Recall our discussion of the hand and the handle, or big L and little L, in section 5.2. Here we are using 'artificer' in a wide sense, not just a human or human-like agent who intentionally makes things, but any causal process more generally: whatever we must 'take into account', or 'make reference to', in order to understand the existence of some entity or the occurrence of some event (with all their particular qualities).

Such an issue is perhaps more likely to arise when we are focused on individuals or specimens whose identity is singular. That is, it comes to the fore not so much when we are trying to assay whether some substance is gold, or whether some person is a police officer; but especially when we are trying to assay whether this person is Margaret Thatcher, or whether that gun was the one used to assassinate Abraham Lincoln. In particular, an individual's biographical presence in the world, itself causally generating a wake of micro-cascades of spatiotemporal distributed effects, themselves preserved in social and material differences, as embodied in the indices of other individuals, is perhaps the ultimate non-feignable (and non-maskable) signature of its singular identity. This is where non-virtuality intersects with authenticity, emblemeticity with aura, and the ideas of Charles Sanders Peirce with those of Walter Benjamin. (Recall our discussion of the trace in section 5.1 and again in 5.4.) What is particularly revealing about this framing is that it implies the authenticity, actuality, or non-virtuality, of a singular entity (be it person or thing, or anything else outside or in-between) is ultimately secured only in its relation to other entities. To build a virtual object that really approaches the non-virtual or 'real', or simply to hold onto an auraric object that remains true to itself, would thereby entail building an entire (virtual) world.

6

Computation, Interpretation, and Mediation

6.1. Sifters and Shifters

Sieves are often defined as mechanical devices that separate desired materials from undesired materials.[1] For example, devices like gold pans and sluice boxes are ways of separating more dense and desirable materials (such as gold) from less dense and desirable materials (such as sand, mud, sticks, and so forth). A strainer is a type of sieve that separates a solid (such as pasta) from a liquid (such as water). Somewhat abstractly, the Sieve of Eratosthenes is an algorithm for separating prime numbers from natural numbers. More concretely, norms and laws may sieve (accepting certain behaviors and rejecting others), as may price and infrastructure. In this last framing, devices such as turnstiles and admission fees, gatekeepers and logic gates, and passport checks and prescriptive grammars are sieves as much as sluice boxes. Other important sieving devices include not only Maxwell's demon (sieving for fast versus slow molecules), but also Freud's superego (sieving for acceptable versus forbidden wishes). Other names for sieves include filters, strainers, and sifters. And sieve-like entities with other names include nets, jury selection processes, surgical masks, traps, entrance examinations, air purifiers, trials, assays, and sorting devices of all sorts.

As these examples should attest, sieving has as wide a reach in our cultural imaginary as it does in our material environment. We even have a relatively productive linguistic construction that turns on it: to *separate the X from the Y* (the men from the boys, the sheep from the goats, the wheat from the chaff). Indeed, the last example, which comes from Matthew 3.12, is quite telling: not only does John the Baptist tell us that Jesus will gather the wheat into the barn, but also that he will burn the chaff with unquenchable fire.

Separating substances is thus not just an end in itself, but often a means for further ends. In particular, just as the desirable materials may now be collected, the undesirable materials may now be destroyed. Moreover, it is always useful to remember that what is chaff for someone (say, a person who cannot digest it), may

Paul Kockelman. *The Art of Interpretation in the Age of Computation.* © Oxford University Press 2017

be sustenance for another: for example, a cow who can eat it, the fire that requires it for fuel, or the people who need the fire for warmth, illumination, protection, or divination. That is, just as there is wiggle room as to what has or has not been put through a sieve (i.e., are we at the input end of a sieve, and so still 'aggregated', or are we at the output end of a sieve, and so already 'disaggregated'), there is also wiggle room as to which of the two substances sieved is a bad or a good. In this way, both the outputs of a sieve (wheat versus chaff), and the input-output relation per se (pre-winnowing or post-winnowing), are subject to classic shifts in frame: following Mary Douglas (1966), what is dirt for me may be order (or 'matter in place') for you; and following Gregory Bateson (1972), what is noise for you may be signal (or 'meaning in place') for me.

Notice, then, how sieves are inherently temporal (pre-winnowing and post-winnowing, or aggregated and disaggregated) and spatial (here and there, or accept and reject). In some sense, they constitute a potential indexical ground relative to which both a past and future and a near and far may be constituted. In this way, they are inherently chronotopic.

Finally, it is always useful to remember light polarizers: two polarizers, at right angles to each other, will stop all light from getting through; however, if you put a third polarizer in between them, itself 45 degrees out of skew in relation to the other two, some light gets through. Note, then, that in sieving for a feature, the substances sieved may be affected by the sieving, and thereby come to take on features they did not originally have—in particular, features that allow such substances to slip through such sieves. Think, for example, of Freud's (1999 [1900]) ideas concerning the dream-work. And, more generally, as per the concerns of chapter 2, think of the possibility of recoding and rechanneling any message so as to slip past a censor.[2]

For all of these reasons, it is tempting to introduce a word that points back to anthropology's Boasian heritage (Boas 1889): we apperceive through our sieves as much as we sieve through our apperception. We appersieve, if you will. Or, if you go back to Kant (1965 [1781]), who defined the ego as the transcendental unity of apperception (whatever that means), we are our sieves.

Indeed, and crucially, sieves have to *take on* (and not just *take in*) features of the substances they sieve, if only as 'inverses' of them. A hole in the ground, for example, constitutes a simple sieve: anything with a diameter less than the hole will fall through; anything with a diameter larger than the hole will stay on top. In this way, to sieve a substance, the sieve must often have an (elective) affinity with the substance to be sieved and, in particular, the qualities sieved for—in this case size. In some sense, all sieves are inverted iconic-indices or even shadows of the substances they sort. By necessity, they exhibit a radical kind of intimacy.

Another good example of sieving is natural selection, which is sometimes framed in terms of serendipity (to generate variation) and sieving (to separate more fit from less fit variants). Note, then, that sieves are often happenstance, rather than intentional or telic, devices: their outcomes are as likely to be accidental as designed.

And thus while many sieves are artificed entities, or tools, built precisely for the sake of their sieving function, many are atelic—generating various degrees of order for no good reason at all. (Recall our distinction between instruments and affordances in chapter 1.) And, as natural selection should also make clear, while any particular sieve may grade coarsely, and only for a single feature, each of the sieved groups can be further sieved into groups, and so on indefinitely. In this way, even though any actual division may be incredibly gross and simplistic, the concatenation and ratcheting of such gross and simple divisions can give rise to distinctions of great subtlety and beauty—for example, all the life-forms that surround us.[3]

Note, then, that the ability to sieve can itself be sieved: one can sieve sieves on the basis of their ability to sieve. Such sieve-sieving sieves may range from something as simple as quality-control mechanisms imposed by manufactures of pasta strainers (e.g., which strainers passed the 'countertop-drop test' and so may be sold) to algorithms that use natural selection-like processes to generate more powerful or efficient algorithms.

In one sense, then, a sieve may be understood as the simplest of interpreting agents. See Figure 6.1. Its input can be any sign—for example, strings of any length composed of characters from any alphabet (e.g., text); or indices of any complexity composed of qualia of any kind (e.g., experience); or substances of any type composed of properties of any sort (e.g., things). Its output can be one of two interpretations: yes or no, true or false, accept or reject, stay or go. Such interpretations can be enminded in cognitive judgments (good/bad) as much as embodied in physical actions (open/close); and they may be generated by processes grounded in 'understanding' as much as 'force', or 'culture' as much as 'nature', or 'people' as much as 'things', or 'mediators' as much as 'intermediaries', or 'thirdness' as much as 'secondness'.[4]

Crucially, what the signs in question correlate with (qua features of some significant object), and why that correlation matters (qua interests of some selecting agent), can be as wide or varied as possible. In particular, and returning to Jakobson's categories from chapter 2, these devices are arguably *shifters* (e.g., similar to words like *here* and *there*, *this* and *that*, *I* and *you*), in a much expanded sense: while one can often give a relatively context-free description of their input-output relation, or

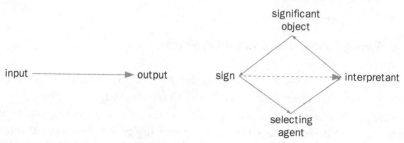

FIGURE 6.1 Secondness and Thirdness Revisited

sign-interpretant pattern per se, their actual meaning (as a relation between the features or values of the object and the interests or evaluative standards of the agent), *if they have one at all*, can only be determined by reference to a larger context, and may thereby shift (or sift) accordingly.[5]

***

We have just seen how the sieve, as both a physical device and an analytic concept, is of fundamental importance not just to anthropology, but also to linguistics, biology, philosophy, and critical theory more generally. As intimated, sieves are also essential to information processing. A variety of more or less powerful 'computers' (in a theoretical sense) may be understood as devices that take in sequences of symbols as inputs and turn out one of two symbols (1/0, true/false, wheat/chaff) as outputs.

This chapter argues that computation (in the machine-specific sense) may be understood as the enclosure of interpretation—an attempt to render a highly messy and stereotypically human process relatively formal, quantifiable, and context-independent. To make these arguments, and heavily qualify them, it introduces some of the key concepts and claims of computer science (language, recognition, automaton, transition function, Universal Turing Machine, and so forth). And it shows their fundamental importance not just to the concerns of linguistic anthropology (as a particular subfield of anthropology), but also to the concerns of context-sensitive and culture-specific approaches to language and media more generally (such as poetics, sociolinguistics, conversational analysis, functional linguistics, comparative literature, media studies, and beyond).

Sections 6.2 and 6.4 describe key concepts of computer science in their own terms, developing the relation between different kinds of languages and different kinds of computers. Readers already familiar with the theory of automata may skim these sections if they wish. Sections 6.3 and 6.5 show the ways these concepts relate to core concerns in linguistics and anthropology, such as interaction versus abstraction and linguistic relativity versus universal grammar. Section 6.6 returns to the path metaphor that was introduced in chapter 1, and developed in subsequent chapters, using it to characterize the inner workings of automata. And the conclusion tacks between the concerns of such otherwise disparate disciplines (and far beyond), highlighting key areas of mutual interest.

6.2. Sieving Symbols and Symbolizing Sieves

A computer (or, automaton more generally) may be abstractly understood as a sieving device that accepts certain strings of characters and rejects others. The set of strings that it accepts is called the language that it recognizes (or, alternately, 'generates' or 'decides'). The rest of this section will develop these ideas at length, as grounded in standard works on this subject (Rabin and Scott 1959; Turing 2004

[1936]; Sipser 2007). It describes the core operations that computers must be able to perform if they are to sieve strings in these ways.

An *alphabet* may be understood as a set of symbol types, or characters. Examples include: {0, 1}, {0, 1, 2, 3, ..., 9, #}, {a, b, c, ..., z}, {the characters of a standard QWERTY typewriter}, {glyphs from an ancient language}, and so forth. Most generally, an alphabet can be any set of types whose tokens are perfectly and reliably readable and writable by the computer in question. A *string* may be understood as a list of characters from such an alphabet (such that a string is said to be 'over' the particular alphabet whose characters it incorporates). Examples of strings, over some of the foregoing alphabets, include: '11110111100', '3#29', 'hullabaloo', 'What did the quick brown fox jump over?', and so forth. As should be clear from chapters 3 and 4, such strings can represent not just words and numbers but all media, DNA and, as will be discussed below, the algorithms that govern the computers themselves.[6] And a *language* may be understood as a set of such strings. Examples include: {the set of all w, where w is a string over the English alphabet that ends in *-ing*}, {the set of all s, where s is a grammatically acceptable sentence in German}, {the set of all pairs $x\#y$, where $y = x^3 + 2$}, and so forth. In this way, with its innards still suitably black-boxed, a computer may be understood as taking in strings as its input (whatever their length or alphabet), and turning out one of two strings, and thereby instigating one of two actions, as its output: 'accept' or 'reject', 1 or 0, 'True' or 'False', 'permit' or 'prohibit', 'stay' or 'go', and so forth. See part (a) of Figure 6.2.

To be able to perform the task of accepting or rejecting particular strings, and thus, ultimately, of recognizing a particular language, a generalized automaton (or *Turing Machine*, as it will be referred to below) must be able to engage in the following kinds of operations: (1) read and write tokens of particular character types; (2) move along some kind of medium (where such tokens are read and written); and (3) both ascertain and update its own internal state. See part (b) of Figure 6.2. At the heart of such a device is a *transition function* that maps a domain of values onto a range of values. And thus, depending on the current state of the device, and the character it is currently reading, the transition function specifies what character to write (if any), what direction to move in (along the medium), and what state to change into. See part (c) of Figure 6.2. In essence, that is all such a device ever does: having been given some string as its initial input (as written into the medium), and having been put in a particular state at a particular position along the string (usually the beginning), it repeats this mapping procedure (a potentially mind-numbing number of times, at a usually mind-boggling speed) until it ends up in one of two particular states as its final output (accept or reject).

Phrased another way, a transition function consists of a finite set of rules which map input values (character read, current state) onto output values (character written, movement undertaken, next state). To *program* such a device is essentially to specify its transition function (usually by giving the device another, more

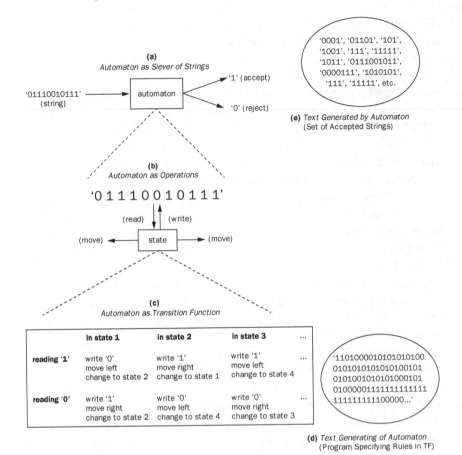

FIGURE 6.2 Automata as Text-Generated and Text-Generating Devices

'primordial' string which encodes the rules in question). See part (d) of Figure 6.2. Such a transition function determines whether or not the device will accept particular strings; and thus, ultimately, whether or not the device will recognize a particular language. See part (e) of Figure 6.2. Crucially, while each rule may be trivial to specify, the list of rules (or 'program') can be quite complicated to formulate, and the overall behavior of such a device (e.g., the particular patterning of the language it recognizes) impossible to predict without actually observing it (if a pattern is even inferable at all).

Framed recursively, computers presume strings and produce languages, where a language is a set of strings, any one of which might be presumed by another computer in its production of a language. If we think of such strings as 'texts', which can contain any amount of quantifiable information and encode any imaginable kind of meaning, then *computers, as both engineered and imagined, are essentially text-generated and text-generating sieves.*

***

Returning to the concerns of chapter 5, the actual material instantiation of such devices is 'immaterial' in regards to the mathematical specification of the language in question. That is, there is nothing inherently electronic (as opposed to mechanical, quantum mechanical, lively, etc.) about computers—even if their practical instantiation, and widespread adoption, had to await a particular technology. What matters, ultimately, is that the device be able to undertake the kinds of tasks listed above (read and write, move left or right, ascertain and update). In particular, people can do each task; and, as often noted, the first 'computers' were indeed people (often women), who carried out lengthy (and tedious) calculations according to a finite set of relatively simple rules (Hayles 1999; Inoue 2011; Kittler 1989 [1986]).

Because such a sieving device is, in some sense, coupled to its input (the string it is initially given) by way of its transition function (which makes reference to the possible characters on a string), the device and the string are 'intimate'.[7] In certain respects, a stringless-device is like an organism without its environment; just as a device-less string is like an environment without an organism. To return to our discussion of Heidegger in chapter 3, neither makes much sense except *in reference to* the other.

Insofar as transition functions presume that such devices can reliably read and write inputs which are tokens of particular types, such devices exhibit the hallmark of digital processes (Haugeland 1981). And, as per the nature of digitality, the types in question, as well as the states and positions, are necessarily discrete: there are no partial types, quasi-states, or half-positions. Needless to say, the discreteness (or 'digitality') of the mechanism, like the discreteness of the alphabet, closely aligns it with classic Saussurean understandings of the 'symbolic': value (qua typehood of any token) only adheres in difference. Loosely speaking, a particular character or symbol can be instantiated however we like, so far as it is distinguishable, in both reading and writing, from the other characters with which it contrasts. Crucially, this does not entail that the meaning of such devices is 'arbitrary' or conventional (as opposed to 'natural' or motivated). As argued in section 6.1, such devices are shifters (in an expanded sense), and thus 'indexical symbols'. And, as should be clear from the arguments of chapter 4, the texts in question, or bit strings, are often highly diagrammatic, and hence iconic-indices. Indeed, it is partly the tension between such grounds (and politicized claims as to the priority of one ground over the other) that make such devices interesting objects of analysis. Loosely speaking, where we draw the line between the symbolic and the iconic-indexical (or the arbitrary and the motivated), is itself grounded in convention (or so say the culturalists), which might itself be grounded in nature (or so say the realists).

In light of these issues (materiality, intimacy, motivation), several other interrelated tensions become immediately apparent.[8] First, claims to a timeless disembodied abstraction in relation to a history of particular material instantiations. Second, the relation between people and machines (as ontologized by any particular community, or imagined in terms of a particular technology) in relation to the relation between different kinds of people (e.g., genders, classes, ethnicities, nationalities, and so forth). Third, the kinds of computational tasks asked of sieving devices and their relation to politicized notions like labor, work, and action (not to mention often highly idealized and romanticized notions like creativity, contemplation, and communication). And finally, the relation between such artificial languages, or 'texts' (both generating and generated), and so-called 'natural' languages. We will explore many of these tensions in what follows.

6.3. Linguistic Anthropology in the Age of Language Automata

Having characterized some of the ways computer scientists understand languages and computers, and having indicated a number of ontological tensions, we may now begin to sketch a linguistic anthropology of strings, and the devices that sieve them. In part, this is done to show how the tools of linguistic anthropology can be applied to the concepts of computer science (as well as to the objects of computer engineering). And, in part, this is done to show and soften the fundamental tension between the culture of linguistic anthropology and the concepts of computer science—a tension that is otherwise almost laughably overdetermined in its binary simplicity. As will be seen, the title of this section is meant to be ironic. For, in fact, linguistic anthropology came of age in the time of language automata, but somehow managed to studiously avoid what it is arguably destined to embrace. As will be seen, the issues raised here don't just go to the heart of the tension between computer science and linguistic anthropology, but also to the heart of the tension between relatively reductive and nonreductive approaches to human behavior more generally.

As described in section 6.2, automata are exemplary instances of relatively black-boxed, rule-bound, and deterministic intermediaries. Recall Figure 6.2. In particular, both the localized mapping of values (from character read and current state to character written, move made, and next state), and the global input-output relation per se (from string inputed to decision to accept or reject), are radically deterministic, such that there seems to be a maximally rigid and predictable (as opposed to flexible and contingent) mapping between inputs and outputs.[9] This characteristic puts them at odds with anthropology's strongly humanistic imaginary, which sees human agency as maximally flexible, or nondeterministic.[10] For example, people are usually understood to be norm-abiding, culture-inhabiting, context-sensitive, interactionally emergent, and reflexively conscious agents (not to mention fickle creatures with volatile tempers); and thus radically nondeterministic in their practices. And so it is not surprising that linguistic anthropologists have been extremely wary of disciplines (such as cognitive science and formal linguistics) that have invoked computational metaphors in their attempts to understand key features of human behavior.

Indeed, an enormous amount of energy has gone into trying to refute any claim that people are in any way automaton like. Forty years of anthropology has spent its time trying to show that each and every social form (such as a practice, sign, identity, behavior, movement, value, institution, or belief) is 'emergent', 'contested', 'fluid', 'embodied', 'non-deterministic', 'dialogic', 'constructed', 'distributed', 'context-bound', 'reflexive', 'mediated', and so forth. In some sense, computers (or rather a widespread folk-theory of computers), have been the favorite bogeyman of anthropology (and social scientists more generally). The mantra goes something like this: where there are rules, give us practices; where there are symbols, give us indices; where there is truth-conditioning, give us poetry and performance; where there is mind, give us body; where there is abstraction give us interaction; where there is form or content, give us context; where there are ideal languages, give us forms of life.[11]

The history of these divisions is institutional as much as intellectual, and deserves a chapter of its own; but some of the key moves are easy enough to sketch. Descartes versus Heidegger in continental philosophy.[12] Early Wittgenstein (1961 [1921]) versus late Wittgenstein (1958 [1953]) in analytic philosophy.[13] The structuralism of Levi-Strauss (1969 [1949]) versus the practice theory of Bourdieu (1977 [1972]) in anthropology. Saussure (1983 [1916]) versus Peirce (1955abc), and hence semiology versus semiotics, in theories of meaning. And formalism (Chomsky 1965) versus functionalism (Greenberg 1980 [1966]) in linguistics.[14] Insofar as modern linguistic anthropology sits downstream, as it were, of all of these currents, it has adopted most of their claims; such that its understanding of interpretation (and meaning) is essentially contrastive with stereotypes about computers (and information). As such, it is worth examining one of its key foils with a renewed empathy built on fifty years or so of enmity.

***

While Latour (2005, 39) is often cited in relation to this distinction between *intermediaries* (or whatever 'transports meaning or force without transformation: defining its inputs is enough to define its outputs') and *mediators* (whose 'input is never a good predictor of their output; their specificity has to be taken into account every time'), Michel Serres (2007 [1982]) is the more originary figure. And, as we saw in chapter 2, Serres was himself simply developing certain ideas of Claude Shannon (in regards to noise and enemies). As we also saw in chapter 2, a much earlier definition was offered by Peirce, when he distinguished between *secondness* and *thirdness*: "a straight road, considered merely as a connection between two places is second, but so far as it implies passing through intermediate places [themselves possibly connected by other paths to further places] it is third" (1955b, 80).

That said, the distinction between secondness and thirdness, or machine-specific forms of computation and human-specific modes of interpretation (as stereotypically understood), is really much more general and variable (not to mention illusory). Figure 6.3, for example, shows how a wide variety of seemingly simple relations (origin-destination, input-output, signifier-signified, and stimulus-response)

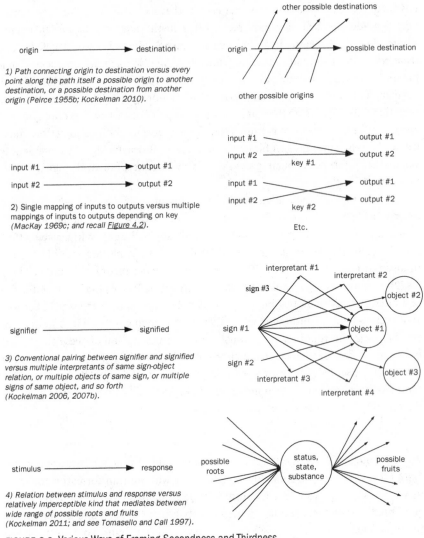

1) Path connecting origin to destination versus every point along the path itself a possible origin to another destination, or a possible destination from another origin (Peirce 1955b; Kockelman 2010).

2) Single mapping of inputs to outputs versus multiple mappings of inputs to outputs depending on key (MacKay 1969c; and recall Figure 4.2).

3) Conventional pairing between signifier and signified versus multiple interpretants of same sign-object relation, or multiple objects of same sign, or multiple signs of same object, and so forth (Kockelman 2006, 2007b).

4) Relation between stimulus and response versus relatively imperceptible kind that mediates between wide range of possible roots and fruits (Kockelman 2011; and see Tomasello and Call 1997).

FIGURE 6.3 Various Ways of Framing Secondness and Thirdness

turn out to be far more complicated when examined carefully and in context. All one needs to do is add parasites (enemies or noise) to paths, semiotic processes to semiological structures, keys or ultimate interpretants to input-output relations, mental states (or cognitive representations) to stimulus-response pairings[15], and so forth.

Indeed, any one of these simplistic shifts from secondness to thirdness might be better framed in terms of *agency*, understood as a multidimensional, graded, distributed, and emergent capacity that underlies highly flexible and accountable behavior. Recall, for example, the way 'agents' were defined in chapter 2. They are (more or less) able to control when and where a sign is expressed. They are (more or less) able to compose what sign is expressed, and what object it stands for. And they are (more or less) able to commit to, or anticipate, what interpretant will be created if such a sign-object relation is expressed in such a space-time location. That is, a given semiotic agent—however distributed—is more or less *flexible* depending on its degrees of control, composition, and commitment. Different semiotic technologies allocate different degrees, to different dimensions, across a wide range of devices. And the more flexible an agent is (or at least is imagined to be) in regards to its semiotic behavior, the more *accountable* that agent is (or at least is often treated as being) for the effects of its semiotic behavior.[16] In short, rather than dividing the world into intermediaries and mediators, or even 'seconds' and 'thirds', one should look at key dimensions of mediation, and the factors that contribute to greater (or lesser) degrees of flexibility along any such dimension (Kockelman 2004, 2007a, 2017a, 2017b).

As noted in chapter 2, a given semiotic technology, or medium, usually turns on a more or less complicated ensemble of such agencies; and such agencies often get personified—not just 'voiced' (for such devices are designed to do much more than speak), but identified and intentionalized, not to mention demonized and fetishized, silenced and seconded, devoiced and denatured—through the projection of complex and contentious sociopolitical identities. Such issues apply not just to all the agents we examined in chapter 2—amplifiers and editors, censors and couriers, enemies and parasites—but to any ensemble of devices, or devicing of an ensemble.

Any entity under the sun, so far as it exhibits one of these dimensions to some degree, or changes the degree to which another agent can exhibit one of these dimensions, is an 'agent' under this conception. That is, just as I am (more or less) agentive insofar as I can (more or less) flexibly undertake an action (including a speech action), any entity that mediates my agency is itself an agent insofar as it makes my actions (more or less) flexible. This means that entities like handcuffs, rules, knives, foremen, assistants, oxygen, friction, algorithms, sieves, and media more generally, are all 'agents'. While I may not be able to throw them all in jail, or punish them or praise them, and thus 'hold them accountable' per se, I can certainly *take them into account* when I act, and thereby try to add them, or remove them, to a given context, such that their effects on my agency, or another's, may be hastened or hindered, mollified or modified. While such 'capacities' (to control, compose, and commit) have multiple and often murky origins (cognitive abilities, legal rights, institutional privileges, technological underpinnings, algorithmic complexities, social relations, material properties, environmental affordances, talents, training, moods, affects, body plans, and so forth), what is being emphasized here are the three dimensions (control, composition, commitment), insofar as these undergird semiotic processes, insofar as these processes are a key factor mediating our relation to objects, others, and ourselves—and hence our relation to the 'world' itself.

Moreover, such modes of mediation couple and compound indefinitely, such that any actual practice is mediated by them in multifaceted ways at multiple degrees of remove. For example, more important than being dismissive of, or trying to circumvent, the rule-like, deterministic, or intermediary nature of computational devices, is to understand the ways allegedly human-specific modes of signifying and interpreting meaning (as grounded in mediators, or thirdness) are mediated by and mediating of allegedly machine-specific modes of sending and sieving information (as grounded in intermediaries, or secondness). In particular, much of the current built environment, qua communicative infrastructure, consists of precisely such devices. And so natural languages, and culture-specific communicative practices more generally, are constantly being mediated by (encoded with and channeled through) such devices. Much of this book is precisely about this kind of mediation.

And finally, the distinction between thirdness and secondness, or mediators and intermediaries, is itself grounded in thirdness: and so there is a culture and history and politics to the ways some community or discipline specifies where machine-like things end and human-like things begin; as well as a culture and history of evaluating what is essential to each, and what is good or bad when breached. Indeed, more generally, *there is also a lot of firstness (or 'ontological wiggle room') in where we draw the line between secondness and thirdness* (Kockelman 2013a:141). We will return to these issues, and how to handle them with care, when we discuss the Turing Test in chapter 7.

In short, rather than ontologize the world in such binary terms, it is much better to: 1) foreground agency as a radically multidimensional, distributed, and graduated process; 2) foreground a variety of practices (including those of many philosophers, critical theorists, and scholars of science and technology) which not only have the effect of enclosing agency as 'agents' but also dichotomizing such agents in terms of distinctions like 'intermediary' and 'mediator'; and 3) genealogize the recent presumption of this dichotomy among scholars. And thus a key task for the linguistic anthropology of language automata is to trace the politics and pragmatics of such thirdable (and often seconded) firstness, or *intermediation*. See Table 6.1.

***

We might end this section with a bit of large-scale historical irony. The art critic and historian John Ruskin often railed against the machine, championing handicraft in the face of widespread industrialization, arguing that latter, insofar as it is mass-produced rather than individually and singularly crafted, loses 'the traces or symptoms of a living being at work' (quoted in Gombrich 1979, 40). Note, then, the relation between Ruskin's ideas and Walter Benjamin's more famous notion of 'aura', as it was interpreted in chapter 5; and note also the relation between replicas and singularities. Interestingly, Rushkin often aimed his critiques at the 'decorative' arts more generally, in their often mechanically produced and repetitive (or highly patterned) nature. This is particularly salient insofar as there is a close linkage between the 'patterns' (qua languages, or texts)

TABLE 6.1

Intermediaries, Mediators, and Intermediation

Secondness	Thirdness	Via Peirce
Intermediary	*Mediator*	Via Serres and Actor-Network Theory
Ideal Language	*Form of Life*	Via Wittgenstein
Universal Grammar	*Linguistic Relativity*	Via Chomsky and Sapir
Machines Talking	*Humans Talking*	Via Turing
Structure	*Agency*	Via Cultural Anthropology
Computer Science	*Linguistic Anthropology*	Via Disciplinary Boundaries
Computing Machines	*Interpreting Humans*	Via Multiple Encodings
Real Imaginaries	*Symbolic Imaginaries*	Via Ontological Mappings
Artificial Languages	*Natural Languages*	Via Possible Objects
Statistics (Math)	*Semiotics (Meaning)*	Via Possible Methods
Enclosing	*Disclosing*	Via Underlying Imperative
Sieving and Serendipity	*Significance and Selection*	Via Semiotic Framing
Redundancy	*Poetry (qua Metricality)*	Via Shannon and Jakobson

Intermediation as Obviation   *As undertaken here.*
1) Secondness and thirdness are poles of a continuum, not positions in an opposition;
2) Boundary between secondness and thirdness is itself grounded in thirdness (and secondness);
3) Each is affecting of, and affected by, the other at various degrees of remove;
4) Whether some process is understood as one or the other is dependent on degree of resolution and frame of relevance;
5) Process of making (or seconding and thirding, as it were), and making seem (like secondness and thirdness), as important as the products made (seconds and thirds, per se).

produced by automata and the patterns produced by decoration-generating mechanisms such as looms (which themselves were, in the age of Jacquard, programmable with punch-cards [Essinger 2004], and thus also generated by text-like patterns).

Crucially, the history of this tension between decorative and representational art probably goes back to the origins of rhetoric (see, for example, Bates 2014): the admonishment to make one's speech simple, and thus less flowery or 'decorated', and thus less poetic and more referential. Note, then, linguistic anthropology's valorization of mediators over intermediaries is itself grounded in the oldest (or at least most famous and widespread) of language ideologies. Ironically, this is, in a certain sense, the converse of its own explicitly articulated sensibilities as to the importance of poetic regimentation and the multifunctionality of language, which we saw Jakobson so forcefully champion in chapter 2.

6.4. Kinds of Languages, Kinds of Computers

Before taking up other important kinds of tensions, it is worth returning to some key claims of computer science. Particular automata (or particular programs running on a universal Turing Machine, essentially a 'computer' in the stereotypic sense) may be characterized in terms of the sets of strings that they accept (and thus the languages that they recognize). And different classes of automata may be characterized in terms of the kinds of languages they can recognize—kinds of languages that can be compared in terms of their relative complexity, and thus classes of automata that can be compared in terms of their relative power.[17] See Figure 6.4.

Three important classes of sieving devices are Deterministic Finite Automata (DFA), Context-Free Grammars (CFG), and Turing Machines (TM). DFAs are the simplest of the three devices. In contrast to TMs (whose inner-workings were detailed in section 6.2), such devices only move in one direction (from the beginning of the string to the end); no characters are ever written; and the medium only ever contains the string in question. Endowed with such capabilities, such devices can recognize the class of *regular languages*, which are essentially all languages recursively definable in terms of three simple functions. (Recall our discussion of recursive closure in chapter 1.) Loosely speaking, the *union* of strings from any two regular languages is itself a regular language; all possible *concatenations* of strings from any two regular languages is itself a regular language; and all possible

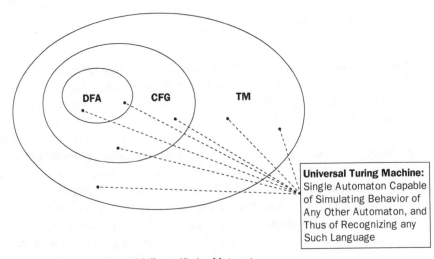

FIGURE 6.4 Relative Power of Different Kinds of Automata

iterations (or 'self-concatenations') of strings from any regular language is itself a regular language.

More carefully, if L_1 and L_2 are two languages recognizable by a DFA (and thus regular languages), the following languages are also recognizable by a DFA (and thus regular languages): $L_1 \cup L_2$ = {the set of all strings w, where w is a string in L_1 or L_2}; L_1 o L_2 = {the set of all strings w_1w_2, where w_1 is a string in L_1 and w_2 is a string in L_2}; and L_1* = {the set of all strings $w_1w_2w_3...w_k$, where k >= 0 and w_i is a string in L_1}. For example, if L_1 = {a, b} and L_2 = {c}, $L_1 \cup L_2$ = {a, b, c}, L_1 o L_2 = {ac, bc}, and L_1* = {e, a, b, ab, ba, aa, bb, abb, aab,...}, where e is the empty string (that is, the string with no characters). And so on, recursively, for languages like $(L_1$ o $L_2) \cup L_1$, $(L_1 \cup L_2)$*, and L_1* $\cup (L_1$ o $L_2)$. In this way, with three relatively simple functions, and some primitive notions like empty strings and singleton languages (or languages with only one string, itself consisting of a single character), one can build up languages with great complexity. Practical applications that implement DFAs include checking passwords, validating field formats, extracting text selections, find and replace functions in word-processing programs, swearword censors, and simple spam-filters; as well as devices like automatic doors, vending machines, traffic lights, and communication protocols. Indeed, insofar as computers are text-generating and text-generated sieving devices, it means that the 'digital age' is essentially a huge corpus of texts, and hence an archive. And regular expressions have proven to be a key tool not just for searching and sorting within this archive, but building up that archive, and using that archive to build. They lie at the heart of 'word processing' in an abstracted and generalized sense.

CFGs not only recognize all regular languages, they also recognize languages like {the set of all strings w#w | where w is itself a string of any length over some alphabet}, which require an infinite amount of memory that is only accessible in a relatively restricted fashion (essentially a kind of 'last-written, first-read' form of storage).[18] In particular, in contrast to DFAs, the domain of the transition function of a CFG turns on not just the current state of the device, and the character currently being read from the string, but also (potentially) the character currently being read from the top of the 'stack' (its restricted memory). And the output involves not only updating the state of the device, and moving to the next character on the string, but also (potentially) writing some other character onto the top of the stack.

When understood as generating languages (as opposed to recognizing them), CFGs should be immediately familiar to linguistic anthropologists in terms of the rewrite rules (or 'tree structures') of formal models of language. For example, a particular set of rules (such as S => NP-VP; NP => DET-ADJ-N; VP => V-NP; DET => *a, the*; ADJ => short, tall; N => boy, girl; V => pinched, ticked) may be understood to generate a particular language (which would include the following strings: *the short girl pinched the tall boy, the tall girl tickled the short girl*, and so forth). Such languages exhibit another kind of recursion when the output of a rule ultimately makes reference to the same variable that constitutes its input (for example, PP => Prep NP, NP => N PP).[19] Practical applications that implement CFGs include most parsers (involved in compiling or interpreting the algorithms that are run on Turing Machines [about which, more below], and thus the texts that specify their transition functions), as well as many applications that either simulate or process natural languages. Indeed, as will be discussed at length in section 6.4, many of Chomsky's early intuitions about language (themselves a key foil for functional linguists and linguistic anthropologists for the last fifty years) were grounded in the structure and logic of CFGs (and their possible 'transformations'). Section 6.7 will show how most classic moves in critical theory may be generated by a sort of context-free grammar.

Finally, TMs not only recognize all languages recognized by CFGs (and thus, all languages recognized by DFAs), but also languages like $\{w \mid$ where w is an integer root of the polynomial $x^3 + 3x^2 + 8x = 0\}$.[20] Indeed, the Church-Turing Thesis postulates that such devices are definitionally equivalent to algorithms: they can recognize any language that can be specified in terms of a finite deterministic procedure (loosely speaking, an iteratively applied, easily followed, and simply stated set of rules for undertaking a longer and more complicated calculation).[21] Not only do they have an infinite amount of memory but, in contrast to CFGs, their memory is unrestricted in its accessibility. Finally, as already mentioned, a *Universal Turing Machine* (essentially a modern day computer with infinite memory) is an automaton that can be programed (by giving it a string that encodes the set of instructions that specify its transition function) to model the behavior of any particular Turing Machine.

***

In some sense, then, a Universal Turing Machine is the one automaton that can take the place of any other automaton. Or, to invoke a comparison that will need some unpacking, and should echo Marx's (1967 [1867]) notion of universal money, it is also akin to a universal language: the one language whose expressions can be used to translate the meaning of any expression from any other language (Kockelman 2006, 100). A Universal Turing Machine is thus the most *portable* of machines. Not portable in the sense that it may be carried anywhere, and used by anyone[22] (though, nowadays with graphic interfaces, cellphones, byte-code, and the like, there is that too), but in the sense that it may undertake the labor, or simulate the behavior, of any other machine.

To return to our discussion of Ruskin, Marx famously spoke of Watt's genius for inventing not so much the steam engine, as 'an agent universally applicable in mechanical industry' (1967, 263–264).[23] That is, prior to the 'universal media machines' (Kay and Goldberg 1977) we now have, such as our laptops and cellphones, we used to have (and still do) universal mechanical machines. Moreover, many of the key features posited of such newer forms of media, such as those described by Haugeland (1981) and Manovich (2001) in their discussion of digital media, arguably apply to these older industrial machines, at least as they were imagined by Marx.[24]

For example, both kinds of universal machines (media and mechanical) are radically automated, and so tend to remove the human element (insofar as this element was understood as slow and error-prone), all the while requiring it (insofar as this element was understood as imaginative, free, non-deterministic, and value-creating). Both render the world in numerical terms: just as every medium becomes digitized; every entity becomes commoditized. Both stand between, and must take into account, the capacities (and limits) of people and the capacities (and limits) of machines—a fact Manovich referred to as 'dual encoding' in the case of digital devices. For example, just as a computer program must be readable/writable by a human, it must be runable/storable by a machine; and just as an industrial commodity must be useful, or desirable, to a human, it must be producible with a machine. Both kinds of devices scale and embed in modular ways: larger algorithms (or data structures) as wholes can incorporate shorter algorithms (or data structures) as parts; any given large machine incorporates many smaller machines, in a complicated machinist division of labor. In this way, both kinds of devices allow one to easily manage greater and greater degrees of complexity; or, as we would now say, they *scale*.

Finally, and perhaps most pointedly, the laws of thermodynamics emerged with the introduction of steam engines; and a central equation in these laws (Boltzmann's definition of entropy) turned out to be perfectly suited, aside from a few tweaks, for calculating information content—that ur-commodity of the digital age, that most portable mode of meaning.

Curiously, Marx's notion of 'world money' (*Weltgeld*), a kind of universal currency, was directly related to Hegel's notion of the 'world spirit' (*Weltgeist*). All of which make it likely that we need a third term to capture such extreme forms of portability, however putative: not so much *Wortgeist* ('word spirit'), or even *Wortgeld* ('word money'), but rather *Weltwortgeldgeist* (or 'world-word-money-spirit').[25]

6.5. Universal Grammar and Linguistic Relativity

Crucial to the theoretical imaginary surrounding Turing Machines is the fact that various adjustments to their basic capacities do not affect their functioning. For example, there are TMs that can stay in place at any transition (in addition to moving left and right); there are TMs that use more than one tape (where characters may be read or written); there are TMs that move in two dimensions rather than one (and thus accept two-dimensional 'sheets' of text rather than one-dimensional strings of text); there are TMs that enumerate languages rather than recognize them; and so on, and so forth. And not withstanding such differences, all of these devices can be shown to be *equivalent* to the others, in that they all recognize the same set of languages. Understood another way, any algorithm written in one computer language (say, LISP) can be written in any other (say, Java); and, with suitable modifications and some caveats, any program that can be run on one machine can be run on any other.

Because TMs are so incredibly 'robust' in this way, computer scientists consider the class of languages that they recognize (in particular, the set of algorithmically solvable problems) to be relatively *natural* (Sipser 2007, 128–133). This is another way of framing the claim, introduced in the last section, that such devices are 'universal'.

One issue of fundamental importance to linguistic anthropologists is closely related to this fact: the tension between universal grammar and linguistic relativity. To see how, recall our discussion in chapter 3 of Sapir's (1949 [1924]) important claim: while all languages are arguably 'formally complete', in that they are able to represent the same set of experiences (qua reference), each has its own 'secret', which involves not only a way of orienting to a referent (qua 'sense') but also an associated feeling of orientation (qua 'sensibility'). While one may or may not be particularly committed to this claim, it is worthy of careful consideration because of the foundational disciplinary tensions it brings to light.

As we saw in the discussion surrounding Sapir's claim, both Cartesian coordinates (x, y) and polar coordinates (r, θ) may be used to represent the same set of points (all points in a two-dimensional plane). Recall Figure 3.1. And any expression in either system may thereby be translated into the other system (through equations like $x = r \cos \theta$ and $y = r \sin \theta$). But that said, the equations of particular entities may be more or less aesthetically elegant when expressed in one system rather than the other (e.g., lines are relatively simple entities in Cartesian coordinates, whereas circles are relatively simple entities in polar coordinates). As physicists know (Arfken and Weber 1995), certain problems may be more or less easy to solve in one system rather than the other (insofar as the symmetry of the problem matches the symmetry of the system). And finally, as a function of such symmetry and solvability, the intuitions and achievements of problem solvers may be more or less enabled or constrained. In this way, while the two systems may be equivalent at the level of reference, they are nonequivalent at the level of sense and sensibility. As we phrased it in chapter 3: while different systems may allow us to 'touch' the same worlds, the worlds so touched may be nonetheless 'felt' in distinctly different ways.

Understood in such terms, three points may now be made. First, while Sapir was, of course, talking about (so called) natural languages, such claims may also be understood to hold for (so called) artificial languages. In particular, while any program written in one programming language may be written in another programming language (as per our discussion of Universal Turing Machines), it is likely that different programming languages (not to mention interfaces, platforms, applications, protocols, architectures, and so forth) have different 'secrets'.[26] That is, they have different symmetries built into them (that make certain problems easier or harder to solve, not to mention notice and communicate), and different sensibilities disciplined by them (as embodied in those who habitually program in them, or heed and wield their affordances more generally). While this claim is a low-hanging fruit, it is worth making insofar as it shows another site where classic techniques of linguistic anthropology can be applied to classic objects of computer science—the texts that generate computation (qua programs) as much as the texts generated by computation (qua languages, in the technical sense discussed above).

Second, given the relation between the languages generated by context-free grammars and natural languages (like Spanish, Nahuatl, and Japanese), given the 'naturalness' of the class of languages recognizable by Turing Machines, given the strong referential equivalence of natural languages (qua 'formal completeness'), and given the close initial disciplinary linkage between computer science, cognitive science, and formal linguistics, it is not difficult to empathize with the desire of early generative linguists to discover a 'universal grammar' underlying all natural languages. Nor is it difficult to empathize with their intuition that it should be equally discoverable through any particular language (say, standardized English) if analyzed closely enough. In other words, if all coordinate systems (qua systems of signs) are equivalent (in that any one may relate to the others as interpretant to sign, and thereby represent the same world of objects), why not just use one of them to understand the key features, or essential semiotic affordances, that any equivalent system must thereby contain?

And third, just as it is easy to foreground equivalence of reference (as a disciplinary focus), it is also easy to foreground nonequivalence of sense and sensibility. In particular, having just characterized some key ideas underlying the analytic imaginary (or disciplinary culture) of generative linguists, it is easy to see where some of linguistic anthropology's own contrastive commitments come from. For example, if universal grammar may be understood to foreground 'formal completeness', linguistic relativity may be understood to foreground 'secrets'. And while early linguistic anthropologists like Whorf (1956 [1939], 1956 [1937]) and Sapir (1985 [1927], 1985 [1945]) could comfortably shift between both perspectives (indeed, notwithstanding contemporary misreadings of them, Sapir and Whorf highlighted linguistic *invariance* as much as linguistic *relativity*), the latter perspective has come to take center stage in the discipline. For example, Hill and Mannheim (1992; and see Lee 1996), have gone so far as to argue that linguistic relativity should be understood as an 'axiom' of linguistic anthropology rather than a hypothesis. In this way, two sets of scholars have passionately rallied around flags of complementary colors, themselves placed in contiguous and often overlapping terrains, that were originally staked out by the same surveyors.

6.6. Virtuality, Happiness, and Secret Roads to Recognition

In previous chapters we used the metaphor of a path to understand the relation between objects and signs (qua code) and signers and interpretants (qua channel). We are now in a position to see how this metaphor may also be used to understand the relation between signs and interpretants (qua computation). To show this, we will first work through the relatively simple example of a deterministic finite automaton, and then work through the relatively complicated example of a Turing machine.

As seen in Figure 6.5, a DFA may be easily diagrammed. In particular, such a device may be represented as a set of directed paths (the lines, or relations) through a space of possible states (the circles, or nodes).[27] A given string, as a list of symbols, may be understood as moving through such a space, by taking a particular route (from state to state). Such a route is determined, in part, by the particular arrangement of nodes and relations that constitute the device; and, in part, by the particular ordering of symbols that constitutes the string itself. As may be seen, almost every state is both a destination (that can be arrived at from other states) and an origin (that can be departed from to other states).

We begin at the initial state of the device (the circle on the far left, which is marked by an incoming arrow). To decide which path to take, we look at the first (or left-most) symbol in the string. If it is the letter 'a', we move along the path labeled 'a', in the direction indicated, to the next state (another circle, or node). If it is the letter 'b', we move along the path labeled 'b', in the direction indicated, to the next state. Once in the new state, we look at the next symbol in the string. We then move along the path labeled with that symbol in the direction indicated. Moving from state to state, while moving along the symbols in the string, we continue doing exactly this same procedure until we get to the end of our string. At that point, if we happen to be in an 'accept state' (any state that is colored black), the string is accepted. If we happen to be in any other state, the string is rejected. Note, then, that the path we take may be incredibly complicated (especially if the string is long); and different strings may take very different paths. But, at the end of the journey, what matters is the state one ends up in—regardless of how long it took to get there, or what route was taken. (Recall our discussion, in chapter 3, of multiple senses with a single referent.) As can be seen, this DFA accepts any string that is of the pattern: *ab, ba, aba, bab, abab, baba,* and so forth.

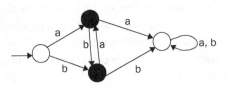

FIGURE 6.5 Example of Deterministic Finite Automata

In the case of Turing Machines, we might consider the string to constitute an environment, and the device to constitute a kind of organism that is positioned in that environment. Recall our discussion of beetles and sandy planes in chapter 2. Such an organism can 'sense' the external environment (in particular, what symbol it is currently positioned at); and it can 'sense' its internal environment (in particular, what state it is currently in). As a function of its transition function (a kind of habit, genome, mind, culture, or program), the organism can transform its external environment (by writing a new symbol), transform its position in that environment (by moving up or down the string), and transform its internal environment (by changing its current state). Such an organism, then, does not just sense and instigate: it instigates as a function of what it senses (and what state it is in); and it senses as a function of how it instigates. (Note, by the way, the relation between internal states and the 'keys' of McLuhan, or the ultimate interpretants of Peirce, as described in chapter 4.) Moreover, the organism itself changes as it senses and instigates (via its updating of its own internal state); and the environment itself changes as the organism moves through it (via the new symbols that are being written there). In terms of section 6.2, the environment and the organism are intimate; in terms of chapter 2, both entities are akin to self-channeling channels (and even source-dependent channels); and in terms of chapter 5, we have a relatively deterministic, but nonetheless incredibly complicated, envorganism.

Note, then, that in both cases (DFA and TM) the automata can be understood as a black box, as well as a sieve: put a string in, and see whether it is accepted or rejected. With the path metaphor, we are in effect opening up the black box, and seeing that *inside the black box is a complicated space of potential paths.* The route taken, itself some particular concatenation of shorter paths, stepping through certain states is, in part, a function of the space itself and, in part, a function of the inputed string. Together, *the fate of the string* is 'determined'—whether it will be accepted or rejected, whether it is deemed wheat or chaff, and hence whether it is part of the language 'recognized'.

Such a device is precisely a means of assaying strings to find out if they do indeed 'belong'. To return to our parasite metaphor: the device intercepts those strings that don't take the right route; or inversely, it accepts those strings that do. To return to our notion of *eudamonia* from chapter 2, Friedrich Kittler (1996) once perversely and provocatively intimated that to perceive such routes, such circuity, is to 'find happiness' (xli), understood here as *the secret path to acceptance, the hidden way to recognition.*

If we think of all the different strings we could put in the device, and all the different paths they (and the device) might take, with all the various destinations they might arrive at, we see how those strings that are accepted have an essential— or *virtual*—similarity, however much they may otherwise differ from one other (in terms of their symbol sequence or in terms of their path structure). Crucially, such a virtual similarity among strings is device specific, and hence context-dependent, and so may shift accordingly. Such happiness, then, is fickle and fleeting.

***

In short, across a wide range of different domains—codes, channels, computers—this notion of a path, of a journey, of a sense, of a secret, is key. Such a metaphor is not used lightly. It seems to be the most widespread of ideas, such that most of the world's languages and cultures have domains that are organized by its logic. And it is essential to modern infrastructure—a key idea organizing not just our imaginary of technology, but also the engineering of the technology itself. As introduced in chapter 1, the mathematical field devoted to this powerful metaphor is called graph theory; and, somewhat ironically given the arguments of chapter 2, the first key work in this field was Euler's famous paper of 1736, "The Seven Bridges of Koenigsberg."

As in the case of codes and channels, such paths constitute the secret of computation: they may be rendered in other terms (e.g,. functions calling functions calling functions . . .), but they lie black-boxed between the more readily available inputs and outputs they bring into relation. Just like the secrets of channels and codes, their inherent symmetries lend themselves to different sensibilities. And, like all generative mechanisms, there are ways of bringing them and the virtual similarities they intimate (more or less) into intuition.

6.7. Intermediation as Topic and Technique

Recall our opening example of *interpretation*: a boy turning to look at the object of his mother's interjection. And recall our extended discussion of interpretation in chapter 5: the multiple grounds underlying any semiotic process—from Grice to Freud, from archeology to astrophysics, from ripples in rivers to traces of aura, and far beyond. With these context rich, culture-bound, frame-specific, abductive, and often radically *unruly* interpretations in mind, one way to reframe some of the foregoing claims is as follows: *computation is the enclosure of interpretation*.

In part, this means that computation is a species of interpretation that has been relatively mediated by technology, science, and economy (as per our discussion of value at the end of chapter 2). In part, this means that computation is a species of interpretation that is relatively regimented as to its use-value, truth-value, exchange-value, deontic value, and epistemic value (as per our discussion of value in chapter 4). And in part, this means that the values in question become relatively portable: not so much independent of context, as dependent on contexts which have been engineered so as to be ubiquitous, and hence seemingly context-free. In effect, the mediation is so great that it appears to be unmediated—and thus a mere intermediary. For the average denizen of such an environs, or organism in such an environment, thirdness often goes about as secondness (and vice-versa).

This claim was already generalized. While the focus in this chapter was on the relation between computation and interpretation (and thus the input-output, or sign-interpretant relation per se), we also focused on the sign-object relation, and argued that information is the enclosure of meaning (chapter 4). And we focused on the signer-interpreter relation, and argued that infrastructure is the enclosure of interaction (chapter 2). In this way, we focused on *a set of concomitant processes whereby semiosis gets not only automated, but also formatted and networked.* If all such relations are grounded in path metaphors (sign to object, or code; signer to interpreter, or channel; sign to interpretant, or computation), then we have relatively enclosed paths. To return to our discussion of coordinate systems, we have something somewhat akin to a linear circle or a circular line. *Descartes among the polar bears, in a saddle and with a sombrero.*

Such a claim was also already called into question *many, many times.* For hand in hand with the real-time practices and *longue-durée* processes though which such a transformation occurs, or at least seems to occur, is a kind of reflective understanding of its occurrence—itself usually radically refracted (or so the story goes). In each kind of enclosure, a great degree of agency (power, flexibility, meta-reflexivity, progress, calculability, etc.) seems to be gained—and so there is celebration and speculation. And a great degree of authenticity (context-dependence, historical uniqueness, cultural specificity, etc.) seems to be lost—and so there is nostalgia and mourning. Recall the admonishments of Rushkin.

Needless to say, such refracted reflectivity should be all-too-familiar to anthropologists, as they are themselves grounded in a particular imaginary that is found again and again in critical theory (Kockelman 2007b): from Aristotle and Marx (e.g., substance and form, quality and quantity), through Maine and Toennies (e.g., status and contract, community and society), to Levi-Strauss and Bourdieu (e.g., raw and cooked, practice and structure). Indeed, anthropology has always been, in part, the disciplinization of precisely such refracted reflections: in its more sophisticated variants it proposes them; in its less sophisticated variants it presupposes them. From this perspective, celebrations of cyborg futures are just as misplaced as lamentations about authenticities lost.

***

Let's return to Aristotle's long list of complementary entities, as reviewed and reinterpreted in chapter 1. Recall that he judged one such entity relatively mediate, and its complement relatively immediate: man and woman, human and animal, reason and passion, voice and sound, *bios* and *zoe*, and so forth. As argued there, a key trend in anthropology has been to revisit such distinctions, where such a revisiting sometimes has the intended effect of perturbing or dissolving the distinction, but more often has the unintended effect of presupposing and thereby reproducing the distinction.

A similar logic is often at work in the study of science and technology. On the one hand, many scholars still want to safeguard the 'uniquely human' in the face of technological encroachment (the robot, the chatbot, the simulation, the algorithm, the virtual); on the other hand, many scholars are constantly drawn to what they deem to be the most novel, advanced, or cutting-edge technology (because that is where the putative encroachment seems so stark, the political stakes seem so high, and the funding potential so great).

Or, phrased in a slightly inverted fashion: whenever someone (such as the 'humanist') says there is something a human can do, but an algorithm (machine, automaton, etc.) cannot, someone else (such as 'the non-humanist') says: if you can precisely state what it is you don't think an algorithm can do, I can certainly write one that will do it; and if you cannot state what it cannot do, then you don't know what a human can do that a machine cannot (and so why are we even arguing?).[28] And yet, with each new algorithm, there will be a new encroachment (however illusory), and so a new line to be drawn (however imprecisely), and so a new argument to be had (however unproductively). We will return to these important issues in chapter 7, for the temporal dynamics underlying transformations in ontologies and worlds are as wily as our understandings of them are woolly.

***

With these claims and caveats in mind, we may now sketch some topics and techniques for a linguistic anthropology of automatized (formatted and networked) languages; one which focuses on *intermediation* (or firstness) rather than constantly trying to counter intermediaries by reference to mediators, or secondness by reference to thirdness; and thus one which seeks to empathize with machines (and their makers), as much as with humans (and their makings).[29] Recall Figure 6.3 and Table 6.1.

One important relation that shows up again and again in computer science, among other places, might be called *ontological isomorphisms, cross-domain diagrams,* or even *real imaginaries.* By this is meant that a set of relations found in one domain is found in another seemingly disparate domain, such that insights from one domain may be used to generate insights about the other, in ways that often license large-scale theoretical and technological innovation. For example, just as Boole (1958 [1854]) worked out the relation between binary numbers and truth conditions (and thus math and logic), Shannon (1937) worked out the relation between truth conditions and electrical circuits (and thus logic and engineering).[30] And actual material instantiations of Turing Machines, such as the standard desktop computer we now have, itself not much different from the architecture initially proposed by von Neumann (Ceruzzi 2000; Petzold 2000), exploit precisely these relations. Also well-known, as noted at the end of section 6.4, is the ontological isomorphism between entropy and information, and hence thermodynamics and computer science. More generally, we saw in the last chapter how different systems (a pendulum and a planet and an atom) may have similar dynamics through phase-space, insofar as the singularities that structure their differential equations are topologically equivalent. Finally, as just reviewed, this entire book has been organized around a particular metaphor, the path or graph, and its various extensions and perturbations. Recall Figure 3.1.

While closely related to metaphor (and thus able to be studied, in part, using the techniques of trope analysis), these mappings are not metaphors in the conventional sense of, say, Lakoff and Johnson (1980). This is for two crucial reasons. First, there is no distinction between concrete and abstract domains (each domain is on equal par, as it were). And second, it is not, strictly speaking, a linguistic or conceptual phenomenon: the parallels are not projections, but actually exist in the domain of reference, and may be pointed to with any kind of sign. But that said, while certain mappings may be well-founded and referentially motivated, other mappings may be more whimsical, unfounded or performative—licensed by particular imaginaries and symbolics, as much as by particular reals. In particular, a key kind of relation between relations to study is the relation between these real imaginaries (i.e., cross-domain diagrams) and symbolic imaginaries (i.e., metaphors in their more conventional sense, and textual and technological aesthetics more generally). These are key sites where the promises and pitfalls of automatized languages, as well as the interfaces they present to the world, and the infrastructures they depend on in the world, get refracted in reflection (as well as redacted, diffracted, enacted, and beyond).

***

Intersecting the phenomenon of cross-domain diagrams is *dual encoding* as was introduced at the end of section 6.4, following Manovich's (2001) characterization of the key principles of new media: the way a given computer language (or technology more generally) is subject to the demands and abilities of the machines that compute with it as much as of the humans that interpret with it.[31] For example, the texts that tell computers what to do (i.e., 'programs'), such that they may generate further texts (i.e. 'languages') can be more or less easily 'read' by humans and, concomitantly, less or more easily 'read' by machines. And so there are programming languages like Assembly and Machine which stay very close to the structure of the machines that run them; and there are programming languages like Python and C which are, relatively speaking, more amenable to the intuitions of people who write in them, and which have to be interpreted or compiled before they can be run by a computer. Phrased another way, algorithms are 'boundary objects' in a sense much extended from that of Star and Geisemer (1989): they stand at the intersection of two kinds of agents, the machines that run them and the people that program them. And, as such, they allow machines and humans to collaborate on common projects, all the while maintaining their respective 'autonomies'.

Framed more generally, to serve a single function (or have a particular object) a given sign must be amenable to the ontologies (capacities, codes, habits, cultures, protocols, etc.) of several interpreting agents at once. Crucially, this means that each kind of interpreting agent might understand it in different ways, and so there can be issues of translation, the division of labor, relative perspicacity of encoding, and so forth, with all the usual tensions at the intersections. And yet, from another perspective, or at a different scale, there must be a commonality or complementarity of materials, uses, ideas, affordances, or ends. Such an issue is directly related to a much more timeless and variable topic: how a tool (idea, sign, institution, etc.) is (more or less) crafted to the demands of the world, the body, the mind, and the society all at once (for better or worse); or how a practice is regimented by cultural norms and natural causes simultaneously; or how a dream may be interpretable in regards to both its manifest and its latent content at the same time; and so forth.

The issue, then, is not just 'dual encoding' but also *multiple interpreters* or, in light of chapter 5, *multiple grounds*. Recall Figure 5.3, and the discussion surrounding it. Each of us is regimented by multiple imaginaries, interactions, institutions, infrastructures, interfaces, and instincts. And so our forms and formulations, our dreams and deviations, our functions and failings, our affects and effects, reflect such multiple regimenting agencies, such manifold conditions of possibility. And algorithms and automata are no different (or at least not much different).

To put this in a more critical perspective, such issues point to a related set of tensions that were first foregrounded by Marx: the degree to which an instrument is designed to fit the requirements of a user (e.g., a 'tool'); or a user is disciplined to fit the requirements of an instrument (e.g., a 'machine'). And this relation may itself be reframed in semiotic terms. There is *iconicity,* via Saussure and Peirce: the degree to which a sign (and, concomitantly, a signer) takes on features of its object. And, conversely, there is *projection*, via Sapir and Whorf: the degree to which an object (and, concomitantly, an interpreter) takes on features of its sign. Again, the relevance and reach of these issues for linguistic anthropologists, and similarly committed scholars, should be clear, especially given the discussion of reference, sense, and sensibility in section 6.5 (and recall chapter 3), and given the discussion of affordances and instruments in chapter 1.

***

As mentioned in section 6.4, critical theory may not only be applied to algorithms and automata, it may also be generated by an algorithm or automaton. While such a topic deserves an essay in itself (Kockelman 2014a), it is useful to sketch a few of the key moves insofar as they also offer an ideal typological account of mediation.

Suppose, by mediation (M), we mean one of two relations: some entity *represents* another entity, or some entity *conditions* another entity. The first type of relation (-) might be understood as a sign standing for an object (S-O), or an assertion representing a fact, or a belief representing a state of affairs, or a dream representing a past experience, or an ideology representing a world, and so forth. The second type of relation might be understood as a cause giving rise to an effect (C-E), or one event conditioning another event, or a forcefield channeling one happening into another, or a sign giving rise to an interpretant, and so forth.

In this way, the first kind of relation (S-O) relates to the second kind of relation (C-E) in a variety of ways, depending on the inclinations of the analyst, and the particularities of the mode of mediation in question: code to channel, knowledge to power, representation to intervention, object-sign relation to sign-interpretant relation, relatively conventional grounds to relatively causal grounds, third to second, and so forth. And, as such, the relata in question can be any kind of 'object' under the sun: dreams, desires, qualia, processes, events, affordances, actions, worlds, ontologies, beliefs, grammatical categories, books, and beyond. In effect, then, we have the first two rules of a context-free grammar: M => S-O and M => C-E. That is, just as a sentence (S) may be rewritten as a relation between a noun phrase (NP) and a verb phrase (VP), any mode of mediation may be written as a sign-object relation, or as a cause-effect relation. Phrased another way, we have two kinds of 'bridges' (-), with their respective 'banks' (S and O, or C and E). See Table 6.2a.

Crucially, any such entity (qua relatum) can itself be a relation between relata. And so we get four more rules that enable *embedding*: S => M, O => M, C => M, and E => M. See Table 6.2b, where subscripts and parenthesis show the relation before the embedding.[32] Next, note that a mediating relation of type S-O can be *reframed* as a mediating relation of type C-E, and vice-versa. That is, relatively causal processes can be understood semiotically (however fetishizing such an understanding may be); and relatively semiotic processes can be understood causally (however reifying such an understanding may be). Recall Figure 5.2, and the discussion surrounding it. And so we get two more rules: S-O => C-E and C-E => S-O. See Table 6.2c, where subscripts and parentheses show the relation before the reframing. Finally, any such relation (-), or movement, can be intercepted, and so fail to arrive at its destination (|); or it can be interfered with, and so arrive at a different destination (~). See Table 6.2d, and recall our definition of the parasite from chapter 2.

Table 6.3 shows a range of even more elaborate expressions that may be generated with this small set of deterministic rules, or 'intermediaries'. There are *conditioned disturbances* (a), such as the conditions and consequences (or causes and effects) of misrepresenting an entity, or being unconscious of an idea. Similarly, we may inquire into the conditions and consequences, or roots and fruits, of unintended effects and failed efforts. There are *embedded disturbances* (b), such as misunderstanding, or being unaware of, the conditions and consequences of various representations, or various conditionings. For example, depending on how one understands a wish or desire (say, as a mode of intentionality or as a causal drive, and thus in terms of representation or in terms of conditioning), Freud's (1999) unconscious can be understood in either way. There are *circular disturbances* (c), such as distorted (or blocked) representations of the conditions of possibility for precisely that distorting (or blocking) of the representation. Loosely speaking, what I cannot envision is precisely that which blocks my vision. And there are *disturbed frames* (d), such as 'reification' (a sign-object relation is misrepresented as a

TABLE 6.2
Critical Theory as Context-Free Grammar (part 1)

	Expression	Paraphrase	Examples
a) Basic Modes	S-O	Sign stands for object, or representation has some representatum	Grammatical Category Stands for Semantic Feature, Mental State Represents State of Affairs
	C-E	Cause gives rise to effect, or condition has some consequence	Discursive Practice Leads to Grammatical Structure, Mode of Communication Conditions Mode of Consciousness
b) Embeddings	$S\text{-}(S\text{-}O)_O$	Object of sign is sign-object relation	Meta-language, Paraphrase, Reported speech, etc.
	$C\text{-}(C\text{-}E)_E$	Effect of cause is cause-effect relation	Meta-Control, Conducting Conduct, Keys, Switches, etc.
	$S\text{-}(C\text{-}E)_O$	Object of sign is cause-effect relation	Physics Equation: $F = ma$ Warning Sign: Harmful if Ingested
	$C\text{-}(S\text{-}O)_E$	Effect of cause is sign-object relation	Grammaticalization, Regimentation, Conventionalization, Enregisterment
	$(S\text{-}O)_S\text{-}O$	Sign-object relation is sign of object	Language You Speak Is Sign of Your Identity
	$(S\text{-}O)_C\text{-}E$	Sign-object relation is cause of effect	Any Interpretant of Sign-Object Relation
	$(C\text{-}E)_S\text{-}O$	Cause-effect relation is sign of object	One's Reaction to a Situation itself an Index of One's Mood or Emotion
	$(C\text{-}E)_C\text{-}E$	Cause-effect relation is cause of effect	Phylogenetic Interpretants
c) Reframings	$(S)_C\text{-}(O)_E$	Sign relates to object as cause to effect	Performatives (token level) Projection (type level)
	$(O)_C\text{-}(S)_E$	Object relates to sign as cause to effect	Constatives (token level) Iconicity (type level)
	$(C)_S\text{-}(E)_O$	Cause relates to effect as sign to object	Clues, Symptoms, or Forces (Understood Protentively)
	$(E)_S\text{-}(C)_O$	Effect relates to cause as sign to object	Clues, Symptoms, or Forces (Understood Retentively)
d) Disturbances	S | O	Blocked or unknown representation	Not Conscious of Some Object Cannot Articulate Some Object
	S ~ O	Distorted or false representation	Representation of Object Incorrect or Distorted
	C | E	Effect stopped, path blocked	Thwarting of Action Capping of Channel
	C ~ E	Effect redirected, path rerouted	Coopting of Action Redirecting of Channel

TABLE 6.3
Critical Theory as Context-Free Grammar (part 2)

	Expression	Paraphrase
a) Conditioned Disturbances	$C\text{-}(S \mid O)_E$ or $(S \mid O)_C\text{-}E$ $C\text{-}(S \sim O)_E$ or $(S \sim O)_C\text{-}E$	Conditions for, or Consequences of, Unrepresented or Distorted Object
	$C\text{-}(C \mid E)_E$ or $(C \mid E)_C\text{-}E$ $C\text{-}(C \sim E)_E$ or $(C \sim E)_C\text{-}E$	Conditions for, or Consequences of, Blocked or Redirected Effect
b) Embedded Disturbances	$S \sim (S\text{-}O)_O$ or $S \mid (S\text{-}O)_O$ $S \sim (C\text{-}(S\text{-}O)_E)_O$, etc.	Misrepresented, or Unrepresented, Representations (and Their Conditions and Consequences)
	$S \sim (C\text{-}E)_O$ or $S \mid (C\text{-}E)_O$ $S \sim (C\text{-}(C\text{-}E)_E)_O$, etc.	Misrepresented, or Unrepresented, Conditionings (and Their Conditions and Consequences)
c) Circular Disturbances	$Si \mid (C\text{-}(Si \mid Oi)_E)_{Oi}$ $Si \sim (C\text{-}(Si \sim Oi)_E)_{Oi}$	Distorted (or Blocked) Representation of Conditions for *That* Distorted (or Blocked) Representation
	$Si \mid ((Si \mid Oi)_C\text{-}E)_{Oi}$ $Si \sim ((Si \sim Oi)_C\text{-}E)_{Oi}$	Distorted (or Blocked) Representation of Consequences of *That* Distorted Representation
d) Disturbed Frames	$S \sim ((S)_C\text{-}(O)_E)_O$	Sign-Object Relations Misrepresented as Cause-Effect Relations, or 'Reification' (in one sense of the term)
	$S \sim ((C)_S\text{-}(E)_O)_O$	Cause-Effect Relations Misrepresented as Sign-Object Relations, or 'Fetishization' (in one sense of the term)

cause-effect relation) and 'fetishization' (a cause-effect relation is misrepresented as a sign-object relation).

When one is really fluent in this language, one doesn't just claim that others' theories (that is, their representations) of mediation are mediated, one also claims that one's own account of mediation is mediated. Indeed, many articles by critical theorists, and similarly situated scholars, are precisely complicated signs (qua texts) that represent conditions for (and consequences of) particular sign-object relations, where such conditions and consequences, qua causes and effects, are themselves other sign-object relations (such as other scholars' texts), and may themselves have other conditions and consequences. For example, $(\text{Text})_S\text{-}((S\text{-}O)_C\text{-}(S\text{-}O)_E)_O$. And so on, and so forth.

Crucially, all the expressions shown in Table 6.2 and Table 6.3 are simply strings, or sequences of symbols, that may be generated with the rules of our automaton (which is more or less a context-free grammar (CFG), as described in section 6.4). The semantics of such strings were just described (that is, what they refer to, or represent, qua modes of mediation)); and the details of many such modes of mediation were taken up in various parts of this monograph. The entirety of strings generated by such an automata, or the language recognized by that automata, might best be labeled not 'English', 'Nahuatl', or 'German', but simply *Critical Theory* (in one of its guises).

Such a language should have all the mystery and mustiness of New Latin, that other maximally portable 'artificial language', or *lingua franca*, so favored by scholastic humanists otherwise enclosed in their monasteries, polities, and universities. Finally, like any good language, this one also functions as a *shibboleth*: if you can speak it (more or less fluently) you will be 'recognized' by other speakers, and thereby accepted into their disciplinary enclosures and journals (Kockelman 2014a).[33] (It also, of course, functions like a *cipher*—ensuring that nobody else will really understand what you all are saying.)

***

Finally, a more obvious topic of interest to linguistic anthropologists, and similarly directed scholars, is the *Turing Test*, and attempts to make computers speak (and interact more generally) in ways that are more or less indistinguishable from human speech and interaction (Turing 2004 [1950]; and see French 2000 and Saygin et. al. 2001). One relatively indirect route to this topic would be to study the intersection of several text-building processes. First, the texts (qua computer programs), and practices of textualization used to make computers 'speak' (if only virtually, following our discussion in chapter 5). Second, the 'texts' (qua rules, protocols, norms, constraints), and practices of textualization, used to make people speak in ways that are deemed appropriate and effective (by teachers, parents, employers, states, and so forth). Third, the texts (qua human-machine dialogues), and practices of textualization, generated through interactions between these programs and these people. And fourth, the texts (qua meta-language) by humans and machines about these dialogues and programs and norms (describing them, theorizing them, categorizing them, evaluating them, commodifying them, vilifying them, textualizing them, contextualizing them, and so forth). More generally, these kinds of (minimally fourfold) intertextual processes are at work in a multitude of natural language processing projects. And so there are ample opportunities for scholars who want to study the tensions among such texts and practices of textualization.[34]

As intimated above, one relatively direct route to this topic is through the lens of ontology and transformativity. As used here, *ontology* refers to an agent's assumptions as to the behavioral propensities of various kinds (such as 'person', qua autonomous agent, versus 'machine', qua automaton), insofar as these assumptions license particular inferences, or interpretations, when brought to bear on particular indices (such as syntactic patterns, conversational moves, and semiotic processes more generally). *Transformativity*, in turn, refers to the various ways an agent's ontological assumptions change over time through their indexical encounters with individuals (who seem to instantiate such kinds), as well as through their informative encounters with other agents (who characterize the indexical propensities of such kinds, however incorrectly, prejudicially, or performatively). These issues are so important that chapter 7 will be devoted to them, in a much generalized sense. As will be seen, determining whether one is speaking to a human or a machine is not much different than determining whether a message in your inbox is ham or spam; and so is not much different than judging whether an entity is 'real' or virtual, or sieving for wheat versus chaff, or listening for 'shibboleth' versus 'sibboleth'.

7

Algorithms, Agents, and Ontologies

7.1. The Sabotaging of Sieves

As we saw in chapter 6, sieves are essential to information processing. That said, a machine such as the combine harvester (which not only reaps and threshes, but also winnows—by removing chaff from grain), should remind us that agricultural and industrial economies rely on sieves as much as information economies. Returning to our discussion of the value of information in chapter 4, rather than thinking about *work* as the giving of form to substance for the sake of function, it may often be usefully understood as *the organization of complexity for the sake of predictability*.

Take, for example, a gas in a container. We may do work on the gas by compressing it (applying a force through a distance and thereby decreasing the volume of the gas); and, in so doing, we obtain more information about the position of the molecules that make up the gas (in that they are now located in a much smaller volume than previously, and so we can point to their location with greater certainty). Phrased another way, by exercising a power (i.e., moving a piston), we increase our knowledge (of where the gas is located in the container). What sieves really produce is patterns, and hence predictability (perhaps no more and no less than poetry or peoples). And thus it's not so much that all work is done through sieves (though that may be the case, or certainly may be more and more the case)—but rather that *all sieves do work*.

Except when they 'don't work', an expression that is ambiguous in precisely the right way—for, as we will now see, the sieve, while in some sense the prototypic parasite (as per our definition in chapter 2), is itself an unwitting host to a variety of parasites. For example, and somewhat ironically, before you can sieve a substance you usually need to make sure the substance has already been sieved, so that it constitutes appropriate input in the first place. And thus, *Weapons of The Weak* fans (Scott 1985), if you want to 'gum up the works' of a sieve the best

Paul Kockelman. *The Art of Interpretation in the Age of Computation.* © Oxford University Press 2017

thing to do is to give it input that is neither here nor there: for example, strings of symbols from an alphabet it does not recognize or indices unidentifiable in its ontology. The more singular your sign, in other words, the less likely it is that there is a sieve out there that has its qualities built into its design. (Recall our example of the hole, and the strange intimacy sieves have in regards to the substances they sort.)

For our second example, and as per the Hollywood image of a computer exploit, you can give a sieve input (say, particular strings, qua snippets of code) that commandeer its processor, or interpreting agent, for other ends. We needn't focus on this all too often celebrated (or reviled) parasite except insofar as it resonates with the expanded definition of a shifter offered in chapter 6: that which has no object and serves no purpose, and so can be coupled to any object and used for any purpose (depending on the context in which it is put—a context which includes the contents of its own input).

As a third example, and more technically, there is also the possibility that sieves of the Turing Machine sort (i.e., computers) cannot 'decide' or 'select', and hence cannot stop or 'halt', but merely cycle on infinitely or at least indefinitely, unable to make a decision as to the status of a string: acceptable or unacceptable. To invoke the categories of Hannah Arendt (1958), your *actions* can ensure such a machine never *works* by making sure that it is always in *labor*.

As a fourth example, and somewhat more decisively, we can always just mix—which is, in some sense, the opposite of sieving: simply shake, aggregate, amass, spill, muddle, muddy, infiltrate, slip by, and more generally strategically discombobulate.

And finally, if sieves are machines that ensure that things are either *here* or *there*, we might just make sure that we only make things (and say things) that are 'neither here nor there'. This reminds us that 'meaning'—ensuring that something is either here or there, in the sense that it makes or has sense—is the quintessential form of sorting. *His reply to my question was neither here nor there* (and so failed to sort the world for me). Or, as particularly pertinent to the history of anthropology, questions like: *is this permitted, may I eat at your table, can we marry each other, is he a witch, am I predestined?* In other words, given that we are all, in part, just sieves ourselves, we might all just stop making sense (if only in the sense of trying to make sense of it all).

See Figure 7.1 which, as shown in chapter 2, owes as much to Claude Shannon's understanding of enemies and noise as it does to Serres's account of parasites as it does to Peirce's theory of thirdness.[1] In short, if we think of an entity's parasites as whatever implies other ends the entity could be used to serve (besides its intended purpose or function per se), or implies any way the entity might fail to serve its end (be it original or derived), these are some of the parasites of sieves—*parasieves*, in fact. Of course, if many sieves are not designed, and thus cannot fail to achieve an end nor be diverted from an end (for they have no end), then they are in essence parasiteless creatures, and thus unexploitable entities—the lucky little devils.

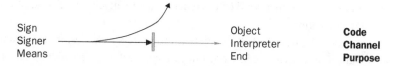

Sign	Object	**Code**
Signer	Interpreter	**Channel**
Means	End	**Purpose**

An object (action or sign) considered as a means to an end (or infrastructure considered as a path to a destination) is a second (or intermediary), but insofar as it implies (embodies or indexes) other ends it might be diverted to serve, or indeed implies any way it may fail to serve an end (whether original or diverted), it is a third (or mediator). The parasite is whatever inhabits such implications. That is, parasites reside in as much as off such systems, where their residence perturbs systems, pushing them off of old paths, and sometimes even pulling them onto new paths.

Indeed, the possibility of going awry, or at least of being judged so, is arguably the essence of such processes. Focusing on codes or representations, there is unconsciousness (being unable to represent some particular object) and misrepresentation (representing something incorrectly, or in a highly refracted fashion). Focusing on channels or conditioning, there is repression (stopping a cause from having its effect) and rechanneling (creating conditions for causes to have unusual or unintended effects).

FIGURE 7.1 Parasite Defined and Exemplified in Terms of Code, Channel, and Purpose

***

This chapter is ostensibly about *spam filters*, algorithmic devices that separate desirable messages from undesirable messages. Such filters are a particularly important kind of sieve insofar as they readily exhibit key features of sieving devices in general, and algorithmic sieving in particular.

In analyzing the inner workings of spam filters, this chapter also describes some of the key presumptions, possibilities, and pitfalls of a paradigm that might be best called *Bayesian anthropology*, or even *Machinic Culture*. It is meant to stand as a case study of some of the concerns outlined in chapter 6—regarding how to offer careful anthropological accounts of mathematical and computational objects.

As will be shown, while the key categories developed here are embodied in the technological and mathematical objects in question (in particular, spam filters and Bayesian statistics), they have the potential to be usefully and critically applied to other domains (when radically perturbed or 'tweaked').[2] Such domains range from the interactional orders of Goffman (e.g., the dynamics of selfhood and semiosis in face-to-face interaction) to the epistemes of Foucault and the historical ontologies of Hacking to machine learning more generally.

Section 7.2 returns to some of the categories introduced at the end of chapter 5, using these to analyze the relation between ontology (assumptions that drive interpretations) and inference (interpretations that alter assumptions) as it plays out in the transformation of spam as a kind of message style. It also shows the relation between spam filters, museum displays, and identifying practices. Section 7.3 uses this analysis to track some of the unstable processes whereby identifying algorithms, identified styles, and evasive transformations are dynamically coupled over time. And section 7.4 applies this analysis to the Turing Test, or the indexical styling of the human kind. It argues that most thought about this scenario has focused on a very limited kind of inference, and a relatively trivial kind of ontological transformation.

Section 7.5 carefully walks readers through Bayes's Equation, a mathematical formulation that lies at the heart of not just spam filters, but a wide range of other powerful computational technologies. It shows the limits of mathematical formulations through the formulations themselves by foregrounding some of the aporia of sieves. Along the way, it theorizes various kinds of *ontological inertia*, showing how certain assumptions are 'deeper' and so more difficult to historically transform. Concomitantly, it theorizes various kinds of *algorithmic ineffability*, showing how certain processes are more difficult to mathematically capture. More than anything, and in conjunction with the other sections, this section shows how equations and algorithms can simultaneously be subject to and contribute to anthropological analysis. And so while this chapter focuses on a certain kind of classification (spam versus ham), and a certain type of algorithm, most of the issues foregrounded and theorized are easily ported to other kinds of classification and other kinds of machine learning.

And the last two sections show the repercussions of the foregoing arguments and analytics for understanding key issues in political economy, human evolution, and art history. Section 7.6 returns to the relation between virtuality and actuality, showing how virtuality relates to fetishization, as the systematic misrecognition of the origins of value. And section 7.7 highlights the strange relation between meaning, mathematics, and meat by reviewing the inspirational origins of psychoanalysis, and the 'work of interpretation'.

7.2. The Ontology of Spam, Meteorites, and Huckleberry Finn

The term spam usually refers to unsolicited commercial bulk email, and the like.[3] In terms of chapter 2, it is a quintessential form of *noise*. As used here, a spam filter is just a particular kind of sieve, one that uses mathematical algorithms to identify particular email messages as spam (or, conversely, as 'ham', in the sense of desirable, as opposed to undesirable, email) as a function of the kinds of features such messages incorporate (such as their word frequencies, and genre conventions). As will be discussed, such algorithms usually assume (in a manner that may be easily updated through 'experiential learning') that typical or average features of spam and ham messages are already known, and base their identification on such statistical assumptions. When they identify a message as spam, or likely to be spam (above, say, a certain specifiable threshold of certainty), they can push the message into a special folder (often outside the user's view). And, as a function of how often a particular filter creates 'false positives' (incorrectly identifying ham as spam) or 'false negatives' (incorrectly identifying spam as ham), the statistical assumptions themselves can be updated. Indeed, in cases like intentional deception (e.g., when senders of spam start packing their messages with features designed to dupe spam filters), not only may such statistical assumptions need to be updated, but the relevant features to look for may have to be redefined, and the actual algorithms used for filtering may have to be redeveloped.

In what follows, after taking some time to make these topics more obviously relevant to the concerns of anthropology and critical theory, we delve into such processes in much more detail, and with much more generality. Readers will detect a Peircean orientation in what follows, but it is the definitions of these terms that matter, not the labels.[4]

The term *index* will be used to refer to any quality, cluster of qualities, or relation between qualities, that is potentially perceivable (to some agent). The term *kind* will be used to refer to any projected propensity to exhibit particular indices. The term *agent* will be used to refer to any entity that can perceive such an index and thereby project such a kind. The term *individual* will be used to refer to any entity that can evince indices to an agent and thereby be a site to project kindedness by that agent. And the term *ontology* will be used to refer to an agent's assumptions as to the indices, kinds, and individuals that constitute a particular world. See Table 7.1 (and recall chapter 5, section 5.7).

Note, then, that so called 'material substances' (gold, water, snow, etc.) are kinds, as are 'social statuses' (speaker, banker, woman, etc.), as are 'mental states' (believing X, fearing Y, etc.). In particular, we interpreting agents can project such kinds onto particular individuals (such as *this stuff, that woman, my dog*) as a function of the indices they express (the clothes they wear, the actions they undertake, the temperatures at which they freeze, the properties they possess, and so forth).

TABLE 7.1

Some Key Constituents of Ontologies Defined and Exemplified

Index	Any quality, set of qualities, or relation between qualities, that is relatively perceivable (to some agent). Spam example: *word-token ('sale', 'sex', 'enhance', 'lose'), address of sender, type of attachment, etc.* General examples: *actions, traits, properties, factors, semiotic processes, etc.*
Kind	Any projected propensity to exhibit particular indices. Spam example: *textual genre (spam versus non-spam)* General examples: *mental states, social statuses, material substances, types, sorts, identities, etc.*
Agent	Any entity that can perceive such an index and project such a kind (itself often an individual). Spam example: *computer program (derivative), computer programmer (original)* General examples: *people, animals, instruments, etc.*
Individual	Any entity that can evince indices (to an agent) and thereby be a site to project kindedness (by that agent). Spam example: *some particular email message* General examples: *some woman, this stuff, that galaxy, an era, my dog, your DNA, etc.*
Ontology	The assumptions an agent has as to the indices, kinds, and individuals that constitute a particular world. Spam example: *set of assumptions as to genres at issue and evidence available* General examples: *culture, worldview, ground, stereotype, imaginary, theory, taxonomy, model, episteme, etc.*

That's gold, she's a banker, he's afraid of the dark. In this way, *ontologies drive inter-pretation*: by one or more of your indices (sign), I infer your kind (object), and thereby come to expect (interpretant) other indices that would be in keeping with your kind (insofar as I have a particular ontology). Recall Figure 6.1.

***

We might exemplify such ontologies with a famous passage from *The Adventures of Huckleberry Finn*. Dressed as a girl, Huckleberry Finn went into town to find out what people were saying about Jim. In this scene, Mrs. Judith Loftus has just 'spotted him for a boy', and she is reporting to him the evidence she used to come to this conclusion.

> *And don't go about women in that old calico. You do a girl tolerable poor, but you might fool men, maybe. Bless you, child, when you set out to thread a needle don't hold the thread still and fetch the needle up to it; hold the needle still and poke the thread at it; that's the way a woman most always does, but a man always does t'other way. And when you throw at a rat or anything, hitch your-self up a tiptoe and fetch your hand up over your head as awkward as you can, and miss your rat about six or seven foot. Throw stiff-armed from the shoulder, like there was a pivot there for it to turn on, like a girl; not from the wrist and elbow, with your arm out to one side, like a boy. And, mind you, when a girl tries to catch anything in her lap she throws her knees apart; she don't clap them together, the way you did when you catched the lump of lead. Why, I spotted you for a boy when you was threading the needle; and I contrived the other things just to make certain.*

As may be seen, Mrs. Loftus has an ontology that she is here making rela-tively explicit. In particular, Huck is the individual in question. Mrs. Loftus is the agent. The indices include particular actions (different styles of throwing and catch-ing things, as well as threading needles, and techniques of the body more gener-ally). And the kinds in questions are boy and girl—though they could have been any sociocultural identities under the sun (e.g. Huck's father could have gone into town trying to pass himself off as rich, sober, or sophisticated). Finally, note that Mark Twain, as the author of this scenario, has a relatively implicit ontology which includes within it assumptions about the ontologies of people like Mrs. Loftus. In particular, what kinds of beliefs does she have about particular kinds, like girl and boy? In this way, many ontologies are inherently meta-ontologies—one may have assumptions about others' assumptions (about one's assumptions about others' assumptions. . .), and so on, and so forth.

More specifically, Mrs. Loftus has a relatively elaborate (and, in part, articu-latable) set of assumptions about which indices are evinced by individuals belong-ing to what kinds with what likelihoods (e.g., 'most always'). And she uses these assumptions not only to infer that Huck is a boy rather than a girl, but also to generate a set of experiments (or 'trials') to check her own hypothesis. Some of these indices are relatively easy to think of and simple to feign (e.g., wearing a bonnet). Others are relatively tacit and embodied, and so hard to predict or hide (e.g., threading a needle). And all are strongly correlated with one social kind rather than another (if only in the mind of Mrs. Loftus), and involve circumstances and behaviors that are more or less public and easy to elicit. Finally, as this example should make clear, it cannot be stressed enough that most indices are only emergent in, and distributed across, the interactions between agents and individuals. Moreover, one and the same behavior (trait, quality, factor, relation, semiotic process, etc.) can be an index of many different kinds to one and the same agent depending on the context in which it is evinced.

Such a set of assumptions might be called a theory (when articulated in relation to a scientific institution, episteme, or disciplinary formation), a ground (in the way this term was used in chapter 5), a stereotype or prejudice (when negatively valenced), a likelihood (when framed mathematically), a heuristic (when framed qualitatively, or as a 'rule of thumb'), an imaginary (when understood in relation to an underlying account or narrative about the prototypic entities involved in the domain being judged), a culture (when more or less intersubjectively shared by a group of people), and even a habitus or 'sense' (when understood as a tacit intuition regarding another's identity via their techniques of the body, styles of speaking, and so forth). The term ontology functions as a cover-all term to capture the ramifications present in each of these framings (Kockelman 2013a).

***

To give another example of the odd and pervasive nature of ontologies, we might turn to a meteorite—a kind of quintessential material substance, however otherworldly it might seem to be. While visiting the Peabody Museum in New Haven, I came across an exhibit that had several meteorites on display—which, to me, looked more or less like rocks. Next to these meteorites was a placard telling the viewer how to identify a meteorite, offered as a list of potentially perceivable qualities: *should have smooth appearance; should be irregularly shaped, not round; should not be full of holes*; and so on and so forth, until it came to the last one, which gave the whole exhibit a decidedly Borgesian twist: *should not look odd*. In terms of the foregoing categories, the viewer of the meteorite is the agent, the meteorites themselves are individuals, each item in the list of potentially perceivable qualities could be an index, and the kinds in question are meteorite and rock (in the sense of a non-meteorite, or more boring everyday sort of stone). But what is really special about this example, however quotidian and pervasive this kind of informative display actually is in our lives, is the way it highlights the reflexive, recursive, frame-dependent, symbolically mediated, and socially distributed nature of human ontologies (Agha 2007; Goffman 1974; Lucy 1993; Kockelman 2005, 2013a).

Note first that indices can themselves be reframed as kinds. In particular, the last index ('should not look odd') presumes that oddness is a sort of perceivable quality. But surely oddness can be understood in many different ways, such that there can be different indices of oddness. For example, odd for a rock is different from odd for a person; or odd in light of one interpretation (if this were a bar, his actions would not be weird) might not be odd in light of another interpretation (but we happen to be in church). In other words, what may be indices in one frame may be kinds in another, as well as indices of one kind rather than another. This is a very general point: not only may indices be reframed as kinds (and vice-versa), but so too may individuals be reframed as agents, indices as individuals, ontologies as indices, and so on and so forth.[5] To offer one more example: meteorites themselves, when framed as kinded individuals, may be treated as indices of gravitational fields, God's wrath, and northern latitudes.

Second, while agents may often have seemingly 'raw' indexical encounters with individuals, they also often have relatively 'cooked' symbolically mediated encounters with individuals, in which another set of signs (such as a list of perceivable qualities, or a placard bearing a name, or a display telling us where to look) does much of the interpretive work for us by telling us how to interpret and what to perceive (with more or less precision).[6] Phrased another way, even relatively immediate indexical encounters are usually symbolically and conceptually mediated—we are always only one or two steps away from the display case, tour guide, web page, literary work, parental point, expert opinion, prophetic pronouncement, sovereign assessment, textbook, scientific atlas, or price tag. In this way, we interpretive agents are radically distributed: it is only me, in conjunction with the display case (itself the communicative trace of another set of actors), that allows me to interpret in this way. And framed yet another way, this example shows that many, if not most, of our ontological assumptions come from communicative practices with 'others' (however objectified) instead of indexical encounters with 'objects'.

7.3. Ontologies in Transformation, Ontologies of Transformation

Returning to our key theme, *styles are often best understood as kinds*. An interpreting agent examines an individual text (or artwork or artificed entity, more generally) and, as a function of the indices that make up the text (from the parchment it is written on, to the forms of parallelism it incorporates, to the language it was written in, to the actions of the characters, etc.), projects a certain kind onto it (Haiku, seventeenth-century Japan; Picasso, early Blue Period, etc.). And, as a function of this projection, such an agent comes to expect other indices from the text that would be in keeping with that kind: expectations as to its contents, authors, readers, contexts of presentation, likely endings, other features of its form, and so forth.

And, to return to our earlier concern, if style is a kind of kind, *spam is a kind of style*. In particular, and prefiguring many of the concerns of section 7.6, filters designed to stop spam from reaching your inbox embody an ontology as to the propensity for an individual spam message to evince particular indices (in contrast to a non-spam message). See Figure 7.2. Such propensities can be figured in many ways, but a widespread approach (Graham 2004) frames them in terms of likelihoods: in particular, the probability that a spam message contains a certain word (or quality more generally). Such likelihoods are usually found by doing frequency counts over particular words found in large corpora of known instances of spam (and non-spam) messages. Any new message is then 'assayed': one takes from it a number of words (or qualities) at random, gauges how likely these would be if the message was spam or not, and thereby updates one's certainty as to the spaminess of the message in question: say, from 50% uncertain (before the assays, qua a priori probability) to 96% certain (after the assays, qua a posteriori probability). In some sense, Mrs. Loftus was engaged in a similar kind of assay, or trial, however different the techniques she employed, via the little tests she "contrived just to make sure." And, similarly, the museum exhibit was, in some sense, a primer on extraterrestrial rock assayal.

All that is fine and good: ontologies license an agent's interpretations as to an individual's kinds, be those kinds social statuses, material substances or spam/non-spam messages; be that individual a person or thing, an artwork or text (or anything outside or in-between); and be that agent an interpreting human or a sieving machine. But rather than focus on how *ontologies license interpretations*, we are also interested in how *interpretations license ontologies*—and, in particular, we are

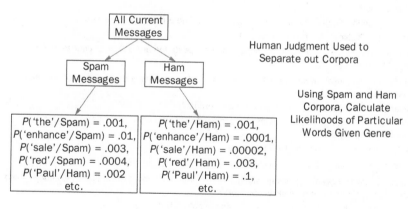

FIGURE 7.2 Some of the Key Steps in One Approach to Spam-Filtering

interested in the coupling of these processes as it gives rise to the processuality of style. While there are many 'natural histories' and 'historical ontologies' (Silverstein and Urban 1996; Hacking 2002) waiting to be written of such interpretation-driven ontological transformations (in the full flush of their worldly unfoldings, as it were) it is worth theorizing some of their key dynamics.

***

Table 7.2 lists five kinds (!) of ontological transformativity—whereby an interpreting agent's ontology transforms via mediated encounters with an individual. The first kind of transformativity is simply causality in a generalized sense: some index (icon, symbol, evidence, token, relation, interaction, etc.) may change an individual's kind more or less independently of some particular agent's assumptions about it.[7] Here go all the usual processes that produce kinded individuals in the first

TABLE 7.2
Some Key Dimensions of Transformativity Defined and Exemplified

1) **Indices (and signs more generally) may change an individual's kind [MORE OR LESS] irrespective of an agent's ontological assumptions.**

   Examples: all processes in world (chemical reactions, material processes, speech acts, etc.) that produce individuals of particular kinds.

   Ontological Inertia (in case of spam): occurs any time a message (spam or non-spam) is written and sent (whether by a person or a machine).

2) **Indices may change an agent's ontological assumptions regarding the kinds that constitute a particular individual.**

   Examples: update certainty of individual's message type (spam or non-spam) in terms of words it contains.

   Ontological Inertia (in case of spam): occurs each time a message is received.

   Inferential Profile: often relatively deductive.

   Mathematical Case: a priori probability becomes a posteriori probability, or change in P(Kind) to $P_{Index}(Kind)$.

3) **Indices may change an agent's ontological assumptions regarding the indices that constitute a particular kind.**

   Examples: likelihood of words in genre given corpus.

   Ontological Inertia (in case of spam): occurs as statistical profile of corpus of assayed messages changes.

   Inferential Profile: often relatively inductive.

   Mathematical Case: change in likelihoods, or change in $P_{Kind}(index)$.

4) **Indices may change an agent's ontological assumptions regarding the indices, individuals, kinds, and agents that constitute a particular world.**

   Examples: update indices and kinds included in calculations.

   Ontological Inertia (in case of spam): occurs as filter stops functioning correctly (e.g. too many false positives or false negatives).

   Inferential Profile: often relatively abductive.

   Mathematical Case: change in indices and kinds which are included in calculation, or changes in individuals assayed and techniques of assaying.

5) **Changes in an agent's ontological assumptions about a world (in foregoing ways) may change the world about which the agent makes assumptions.**

   Examples: looping effects (Hacking), internalization (Goffman, Mead), performativity (Austin, Arendt), etc.

   Ontological Inertia (in case of spam): occurs as sending or receiving agents can internalize ontologies of receiving and sending agents (respectively).

place, from chemical reactions that produce reactants to marriage ceremonies that produce husbands and wives, from performative utterances to contractual agreements, from socialization practices to evolutionary processes. Needless to say, the world is chock-full of kinded individuals (species, natural kinds, fundamental particles, personalities, social groupings, diseases, etc.), grounded in natural causes as much as social conventions, regimented by 'forces' as much as by 'understandings', with various degrees of historical stability and geographic spread, and with various degrees of uptake and explicitness in the assumptions that constitute human and nonhuman ontologies. And there are whole disciplines devoted to studying transformativity in this sense: physics, anthropology, chemistry, biology, and so forth.

The second kind of transformativity is perhaps the most quotidian, and often seems relatively deductive: indices may change an agent's ontological assumptions regarding the kinds that constitute a particular individual. For example, from your ring, I infer you are married; from its word frequency, I infer it is spam. This is where Mrs. Loftus aimed her inquiry. In some sense, the individual-kind relation (is it a dog or a wolf) transforms by reference to the individual-index relation (it bayed at the moon), while the kind-index relation stays constant (wolfs bay at the moon, but dogs do not).

The third kind of transformativity often seems relatively inductive rather than deductive: indices may change an agent's ontological assumptions regarding the indices that constitute a particular kind. For example, from your behavior, I infer that married people don't fool around; from its word frequency, I infer that spam messages have different likelihoods than I thought. Had Mrs. Loftus, in her encounter with Huck, changed her assumptions about the throwing and catching abilities of boys and girls, this kind of transformativity would have been operative. In some sense, the kind-index relation transforms by reference to the individual-index relation, while the individual-kind relation stays constant.

The fourth kind of transformativity often seems relatively abductive: indices may change an agent's ontological assumptions regarding the indices, individuals, kinds, and agents that *constitute* a particular world (as well as regarding the possibilities of other worlds that could be constituted). For example, from your behavior, I hypothesize a new social status (say, the adulterer); from its word frequency, I hypothesize a new style (say, spam worth reading, or non-spam not worth reading). Had Mrs. Loftus hypothesized a new status—say, the transvestite (or something even more surprising to her (in the sense of unconceptualized or unconventional)—this kind of transformativity would have been operative. In some sense, the types of individuals, indices, and kinds we take into account in our ontologies are themselves transformed.

Finally, there is a fifth kind of transformativity that may involve any of the other four kinds to various degrees: in particular, an agent's assumptions about the world (as to its individuals, indices, and kinds) may transform the world about which that agent holds assumptions.[8] In the case of spam, this dimension is essential: makers and senders of spam are often trying to second-guess the ontological assumptions of receivers and sievers of spam, and thereby pack their messages with indices that enable them to pass through such sieves. In other words, built into its ontology are assumptions about the other's assumptions about its own ontological assumptions. If Huck internalized part of Mrs. Loftus's ontology, and so came to act more (or less) in line with her assumptions, or came to raise his own daughter or son to throw and catch differently, this kind of transformativity would be operative.

***

The first and last kinds of transformativity (1 and 5), in various guises, have received a huge amount of attention in anthropology, and critical theory more generally. In contrast, the middle three transformativities (2–4) are relatively under-theorized, and so will be the focus in what follows. In particular, these kinds of transformations not only have relatively different *inferential profiles* (e.g. deductive, inductive, abductive), they also have different *ontological inertias*.[9] For example, in the case of spam, transformativity #2 may occur as often as one receives a message and can assay its indices. Transformativity #3 may occur on a daily or weekly basis, depending on how fast one's corpus of messages grows and changes in statistical profile, such that one updates one's likelihoods as to the relative frequency of particular words in specific genres. Transformativity #4 might never occur at all, until one's spam filters stop working (often for reasons of transformativity #5); and so sievers of spam have to creatively rethink the indices they look for, the individuals that evince them, the kinds that they imagine, or the algorithms they use to sieve them. In this way, as we move from transformativity #2 to transformativity #4, ontological assumptions can be more and more resistant to change; and the kinds of assumptions that are transformed may become 'deeper', or more 'immediate'. More generally, all ontologies embody a range of assumptions which, depending on the kinds of temporal scales in question, may be more or less fluid or fixed, if not unfathomable. Finally, not only do these transformations exhibit different ontological inertias, they may also get progressively more difficult to mathematically formulate and technologically automate, and so the transformations in question seem to turn more and more on human-based significance, as stereotypically understood, and less and less on machine-based sieving.

Note, then, that sieves—such as spam filters—have *values* built into them (insofar as they selectively permit certain things and prohibit others); and they have *beliefs* built into them (insofar as they exhibit ontological assumptions).[10] And not only do sieves have beliefs and desires built into them (and thus, in some sense, embody cultural values that are relatively derivative of their makers and users); they may also be said to have emergent beliefs and desires (and thus embody their own relatively originary cultural values, however unconscious they, and their makers and users, are of them). In particular, the values of the variables are usually steps ahead of the consciousness of the programmers (and certainly of users)—and thus constitute a kind of *prosthetic unconsciousness* with incredibly rich and wily temporal dynamics. Note then that when we make algorithms, and then set those algorithms loose, there is often no way to know what's going to happen next.

Finally, if one is not interested in spam versus non-spam per se, one may just substitute human versus non-human—for the core issues involved in the sieving of spam and the transformation of ontologies are identical to those underlying the Turing Test (not to mention the diagnosis of maladies and the sexing of suspicious guests), and thus the sorting of souls, or the indexical styling of the human kind. But that said, most accounts of Turing's Test are quite a lot like Mrs. Loftus in that they never get past transformativity #2, as we will now see.

7.4. Testing Turing

Let's turn to the famous scenario devised by Alan Turing (2004 [1950]). Imagine you are alone in a room, with a keyboard and monitor, having a text-based conversation, via teletype, with someone (or something) who claims to be a woman, but whose real identity is unknown to you. Indeed, not only may it be a man rather than a woman, but it may also be a machine rather than a human. You can type in whatever you want, and this someone else will reply; and vice versa. And thus the only evidence you can gather as to its kindedness is text-based: what kinds of questions does it ask you (with what kinds of syntax, semantics, and pragmatics); and how does it answer your questions. In some sense, then, you are playing the role of Mrs. Loftus trying to ferret out the identity of a suspicious guest.

What text-based patterns might you look for, or text-based experiments might you run, to determine the identity of this other? If you can or cannot determine the identity of this other via such trials, what does this say, philosophically, about the relation between humans and machines (or men and women)? What does this say, technically, about the relation between computers and their software (or actors and their techniques)? And, more generally, what does it tell us about the potentially unsettling effects of computer-mediated communication in relation to face-to-face interaction?

The aim in what follows is not to answer these questions per se. (Indeed, merely summarizing the rich secondary literature on the Turing Test, and hence over fifty years of thought about this topic, is a book in itself.[11]) Rather, we want to use Turing's beautifully imagined scenario to test the utility of the foregoing analytic framework—itself grounded in a particular theory of the relation between ontology, transformativity, and virtuality. Indeed, given the similarities between this scenario and the situation in which Huck and Mrs. Loftus found themselves (almost identical, aside from the channel), everything said above is immediately applicable— indeed, it was designed precisely to deal with such a scenario. This section, then, will serve as much a summary, as an extension, of the foregoing arguments, as well as of the arguments about virtuality put forth at the end of chapter 5.

For the moment (and quite naively as will be seen below) we may focus on the first issue: the text-based trials one might run to infer the 'true identity' of this other. And we may take as our basic premise the following claim: *it should be able to do to us whatever we are doing to it* (or at least a significant chunk of this). Phrased another way, the key indices for us to look for as signs of its true kind (human versus machine) would turn on its ability to track our indices, as well as on its ability to track our tracking of its indices—not perfectly of course, but to some degree, which is certainly one key feature of humankind (at least in Erving Goffman's [1959] ontology). More carefully put, as per the last section, from the indices we have evinced, it should be able to make inferences about our mental states, social statuses, and material substances—and from such inferred mental states, social statuses, and material substances, it should be able to expect other indices we may evince (and sanction us in the light of those expectations, or draw other inferences from our failures to meet those expectations). In short, it should be able to project kinds onto individuals through their indices via its ontology. In effect, then, we would need to track indices of its ability (qua projected propensity) to track indices of our propensities.

But, of course, this is just one possibility. And while it might be necessary to pass the test, it's surely not sufficient. And so it will forever be tempting to imagine a range of other abilities that would provide necessary and sufficient criteria—and thereby secure some criterial definition of the authentically human. To take just one example, which we might call the singular-humanist criterion, let us suppose that the unknown other should have also an 'individual identity' in some metaphysical sense. This might mean leaving a biographical trace in the mental states and social statuses of others (a notion closely related to Benjamin's concept of aura, as described in chapter 5). It might mean having a standard of values which gives its mental states and social statuses a kind of coherence (as per the arguments of Charles Taylor or Max Weber). It might mean that it has a kind of daimon, soul, or telos that gives its travels through the world a kind of biographical closure (loosely following some ideas of Hannah Arendt). It might require that the entity have reflexive self of the Jamesean sort, such that not only does it have qualities (such as social statuses and mental states, or a ensemble of belongings more generally), but that the flourishing or foundering of such qualities matter to it. Or, indeed, it might mean that its action, or 'life', is subject to rich and multiple interpretations (like any great character in literature or history—such as Huckleberry Finn or Alan Turing). And so on, and so forth. However such a unique identity be framed, perhaps the crucial point here would be that to be human (as a type) is to be both cultural and biographical, or singular with respect to both the community to which one belongs and the life-path along which one travels. In short, it might be argued that a human being (qua material substance) without culture and personality (and thus a historically and personally singular ensemble of social statuses, mental states, and material substances) is not human at all.[12]

We may now turn to the second caveat, which may be understood as a counter to precisely such naive modes of speculation (regarding putative human-specific propensities, such as ontological projection and singular humanism). In particular, the Turing Test is perhaps best understood not as a benchmark for artificial intelligence, but as a diagnostic of what a given group of people at a given point in time think is the essence of the human (or the limitations of the machine)—given the prejudices (or progress) of their era, discipline, expertise, culture, and so on. That is, the Turing Test is really a kind of Rorschach test for the questioner's sense of self, current theories of the brain and body relation, or widespread beliefs about language, culture, and mind per se, the robustness of our knowledge of a population's statistical profile, and more or less fashionable ideas about putative human-specific processes (e.g., recursion, metacognition, subcognition, joint attention, theory of mind, performativity, intersubjectivity, shared intentionality, free-will, singular-humanism, thirdness, deep-teleology, meta-this and mega-that, and so forth). In this way, the real value of the Turing Test is akin to science fiction: it functions not as an augury of the possibilities to come, but as a symptom of the prejudices that are. This very chapter, then, is precisely an assay: an attempt to make maximally public and minimally ambiguous the author's (and/or his discipline's) own personal and cultural prejudices (as to how we may know what kinds of things there might be).

Ironically, such prejudices are essentially what we called ontologies (theories, stereotypes, heuristics, intuitions, likelihoods or imaginaries) in section 7.3. Indeed, somewhat damningly, the foregoing discussion of the Turing Test, and almost all the literature written on it, presumes that transformativity #2 is the central question. That is, given some indices (i.e., actual teletype-based performances of the other, however richly imagined or creatively theorized), let us try to infer the kindedness of our unknown interlocutor. And so there has been no end of discussion as to what constitutes the truly human (as a non-virtual kind), and speculation as to how might we be able to program a computer to mimic it (as a virtual kind). Only partially tongue-in-cheek, one is tempted to say that the crucial index of individuals belonging to the human kind is their so-often-indexed propensity to articulate their own ontological assumptions as to what are the crucial indices of the essential propensities of the human kind . . .

Crucially, however, the most interesting aspect of the Turing Test may not be transformativity #2, but rather transformativities #3 and #4. For example, the point of such an encounter with another might be to generate new indexical propensities for old kinds; or, even better, to generate hypotheses regarding the existence of new kinds, or regarding the existence of hitherto unknown indices (for old kinds), not to mention the value of particular machine learning techniques for exhibiting and identifying such behaviors. That is, the real dialog might not be between me and the unknown other, but rather between 'us' (as an epistemic community, intent on answering such questions) before and 'us' after we have engaged in such a dialog-cum-experiment—such that we learn more about what both things like it and people like us are capable of becoming. Such a stance would represent the marriage of Alan Turing's test with Max Weber's ideal type (1949), and thus the marriage of mechanized circuits and hermeneutic circles: a way to goad humans (and machines) into trying out ever new possibilities for being-human in relation to being-machine.

Finally, there is still that pesky transformativity #5, itself directly linked to transformativity #1: the possibility that the other may internalize our assumptions about it, and thus come to act according to our ontologies; thereby confirming, rather than contradicting—and possibly transforming—our assumptions about it. Indeed, for some, this last scenario may be the most emblematic index that machines are capable of human-being, and perhaps 'kind enough' (and cruel enough) to *be* human: when we internalize our machines' ontologies about us, and thereby come to act according to their assumptions about our behavior. (And vice-versa.)

7.5. Bayesian Anthropology

We have described spam filters, and a variety of other sieving agents, in terms of five dimensions of ontological transformativity. While the folks at McAfee, Barracuda and SpamAssassin may not recognize themselves in the kind of language being used, we have been at pains to render in qualitative terms, and with analytic precision, key aspects of the quantitative operations they design into their algorithms. Their training is in a storied branch of statistics derived from the work of Thomas Bayes (1701–1761), a Protestant minister and English mathematician who first formulated a special case of the theory that now bears his name. While his ideas have undergone a number of twists and turns since his death, Bayesian inference has found applications in fields ranging from machine learning to courtroom decisions, from medical diagnosis to linguistic reconstruction. More generally, it is a key part of many techniques used for mining 'big data'; it has played a key role in dozens of events of historical importance; it has a range of philosophical stances, and counter-stances, associated with it; and weirdos and wizards of all kinds have been infatuated with it, or repulsed by it. As should be apparent by now, and as will be further elucidated in what follows, Bayes's most basic equation has something in common with that other quintessentially modern, radically portable, and infinitely transmutable form: the commodity. Strangely straddling materiality, mathematics, and metaphysics, the practices deploying it and the presumptions underlying it offer insights into conventional and cutting-edge forms of value, as our coin example should now intimate.[13] (And, of course, it's not called '*mining* big data' for nothing. Recall our discussion of 'the matrix' in chapter 4.)

So having discussed the transformational dynamics of ontologies in relatively qualitative terms, we may now discuss the mathematical formulation of Bayesian inference, and thus how it gets mediated by equations involving quantities of various qualities. To do this, let us turn to a scenario that goes back to Laplace (1951 [1820]), who was fourteen when Bayes's theorem was first published (in 1763, two years after Bayes's death), and who was the first mathematician to work with large data sets (McGrayne 2011, 21). (Readers who are already familiar with Bayes's equation, or simply dislike math, may skip the next section.)

***

Suppose that there are two kinds of urns in a room, each filled with a different assortment of coins, but otherwise identical in appearance. In the first kind of urn, 30% of the coins are copper, and 70% are silver. In the second kind of urn, 80% of the coins are copper, and 20% are silver. Suppose further that the two kinds of urn are not equally distributed. Urns of the first kind are more prevalent, constituting about 66% of the urns in the room (so that urns of the second kind constitute the remaining 33%). You come across such an urn and would like to know which kind it is. So you reach in and pull out a coin—which happens to be copper. Given this evidence, what is the probability that the urn is of the first kind as opposed to the second (and thus is filled with one assortment of coins rather than another)?

To answer this question, and understand the logic behind the answer, it is useful to diagram the problem in a particular way. Figure 7.3a shows a square with a unit area equal to 1. This is the space of all possible outcomes (so that the probability of some outcome is 100%). Figure 7.3b shows this same area divided into two parts, one of unit area 2/3 (showing the percentage of urns which are of type 1),

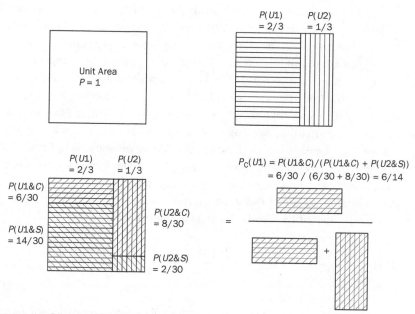

FIGURE 7.3 Diagram of Bayes's Rule

and the other of unit area 1/3 (showing that percentage of urns which are of type 2). These are your *a priori* probabilities: loosely speaking, the probability that the urn is of type 1 or type 2 *before* you pull out the copper coin. They are labeled $P(U1)$ and $P(U2)$, respectively. Note, then, that before you have even reached into the urn, just by way of how the problem was set up, you can say that the probability that the urn is of type 1 is about 66%.

Figure 7.3c shows each of these same areas further divided into two parts, representing the relative percentage of coins which are copper and silver in each of the two kinds of urns. One part is of unit area 6/30 (= 2/3 × 3/10), showing the percentage of coins which are both in urn 1 and copper (and thus the intersection of all coins in urn 1 and all copper coins). Another part is of unit area 14/30 (= 2/3 × 7/10), showing the percentage of coins which are both in urn 1 and silver. Another part is of unit area 8/30 (= 1/3 × 8/10), showing the percentage of coins which are both in urn 2 and copper. And the last part is of unit area 2/30 (= 1/3 × 2/10), showing the percentage of coins which are both in urn 2 and silver. These are labeled $P(U1\&C)$, $P(U1\&S)$, $P(U2\&C)$, and $P(U2\&S)$, respectively. As may be seen, $P(U1\&C)$ is found by multiplying $P(U1)$ by $P_{U1}(C)$, and thus by multiplying the a priori probability that an urn is of type 1 by the *likelihood* that a coin in an urn of type 1 is copper (as per our initial formulation of the problem). That is, $P(U1\&C) = P(U1) \times P_{U1}(C)$, and so forth for the other combinations.

Finally, given such a priori probabilities, and such likelihoods, what you have been asked to calculate is an *a posteriori* probability: the probability that the urn is of type 1 (or type 2) *after* you pull out a coin of a certain metal (which itself constitutes a particular kind of evidence). This may be written as $P_C(U1)$, and so on for other combinations. Figure 7.3d shows a geometric answer to this question: $P_C(U1)$ is equal to 6/14, or the area $P(U1\&C)$ divided by the sum of the areas $P(U1\&C)$ and $P(U2\&C)$, which is equivalent to all the ways of getting a copper coin from an urn of type 1 (6/30) divided by all the ways of getting a copper coin regardless of the type of urn it is drawn from (6/30 + 8/30). In short, before you assayed the urn (by noting the metal of a coin pulled from it), the probability that it was of type 1 was about 66%. And after you assayed the urn, the probability was about 43%. Or, phrased another way, before the assay, you thought it was more likely to be an urn of type 1; and after the assay, you think it is more likely to be an urn of type 2.

Figure 7.4 is another way of showing the information available in Figure 7.3, foregrounding the algebra of the problem instead of the geometry, and so may be more familiar for some readers (though perhaps less intuitive). As may be seen, the key equation, after all is said and done, expresses the a posteriori probabilities in terms of the product of the likelihoods and the a priori probabilities:

$$P_C(U1) = \frac{P(C\,\&\,U1)}{P(C)} = \frac{P_{U1}(C) \times P(U1)}{P(C)} = \frac{P_{U1}(C) \times P(U1)}{P_{U1}(C) \times P(U1) + P_{U2}(C) \times P(U2)}$$

(1)

Such a way of formulating the problem (usually referred to as Bayes's Rule), however canned or trivial it may first appear, turns out to be incredibly general and

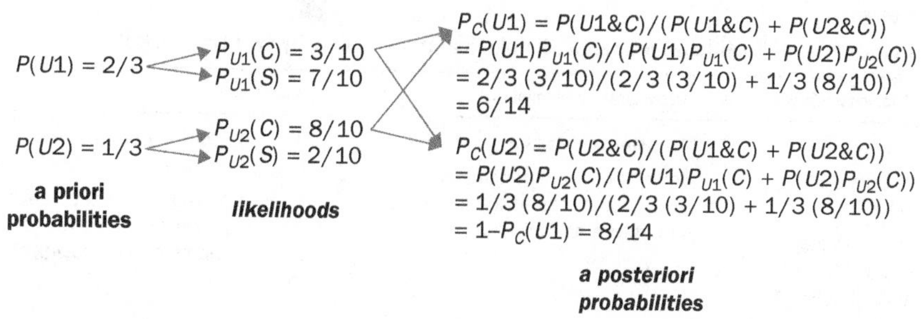

$$P(U1) = 2/3 \rightarrow \begin{matrix} P_{U1}(C) = 3/10 \\ P_{U1}(S) = 7/10 \end{matrix}$$

$$P(U2) = 1/3 \rightarrow \begin{matrix} P_{U2}(C) = 8/10 \\ P_{U2}(S) = 2/10 \end{matrix}$$

a priori
probabilities　　　**likelihoods**

$P_C(U1) = P(U1\&C)/(P(U1\&C) + P(U2\&C))$
$= P(U1)P_{U1}(C)/(P(U1)P_{U1}(C) + P(U2)P_{U2}(C))$
$= 2/3 \, (3/10)/(2/3 \, (3/10) + 1/3 \, (8/10))$
$= 6/14$

$P_C(U2) = P(U2\&C)/(P(U1\&C) + P(U2\&C))$
$= P(U2)P_{U2}(C)/(P(U1)P_{U1}(C) + P(U2)P_{U2}(C))$
$= 1/3 \, (8/10)/(2/3 \, (3/10) + 1/3 \, (8/10))$
$= 1 - P_C(U1) = 8/14$

a posteriori
probabilities

FIGURE 7.4　Relation Between A Priori Probabilities, A Posteriori Probabilities, and Likelihoods

powerful. In particular, to return to the concerns of section 7.3, replace types of urns with kinds; replace coins with indices; and replace particular urns (which may be of one kind or another) with individuals. In this way, we may think of Bayes's rule as a heuristic that an agent might adopt for attributing kinds to individual via their indices, and thus a means for transforming its own ontological assumptions as to the kindedness of the individual in question. In this way, the core equation, in its full generality, may be expressed as follows:

$$P_{\text{index}}(\text{Kind}) = \frac{P_{\text{Kind}}(\text{index}) * P(\text{Kind})}{P_{\text{Kind}}(\text{index}) * P(\text{Kind}) + P_{-\text{Kind}}(\text{index}) * P(-\text{Kind})}$$

$$= \frac{P_{\text{Kind}}(\text{Index}) * P(\text{Kind})}{P(\text{Index})} \tag{2}$$

This equation may be interpreted as follows. On the left-hand side, we have $P_{\text{Index}}(\text{Kind})$, or the probability that an individual is of a certain kind, in the context of its having evinced a particular index. On the right-hand side we have the product of a likelihood (that individuals of particular kinds exhibit indices of particular types, or $P_{\text{Kind}}(\text{Index})$) and an a priori probability (or the probability, however subjective or tentative, that the individual was of that kind before it evinced the index, or $P(\text{Kind})$). And this product is itself divided by the overall probability that the individual evinces the index regardless of its kind, or $P(\text{Index})$. Crucially, while we derived this equation in the context of a world that had only two sorts of kinds with two sorts of indices, it is completely general: one merely needs to sum over the product of likelihoods and a priori probabilities for each possible kind given the index in question.[14]

***

Equation (2) is not just simply a way of expressing Bayes's Rule in terms of our ontology, and thereby showing its relation to kinds as varied as mental states, social statuses, and material substances (as per our more general discussion in section 7.3). It also shows us one way the three middle kinds of ontological transformativity may be understood in terms of one widespread mathematical formulation. (See

TABLE 7.3

Comparison of Traditional Inference, Ontological Transformativity, and Bayes's Rule

Traditional Inference	Ontological Transformativity	Bayes's Rule
Deduction *People die (kind-index);* *And Socrates is a person (individual-kind);* *Thus, Socrates will die (individual-index).*	**Transformativity #2** Indices change an agent's assumptions as to the kinds that constitute an individual.	$\Delta P_{index}(\textbf{Kind})$ (or a priori P goes to a posteriori P) Change strength of hypothesis (e.g. individual-kind relation) in light of evidence (e.g. individual-index relation).
Induction *Socrates (Aristotle, Plato, etc.) is a person (individual-kind);* *And Socrates (Aristotle, Plato, etc.) died (individual-index);* *Thus, people die (kind-index).*	**Transformativity #3** Indices change an agent's assumptions as to the indices that constitute a kind.	$\Delta P_{Kind}(\textbf{index})$ Change likelihoods that are used to calculate changes in strength of hypotheses.
Abduction as Affirming the Consequence (early Peirce) *People die (kind-index);* *And Socrates died (individual-index);* *Thus, Socrates is a person (individual-kind).* **Abduction as Inference to Best Explanation (late Peirce)** Some surprising fact (F) is observed; If some hypothesis (H) were true, F would readily follow; Thus, there is reason to believe that H is true.	**Transformativity #4** Indices change an agent's assumptions as to the indices, kinds, or individuals that constitute a world (or at least to the possibility of other worlds that could be constituted).	Δ**Kind**, Δ**Index** (also Δ**Individual**, Δ**Algorithm**, etc.) Change types of hypotheses (or possible individual-kind relations) and types of evidence (or possible individual-index relations) that are used to calculate likelihoods. Δ ('delta') = change, perturbation, updating, etc.

the third column of Table 7.3, which compares such a mathematical formulation with logical and ontological formulations.)

In this framing, transformativity #2 is described by equation (2) itself, which expresses how a priori probabilities (and thus the strength of ontological assumptions) get changed into a posteriori probabilities, or the change in $P_{Index}(\text{Kind})$ before and after an assay of indexical evidence. For example, holding our assumptions about the indexical propensities of particular kinds constant (i.e., statistical profiles of ham and spam messages), we use these propensities to infer the kindedness of an individual message as a function of the indices it exhibits.

Transformativity #3 is any quantitative transformation in likelihoods, or a change in P_{Kind}(Index), via changes in the statistical profiles of corpora. For example, holding our assumptions about the kindedness of a particular individual constant (this message is spam), we change our assumptions about the indexical propensity of particular kinds (say, spam messages are more likely to be personally addressed than originally assumed).

And transformativity #4 would correspond not only to changes in the types of indices assayed (e.g. perhaps words are not the best indexical types), as well as to changes in the types of kinds entertained (e.g. perhaps there are other genres besides Spam and Ham); but also to changes in the types of individuals assayed (e.g. perhaps spam is not limited to email), and changes in the types of sieving algorithms used in assays (e.g. perhaps Bayesian filters are not enough, insofar as they may easily be duped by spam senders who can internalize the ontologies of spam sievers, and react accordingly, as per our earlier discussion of transformativity #5).

All this is another way of characterizing ontological inertia, as introduced in section 7.3, but now in mathematical terms: as we move from transformativity #2 to transformativity #4, we move from changes in relatively superficial assumptions to changes in relatively deep assumptions. Phrased another way, changes at the level of transformativity #4 necessarily affect calculations at the level of transformativity #3 and #2 (but not vice-versa); and changes at the level of transformativity #3 necessarily affect calculations at the level of transformativity #2 (but not vice-versa). In this way, while the initial definitions of ontology and transformativity were extremely wide, and meant to apply to relatively quotidian modes of semiosis, they also have relatively precise, mathematical analogs that apply not only to the case of sieving spam, but also to any arena in which Bayesian inference is applicable—and thus to an incredibly wide range of processes. This is a key site where two of the foundational currents of anthropology—meaning and mathematics, or semiosis and statistics, and thus the early concerns of Boas and Durkheim—most transparently come together. Together with the theory of ontology and transformativity, it constitutes the basis of what may be called *Bayesian Anthropology*, a potential paradigm that is probably as perilous as it is promising.[15]

7.6. Virtuality and Actuality Revisited

To conclude, it is worth extending a few claims, stressing a few caveats, and speculating on a few possibilities. The categories pertaining to ontology and transformativity, as summarized in Table 7.1 and Table 7.2, are relatively general, and thus widely applicable (Kockelman 2011b, 2013a).[16] They should not be confused with the particular ways such categories are actually formalized (rendered or enclosed) in particular contexts—say, aesthetically (via narratives, qua Huck Finn), instrumentally (via particular technologies, like spam filters), logically (via formal modes of reasoning), and mathematically (via quantifiable qualities related through Bayes's equation). Or, inverting the frame (which follows the actual direction of empirical study), we may say that ontological transformativity, as it plays out in the highly specific context of sieving algorithms designed to stop spam, can be generalized (as an ideal type), and so usefully applied, with many caveats, to a range of other processes and practices.

In short, *do not confuse the enclosures with which we concluded (Bayesian inference) with the processes so enclosed (qua ontology-driven and driving interpretation)—the latter, in their actual unfolding, are often radically distributed and diverse, embedded and embodied, quotidian and quixotic.* Bayesian agents are a tiny subset of possible agents, and so many other kinds of interpretative techniques exist.[17] One only need think, for example, of witch hunting among the Azande, to realize that there are many other ways to justify a particular inference, or ground a particular interpretation.[18] That said, we have simultaneously tried to show that the issues that come to light in this small subset of the possibility space (e.g., the categories developed in Table 7.1 and Table 7.2, and various properties of sieves, and practices of sieving) are quite general and incredibly important.

Framed another way, and such caveats aside, we have tried to introduce ten categories (themselves kinds, and so reflexively part of their own system of categorization) through which one may explore, interpret, know, provoke, create and incite worlds. Such categories are not only meant to be minimalistic, they are also meant to be portable: their meaningfulness and means-ends-fullness should be applicable to many contents and applicable in many contexts.

***

The relation between kinds and indices is legion in social theory. As we saw in chapter 2, they map respectively onto categories like status and role (Linton), *langue* and *parole* (Saussure), competence and performance (Chomsky), power and its exercise (Hobbes), and even essence and appearance (as understood in certain philosophical traditions). Thus, from the standpoint of this chapter, categories like *langue* and *parole* are really ontology-specific (and often discipline-specific) renderings of more general categories. As should be stressed, such discipline-specific categories are by themselves not particularly useful. Rather, they need to be articulated in relation to a broader set of categories (minimally: ontologies, individuals, and agents), and resolutely theorized in terms of their mutual transformations (minimally: the five kinds offered here). That said, such frameworks, however inadequate, are quite powerful in certain ways; and so it is worth noting such connections so that potential conceptual bridges can be dismantled as much as maintained.

As an example of such conceptual bridging, note that there are two incredibly important ways such categories may be framed in terms of economic processes.

From the standpoint of micro-economics, the relation between indices and kinds maps onto the relation between preference relations and utility functions. In particular, one may examine the preferences of an actor (e.g., which commodities did they choose over others in particular situations), infer their utility function (a kind of topological grading of their generalized desire), and come to expect other preferences that would be in keeping with that function. Needless to say, there are great efforts underway to infer various *kinds of consumers*, themselves densely figured in terms of all the other kinds any individual might also belong to (social categories, political beliefs, physical characteristics, etc.), in order to both tap and govern, or exploit and coerce, their utility functions. Data-mining, consumer targeting and political governing are fast becoming indistinguishable—and the algorithmic processes described in this chapter are one particularly important way such processes are carried out. Recall our discussion of enclosure as dispossession in chapter 4.

From the standpoint of critical political economy, the relation between kinds and indices maps onto the relation between labor-power and its exercise. While this move has roots in Hobbes, much of the incredible power of Marx's critique of capital comes from his assumption that the difference between labor-power (or what the capitalist purchases by paying a wage) and its exercise (or what the capitalist recoups, when he sells the products of that power) is not only at the center of veiled inequality within the system (as envisioned by him, with the ontology he had, at the time he was working), but is also at the center of the semiotic mediation that generates (and is generated by) the systematic misrecognition of the origins of value. *This relation between virtuality and actuality, in its generalized form, and not so much the difference between concrete and abstract labor, may be the real pivot of political economy.* In short, one could rethink ontologies and their transformations (as laid out above) from the standpoint of critical political economy (to wit, what more radical modes of mediation link indices to kinds), just as one could rethink critical political economy from the standpoint of ontologies and their transformations. But that would be another book.

7.7. Meaning, Mathematics, and Meat

To conclude, we may return to the original title of this chapter ('Hunting Ham and Sieving Spam'), and take up the venatic origins of meaning. The historian Carlo Ginzburg (1989) entertained the idea that our propensity to read signs had its origins in the necessity of tracking animals. Or in terms of the foregoing categories: our ancestors (qua agents) were sieved on the basis of their ability to correctly infer animal types (qua kinds) from their tracks (qua indices). That is, insofar as one is good at judging from an animal's tracks where it is going, how badly it is wounded, how big it is, and what kind of animal it might be, one is better at securing food (and ensuring that one doesn't become food).

Potentially just a just-so-story, to be sure. In this same chapter, however, Ginzburg described the work of the art historian Morelli, who came up with a new technique for linking unattributed art works to old masters: instead of looking at key motifs as evidence of authorship (an important index-kind relation), he started focusing on minor details, like the shapes of ears, which he thought were more likely to be unconsciously drawn, and so not subject to strategic manipulation. In terms of the foregoing categories, Morelli was engaged in ontological transformativity of the fourth kind. He altered the very evidence scholarly agents look for in their attempts to infer authorship, and thereby inaugurated a minor revolution in art history.

According to Ginzburg, Morelli was a precursor to Freud, who did something similar: moving attention from explicit speech and conscious thought as relatively transparent representations of ordinary beliefs and desires, to dreams and neuroses as evidence of unconscious and undesirable desires (a particularly important kind of projected propensity). He not only introduced a new kind of interpretive agent (the analyst), but his texts trained generations of such agents to do such analysis (his clinical writing being, in some sense, akin to the meteorite display). Indeed, we might add Goffman to this list: he introduced the interactional order, constituted by a hurly-burly of highly contextually contingent, fleeting, and unconscious gestures; and he introduced a new set of kinds (animators, authors, principles, ratified and unratified bystanders, frames, etc.) that were revealed in and consequential to such interaction. In short, one reason scholars such as Freud and Goffman are so important is that they made relatively large interventions at the level of transformativity #4 (with enormous repercussions for the other modes of transformativity as well).

Note, then, that ontologies are held by actors and analysts alike. Weber's *Economy and Society* (1978) is, in some sense, our largest compendium of sociological kinds. And his understanding of the functioning of ideal types in the *Methodology of the Social Sciences* (1949) was, in some sense, a kind of scholarly strategy (and editorial ethos) to help we interpretive agents ferret out indices of bad ontologies (qua sociological imaginaries), push moments of scholarship to their crisis, and thereby transform our ontologies (qua analytic categories). In other words, there is a particularly important kind of kind that should be mentioned: the bad (or good) ontology, in the sense that it is deemed less than adequate to the world it represents (often by reference to another relatively meta-ontology). And, with this kind of kind, there is a crucial kind of index: any sign that indicates our ontology is at odds with a world, or brings the lie of our ontologies to light. *Any symptom of ontological strain (itself such a symptom only in a particular meta-ontological frame)*. Recall our discussion of Figure 5.2. In this way, we may offer one possible framing of what is to be meant by *world*: whatever is potentially represented by, and resistant to, an ontology. It is thus an eerie commingling of firstness (possibility), secondness (resistance), and thirdness (representation). Kockelman (2016b) takes up these issues at length.

Finally, to return to our opening example in chapter 1, ethnography in its most daring undertakings (and as formulated from its very beginnings), has always been about the uncomfortably transformative mediated immediacy of the encounter, an encounter designed—however often it is parasitically diverted from that end—to bring us one step closer to an other's ontologized world (or worlded ontology) and one step further from our own—be that other an interpreting human or a sieving machine, a parasite or a meteorite, Maxwell's demon or Bayes's equation, an interjecting human or a speaking machine.

NOTES

Chapter 1

1. See Enfield (2013) for a different, but related, take on relationality.

2. If the discipline had a watchword, it might be *closer*. Anthropology lives (and dies) in this context as much as its practitioners might protest.

3. While we follow a very different path than Suchman (2007), her work at this interface is particularly important.

4. I don't use the term sharing lightly—it is arguably a gift: my obligation (or desire) to point; your obligation to look where I am pointing; and to point in return.

5. Kockelman (2016) takes up many other modes of enclosure as well.

6. For example, counting numbers (0, 1, 2, 3, . . .) are closed under addition, but not subtraction.

7. As we will see, there is also the closure of instigation ratios, of communication ratios, of cognition ratios (rationality), of affect ratios, and much else besides. Indeed, with each closure of ratios there is arguably an opening of a new 'irratios', or novel ways of being irrational (in regards to such ratios).

8. There is an interesting relation between allegedly portable languages and taboo, where the latter might be understood as a kind of enemy, parasite, or censor. Consider, for example, Freud's (1999 [1899]) account of key dream motifs and their 'universal' symbols. Consider as well Dixon's (1980) account of avoidance registers. For example, so called 'mother-in-law language' is a stripped down, yet insanely serviceable version of the whole language. Finally, think of the ways ideal logical languages attempt to banish ambiguity, and the like.

9. Kockelman and Bernstein (2012), in their description of the portability of measuring systems (clocks, money, languages, weights and measures, etc.), theorized the following dimensions of portability. There is the degree to which such a system, or any of its values, may be used to appropriately and effectively interpret values from other systems (and thereby 'translate' them into its own terms). There is the degree to which a signer and interpreter, or self and other, can communicate effectively across contexts without sharing anything but the system itself (and whatever else is needed may be found in every context, brought to every context, or easily built in every context). There is the relative size or scope of the public that reckons with such a system. There is the relative centrality of a system in a hierarchical chain of calibration (insofar as a greater number of other systems are set in terms of it). There is the relative precision, accuracy, reliability, and repeatability of measurements made with a system (insofar as its values are deemed justified and true). The more the units (and conversions) of a semiotic technology are distributed geographically and historically (and the more the evaluative standards that justify such units and conversions are distributed), the more portable it is. And finally, there is the degree to which

features of other domains are projected onto the domain reckoned (or vice-versa), insofar as the domains are correlated in some way.

10. As will be discussed in chapter 6, such hermeneutics often work, not so much by minimizing the common ground necessary for understanding, but by tapping into allegedly universal common grounds.

11. All this is not a definition of portability. It is an *ideal type* (or pragmatic typology) of some of the key *dimensions* along which the *relative degree* of portability of different semiotic processes, and their various components (sign, object, interpretant), can be compared.

12. Crucially, this is a bare-bones and highly idiosyncratic interpretation of some of his ideas. Colapietro (1989) and Parmentier (1994) offer very careful and helpful discussions of his writings, and stick much closer to his original ideas and terms.

13. As Weaver also notes in that introduction, Shannon's theory of information (which applies to selective information-content) only deals with the first level (even if it may have repercussions for the second and third levels). Chapter 4 will take up this issue at length.

14. Finally, both not only display highly iconic relations between their objects and signs, but also between their signs and interpretants. *The hand meets the handle halfway.* Kockelman (2006b, 2013a) theorizes these relations at length, showing their relation to other key semiotic processes: actions, roles, and identities.

Chapter 2

1. Interestingly, autism was initially understood as a phatic disorder—in particular, the psychological connection between speaker and addressee, or self and other more generally, was thought to be damaged. Autism itself was first considered a kind of childhood schizophrenia. And just as schizophrenics were (erroneously) considered fonts of creativity, or singularities, people with autism were (erroneously) considered fonts of noncreativity, or replicators. Now, of course, there is a new romanticism attached to the so-called disorder, in popular culture, with so called highly functioning autistics, or 'people on the spectrum', often thought to be key contributors to the digital age.

2. Jakobson built on the efforts of previous scholars such as Buehler (1982 [1934]), Malinowski (1936), and Tarski (1944). And through the work of scholars such as John Gumperz (Gumperz and Hymes 1986 [1972]), Dell Hymes (1962) and Michael Silverstein (1976), his ideas laid the groundwork for almost forty years of linguistic anthropology. Also, while Jakobson and Malinowski often get credit for the phatic function of language, Sapir also had relevant insights: "Particularly where cultural understandings of an intimate sort are somewhat lacking among the members of a physical group it is felt important that the lack be made good by a constant supply of small talk. This caressing or reassuring quality of speech in general, even where no one has anything of moment to communicate, reminds us how much more language is than a mere technique of communication" (1985 [1933]:16).

3. Marx, of course, also highlighted the function of infrastructure to *sever connections*, or make certain relations unrecognizable. Phrased another way, infrastructure is as much a 'come between' as a 'go between'. Phrased yet another way, a key question for social theory is not, in the tradition of Benedict Anderson's classic work, what are the conditions of possibility for imagining social relations we have never personally experienced; but rather,

what are the conditions for *not* recognizing social relations that we should otherwise be constantly experiencing. Not: how can I move a person, or a person's mind, that is far away (Munn 1992); but rather, *how can I not be moved by the creatures I see everyday*. This is a key (anti-) function of infrastructure, and media more generally. We will return to this issue when we discuss Hobbes's notion of the fetish in chapter 3.

4. These six factors aren't nearly enough to understand mediation (as should be evident from Figure 1.1 and the discussion surrounding it); but they are enough for now.

5. Kockelman (2006a, 2007a, 2013a) makes these points in greater detail.

6. Goffman, more than anyone, implicitly emphasized this primary sense of channel (with a focus on 'contact') in his essay on the interactional order (1983, 6).

7. As argued in Kockelman (2004, 2007a), this is *not* Goffman's (1981a) distinction between animator, author and principle (though it subsumes that, when suitably reframed). Rather, it is a combination of Peirce's understanding of semiotic processes and Varro's much earlier account of action (1938 [43 B.C.]), which applied to any kind of behavior, not just speech actions; and so captures much more than 'voice'.

8. Even something as seemingly straightforward as a distinction between code and channel only holds in a certain frame. For example, key channels that bind us nowadays are generated by codes—they are called protocols. Also, many indexical relations are physically channeled as causal processes. Moreover, these issues wrap back around in still further ways. For example, if the channel turns on 'contact', then the phatic function is, in part, a focus on 'signs of contact'. Not just between signers and interpreters, but also between signs and objects, beliefs and reality, or representations and the world more generally. That is, a key form of contact is the semiotic ground itself—that which connects signs to objects. And so there can be signs that a ground (worldview, belief system, episteme, ontology, cosmology, etc.) is or is not adequate to some world. Signs that someone, or something, is 'out of touch'.

9. There is also in Shannon's diagram another line, labeled 'key', which connects the encipherer to the decipherer: there is thus another relation, or channel, along which keys may be distributed (which themselves are used in the encoding and decoding process). We will take up such issues in chapter 3.

10. It should be emphasized that Shannon's two models of communication are not meant to be exclusive. Both are ideal types, in some sense, and any actual system of a communication might have safeguards against both noise and enemies (and perhaps multiple sources of noise and multiple kinds of enemies). This means that any actual system might involve messages, cryptograms and signals, as well as sources/destinations, encipherers/decipherers, and transmitters/receivers. As will be discussed in section 2.4, and as presupposed in Figure 1.1, such systems may enchain and embed indefinitely.

11. Indeed, if Shannon saw the third being another (an enemy); Goffman saw the third being a second (that is, the very person you're interacting with is the enemy). And Nietzsche, Freud, and Mead saw the third being a first (the key enemy listening in on your line is you, or at least your *über*-you).

12. And see also Gregory Bateson's (1972) reformulation of Shannon.

13. While we are foregrounding the dependence of Serres on Shannon, and his retracing of Peircean moves, just as interesting is his relation to Heidegger's understanding of tools and breakdowns. See the discussion of references in chapter 3.

14. Whether or not such a critique holds for actor-network theory more generally, I'll leave to the judgment of my readers.

15. Such a definition, it should be emphasized, is independent of the nature of the process of selection, and hence of what kind of 'telos' constitutes the end or destination; it thus includes the emergent effects of 'dumb' sieving. It may thereby engage with natural selection on evolutionary timescales through cultural selection on historical timescales to individual selection ('choice') on biographical timescales (and anything outside or in-between).

16. Indeed, back to Jakobson's original system, we might highlight two emergent duplex categories: *messages about channels*, and *codes in reference to channels*. In the first case, analysis might focus on all the ways interactants both state and show their understandings of the channels that bind them to each other (or bind others to them). In the second case, analysis might focus on all the ways that signs (about other kinds of objects entirely) cannot be interpreted except *in reference to* the channels that connect interactants to each other (in actuality, or as they are imagined to be).

17. As Kripke (1980) originally described it: "Someone, let's say, a baby, is born; his parents call him by a certain name. They talk about him to their friends. Other people meet him. Though various sorts of talk the name is spread from link to link as if by a chain" (92).

18. This essay was also enormously influential; and these four categories are now, in some sense, staple goods of linguistic anthropology (Hanks 1990; Hill and Irvine 1992; Lucy 1993; Silverstein 1976). As will be shown in chapter 3, there is an important relation between this second sense of 'makes reference to' and Heidegger's notion of references (*die Verweisungen*).

19. Indeed, key to communicative infrastructure is the relation between codes and channels. For example, a large part of internet protocols are rules systems must follow in order to communicate through, and about, the channels that connect them. See Goffman (1981b) on 'system constraints'. In a more mundane sense, there are also lots of signs like 'bridge out' and 'channel down'.

20. In each case, the key relation is between a sign event (E^S) and an interpretant event (E^I), where this relation is itself inseparable from Jakobson's (1990b) more famous relation between the sign event (E^S), qua 'speech event', and the object event (E^O), qua 'narrated event'. Returning to our opening discussion of bridges, such co-related events constitute banks—however otherwise distal they are in terms of space, time, or impact. Finally, recall that through our definition of semiotic processes, and the multiple reframings such processes are subject to, the particular 'eventiveness' of any particular event is frame-dependent, and often easily obviated.

21. To be sure, much censorship is more mild, and may even be self-imposed: turning off a cellphone, plugging one's ears, and raising the blinds. Throttling is a closely related function. It involves sending a sign to change how many signs pass through a given channel. Such a sign doesn't change the signs per se, nor does it change where they come from or where they go; it merely transforms the quantity and average quality: how many per unit time pass through a given channel; or what kinds are permitted to pass through a given channel. It is closely related to filtering or sieving, as discussed above. Traffic lights, and all the signs that direct the movement of people, goods, and ideas along infrastructures, serve exactly this function: they may not change the physical channel per se; but they transform its use. Indeed, one of the most famous defecation scenes in literature is Leopold Bloom on the crapper modulating his own bowel movement—for the brain communicates with the ass as much as with the eye. Finally, the function can be enabling as much as constraining. Biochemically, catalysts serve a similar function: their presence allows a certain reaction to more easily occur, such that certain inputs can be converted into certain outputs at a faster

rate, and thereby 'move along' the *path* of a reaction. More prosaically, mailing someone a key, or slipping someone a passport, can achieve the same end.

22. Though narrower in scope than the parasitic function per se.

23. Neurons are often said to have this property: whatever fires together wires together. And some memories may be framed as ways of channeling past experiences into future actions insofar as such actions further entrench such memories. Maps, as artifacts produced by a journey which allow for the retracing of that journey, may serve this function. Indeed, any recounting or description of a journey, so far as it guides or inspires others to replicate the journey, is an instance of this process insofar as such journeys move messages as much as people and goods. If we think of hyperlinks as simultaneously causes of future journeys (so far as they direct others to a site) and effects of past journeys (so far as they are the outcomes of having visited a site), then hyperlinks have path-like properties. And while we think of them as signs, they are simultaneously channels (or 'links') precisely because they are signs whose objects are the addresses of other websites, such that when they are interpreted (by clicking on them), they transport their interpreters to those sites (or rather bring the contents of those sites to these interpreters).

24. If the life-path of an individual turns on a series of transformations in status—from knave to knight, from girl to woman, from tailor to scholar, and so forth—than source-dependent channels (as origin-dependent paths) are akin to social formations that turn on ascribed status: where one goes (or 'how high one rises') is a function of where one came from. In a humanist vein this is considered a tragedy: important ethical systems are attempts to give people access to the same paths and destinations, no matter what their origins. Source-dependent channels, then, are only one pole of a continuum: there are other channels which are indifferent to sources—so long as a sign arrives at one end (no matter how it got there), it will be channeled to the other end; so long as a messenger arrives at the gate, he or she will be permitted into the castle. Insofar as the destination of one path is usually the origin of another (compare topics and foci, and premises and conclusions), channels (institutions and infrastructure) which are governed this way allow for bootstrapping and semiotic cascades of a potentially upsetting or undermining nature. In this way, channels create and consolidate modes of justice and injustice as much as techniques of governance.

25. Crucial to performatives, in Austin's account, are the witnesses of such acts, insofar as they, in recognizing the felicity of the speech act, come to regiment the actors involved as to their new statuses, qua normatively entailed commitments and entitlements. A key communicative agent nowadays is best labeled the *witlessness*: a mindless device that can record, and potentially regiment, social actors and their semiotic transformations, in ways that can be just as 'mindful' as a witness, but in an automated, ever-present way. (Closely related is the kind of witlessness you find in Vegas, or so you hope, such that most of what you do will stay there. Just as machines can be enlivened, people can be inebriated, not to mention 'opiated' in Marx's sense.)

26. In some sense, then, a key enclosure for Austin was 'quotes' or [brackets]: when we quote, or bracket, we no longer point with the word (to a referent), rather we point out the word, or the word-referent relation (as a referent). His theory went as far as such walls, but no further. Recall our discussion of meta-language and reported speech.

27. Phrased another way, each of us is an ensemble of Veblenesque (1899) processes so far as we can commit to others' interpretants of our behavior, and thereby come to shape our behavior for those interpretants in ways that make each party invested in the successful

outcome of a social encounter, such that the unit of accountability becomes the (framed) interaction itself.

28. While the parasite, as an analytic category, gets much of its seemingly productive energy from its accusatory character ('something is taking without giving'), so that 'critical' scholars can now switch to diagnosing parasites rather than unmasking power, that is arguably the least interesting aspect of it.

29. It has already, and perhaps more primordially, been construed in terms of 'interactional value' via the ongoing dynamics of the joint-attentional event that brought it into intersubjective focus in the first place.

Chapter 3

1. That is, this doesn't mean that such entities have no identity outside of their system-specific values: many entities maintain some of their affordances, and some of their functioning, across a wide-range of environs. It means that a significant part of their value—the meanings they have, the functions they serve, the forces they channel, and so forth—are dependent on their contexts and contents. Nothing is pure structure; nothing is pure assemblage.

2. It should be remembered that channels don't have to be communicative media of the stereotypic sort. For example, our neurons, limbs, sense organs, weapons, and telescopes also function to channel experiences in and behaviors out. It should also be remembered that such relations are organized by psychological connections and social conventions as much as physical contacts.

3. As will be detailed in chapter 6, most constructions are far more complicated than this. For example, one element in a construction may itself be a construction with many elements, and so on, recursively, ad infinitum.

4. While encryption practices have changed radically since Shannon wrote his essay, we still live in a world of relatively secure and insecure channels, and so habitually and strategically tack between the complementary affordances of each: what I will tell my sweetheart when we are alone in our bedroom, versus what I will tell him at the dinner table when we are surrounded by friends.

5. Indeed, we can avoid such a mess altogether simply by reading Saussure more carefully, or generously (Kockelman 2011a). Recall Jakobson's revisioning of Saussure, as it was extended in section 2.5 of chapter 2.

6. Kockelman (2009) details frames of relevance and scales of resolution from the standpoint of information theory, and statistical mechanics, focusing on the relation between complexity and organization through the lens of constraint. In chapter 4 we will see the relation between these ideas and MacKay's (1969a) understanding of structural and metrical information.

7. Even physicists can reframe natural systems at will, with more or less strain, depending on the kind of phenomena they are interested in. For example, from the standpoint of a physicist, a simple pendulum has two degrees of freedom: assuming the bar is rigid (and is confined to move in a plane), all we need to know is the angular position and angular momentum of its center of mass. Similarly, a coupled pendulum has four degrees of freedom: the angular position and momentum of both links needs to be known. And so on, and so forth, for coupled pendulums with more and more links. Taking this process to

the extreme, even a single rigid pendulum may be reframed as a non-rigid pendulum, and thus be understood as a long series of (very short) coupled pendulums. In other words, while a rigid bar has only one or two degrees of freedom, the same bar with its rigidity relaxed (if only conceptually) can have many many degrees of freedom.

8. In most cases, though, it is really time that is our undoing.

9. As Sapir put it, "All languages are set to do all the symbolic and expressive work that language is good for, either actually or potentially. The formal technique of this work is the secret of each language" (1949 [1924], 155).

10. Indeed, as will be shown in chapter 6, they also hold for 'computation' (or relations between signs and interpretants, loosely understood as automated input-output processes).

11. Note, then, the issue doesn't just relate to expressions in different languages, but also to different expressions in the same language.

12. Even Benjamin's famous dictum from the *Theses on the Philosophy of History* (1968b) is applicable: Marxism is a version of theology, and "theology is wizened and must stay out of sight." That is, theology and Marxism, however different may be their referents, have very similar senses (in the sense of Frege and Sapir). And it is this very fact that should stay out of sight: it is the similarity of their secrets that should be kept secret (but isn't, ultimately, at least to Benjamin). The secret of Marxism—itself the queen science of positing secrets—is that it has the same secrets as theology, at least at the level of sense: the underlying logic of the system it uses to get at its referents, the grounds it depends on to do its figuring, the interventions it licenses through the interpretations it offers.

13. Recall our discussion in section 3.1 of private and public channels; and note the relation between private spaces and the home, and hence the secret.

14. As Shannon himself glosses the term, an enemy is not so much an unintended recipient of a message, but precisely that whose reception of a message an encryption process is designed to stop. Just as noise, as a kind of thwarting, determines the function of a channel; enemies, as a kind of thwarting, determine the function of encryption (and of secrecy systems more generally).

15. Recall our discussion of signer-directed channels and channel-directed channels in chapter 2.

16. Note, by the way, that one key function of poetry is to *channel* words in certain ways—the sonnet way, the iambic pentameter way, the haiku way. In so doing, poetry offers words the opportunity to overflow, and underfill, such forms. As has long been noted, poetry invites creativity on one front by demanding conformity on another. On the one hand, then, poems ask poets to make their texts predictable, and/or redundant, to work within a shared set of expectations. On the other hand, poems ask poets to violate and perturb such shared expectations. So just as there is a poetics of channels, as we will now show, there has always been a channeling through poetry. In any case, as we noted in chapter 2, redundancy is the flip side of repetition. And so patterning does not just underlie both life forms and forms of life, it also lies at the intersection of information theory and aesthetics. Cybernetics and poetics, like biology and anthropology, have always been fellow travelers.

17. More carefully, if types are, in part, constituted by substitution classes; and if two relations (or paths) are substitutable if they go to, or come from, the same node (qua origin or destination); then simply to successively (iteratively, continuously) take different routes to the same destination or from the same origin, to pass back and forth between the same two points while alternating paths, is to foreground the sense of a network.

18. Indeed, apropos of our discussion of parasites in chapter 2, a key relation between relations is that which interferes or intercepts, that which thwarts or captures. Failure brings into view functioning (at least ostensibly, as we will see in section 3.7, just as nonsense brings into view sense, just as poetry brings into view grammar). Some of the key paths through any network are the paths that enable one to be thrown off the path, or blocked from continuing along the path. How then to iteratively induce these different forms of failure?

19. Moving from relatively instrumental values to relatively existential values, is one route the 'right' course (or the 'leftist' course, or the 'conservative' course, or the 'anarchist' course)? Indeed, just as infrastructure is often taken to be indicative of a collectivity's character or identity, some particular use of it, or routing through it, is often taken to be indicative of the user's identity. That is, the life-course itself is often seen as a channeling of human possibility and frailty, of collective fate and destiny (Kockelman 2010b). One's very soul may be understood to ascend or sizzle depending on the particular path one takes.

20. As will be shown in chapter 5, when we discuss quali-signs and related phenomenona, it also highlights their potential and virtual signs, as well as their potential and virtual objects and interpretants.

21. As our example should also show, it is just as easy to combine Heidegger with Marx as it is to critique Heidegger 'in reference to' Marx. In any case, both thinkers were heavily influenced by Aristotle—not just by his account of relations (in the *Categories*), but also by his account of causes (in the *Physics*), and his account of means-ends chains (in the *Nicomachean Ethics*). Recall our discussion of Aristotle in section 2.6 of chapter 2.

22. While references were designed to account for the immediacies of experience, or being-in-the-world in its classic sense, they readily extend to the three modes of mediation introduced above: channels, infrastructure, and institutions. Indeed, through our reading of Jakobson in chapter 2, we saw how certain duplex categories described in terms of 'in reference to' were precisely those categories that allow for displacement by means of immediacy: our utterances can represent a narrated event (however distal) insofar as we ground them in the speech event. And, more generally, we introduced four other kinds of reflexively-oriented channels to understand such modes of displacement: source-dependent channels, self-channeling channels, signer-directed signers, and channel-directed signers.

23. Indeed, anaphora is a kind of archeology on a sentence-by-sentence scale.

24. Agamben (1998) treats a much more infamous kind of enclosure: the concentration camp. While that is not the focus here, one should note the relation between enemies (and friends), as discussed in section 3.5, and Carl Schmitt's (1996 [1932]) account of the enemy, which Agamben analyzes and critiques so thoroughly, and Agamben's critique of Heidegger (and Heidegger's relation to Nazism).

Chapter 4

1. Instead of events, we may speak of entities, qualities, phenomena, or states of a system, *inter alia*.

2. This may involve prediction: knowing about the cause or circumstance (as sign), an agent may learn about the effect or behavior (as object). Or it may involve retrodiction: knowing something about the effect or behavior (as sign), an agent may learn something about the cause or circumstance (as object).

3. Look for emergent research on 'effacement work', a concept introduced by Shunsuke Nozawa and Gretchen Pfeil, as presented at the 2015 meetings of the American Anthropological Society, in a panel organized by Miyako Inoue and Paul Manning, entitled "Defamiliarizing Communication by Familiarizing the Channel: Linguistic Anthropology Meets Cybernetic Theory."

4. Kockelman (2013b) shows how two influential theorists of new media, Katherine Hayles (1999) and Mark Hansen (2004), misread MacKay, and discusses some of the consequences of their misreading for humanist critiques of cybernetic theory, with their attempts to use MacKay and similar theorists to recover 'the body', 'affect', and so forth.

5. To see why, imagine the 10,000 positions laid out in front of them as square centimeters within a square meter. They ask: is it in the top half of the square meter, or the bottom half? If we answer, the bottom half, they have effectively cut their search space in half. Their next question, then, should be more or less the same: is it in the top half (of that remaining bottom rectangle), or the bottom half? And so on, and so forth. Each answer to such a question cuts the remaining search space in half until there is only one remaining position, which occurs after about thirteen such questions. For more on these issues, Shannon and Weaver (1963 [1949]) is still the canonical text, and there is a wealth of popular accounts and technical treatises on these and related notions. Kockelman (2009) works through some of the mathematical details of information theory, showing their relation to complexity and entropy.

6. The information-content of a single message is the same as the average information-content of an ensemble of messages when all messages are equally probable.

7. That said, anyone who has ever tried to calculate the selectional information-content of a particular message, or ensemble of messages, should know that the calculation is similar to Marx's understanding of how value (or abstract temporality) is to be calculated. And so selectional information-content (which might seem highly 'symbolic', and thus relatively conventional and context-independent) is also highly indexical and iconic: "indexical because in any statistical ensemble each part is related to every other part of the whole; iconic because inversely-proportional as part is to whole" (Kockelman 2006a, 93).

8. To return to the concerns of chapter 2, Bateson's 'slash', or Jakobson's backslash (/), or any bridge, channel, or forcefield more generally, can be found, or produced, anywhere—including, in the case of poetry, text-internally.

9. Marx, for example, was interested in how superficial, inverted, or false correlations (between, say, beliefs about the world and the world itself) were deeply correlated with the world itself (and, in particular, the fact that beliefs about it were superficial, inverted, or false).

10. Note, then, that the theory of meaning that scholars like Hayles (1999) and Hansen (2004) want to recover from MacKay (as a means to offset the negative effects of Shannon's banishment of meaning), is essentially a restatement (and indeed radical watering-down) of the classic pragmatist stance.

11. In this definition Peirce seems indifferent as to whether he means sign (predicate) versus object (quality), or sign (subject) versus object (referent).

12. That is, information for Peirce turned on relation (or 'quantia') as opposed to quantity (Aristotle 2001c; Sapir 1985 [1945]; Kockelman 2016).

13. Peirce's second key definition of information arises most forcefully in his logical typology of ten different kinds of signs (1955a; 1998 [1903], 289–299; and see Kockelman 2013b).

14. Crucially, topic and focus are information-specific terms that need not map onto subject and predicate (as grammatical roles). For example, in a sentence like 'who took out the trash?' the focus is 'who' and the topic is 'took out the trash'. Indeed, such questions are precisely designed to indicate the contours of one's ignorance, so that an addressee can better illuminate it with an answer (compare MacKay on the function of questions).

15. Peirce gets at this idea in two ways. First, as discussed above, each sign (to be subsequently interpreted) may itself be an interpretant of a prior sign. And second, through his idea of the argument, as a sign that is interpreted as being the conclusion of a set of premises through some kind of logical inference. As he puts it, an argument is "a sign whose interpretant represents its object as being an ulterior sign through a law—namely, the law that the passage from all such premises to such conclusions tends to the truth" (1955a, 118–119). If propositions are important because they can be true or false (and thus have truth-value), arguments are important because they offer a reason for their truth-value.

16. All this may also be framed as follows (Kockelman 2007b): Just as Peirce's first definition of information had three interrelated pieces (denotation, connotation, and information), his second definition of information had three interrelated pieces. There is a relatively iconic dimension, or focus (as exemplified by a term). There is a relatively indexical dimension, or topic-focus relation (as exemplified by a proposition that incorporates a term). And third, there is a relatively symbolic dimension, or topic-focus-reason relation (as exemplified by the premises and arguments that lead to a proposition). More generally, there are signs that thematize, signs that characterize (features of a theme), and signs that reason (with this theme-character relation). And most composite signs are wholes that have such smaller signs as parts.

17. As we will see in chapter 7, such issues hold not only for words like 'dog', but also for terms like 'human', 'Edgar Alan Poe', 'spam', and any other kind that might be found in a collectivity's ontology. As we will see in chapter 7, the temporal, cultural, and computational dynamics of the transformations in ontologies that accompany such informational expansions can be far more complicated than these processes would suggest.

18. Things can be far more complicated than this simple example of a database seems to allow. That said, I'm presuming that such a simple example of a relational database (versus one modeled on a hierarchy or network) can illustrate the key concepts, and emphasize the high stakes, without radically misrepresenting the wide range of possible data structures, and their associated algorithms.

Chapter 5

1. To be sure, a wall does this as well. But mirrors typically reflect a much wider range of wavelengths (from around 350 nanometers to more than 900 nanometers, so I'm told) such that any information propagating at such wavelengths from outside the thermos (or from behind the mirror) is lost. Recall our discussion of effacing traces from chapter 4. In this reading, 'self-reflectivity' is not so much a high-end form of cognition, as a low-end form of confinement. The earliest enclosure, after the womb, was probably the cradle, or swaddling more generally.

2. Think of Bazin's (1960) classic discussion of the 'mummy complex'.

3. To be sure, it can also be resurrected: for media not only preserve against death; they also bring back to life (and, more canonically, take life away).

4. Something that may be distinguished provides evidence of something that was extinguished. Indeed, we might define archeology as *the study of whatever can be dug up and put on display without undue deterioration insofar as it provides evidence of the no-longer-living forms of life who developed and deployed it.*

5. And, as a bridge, it brings the banks into being as much as it makes already existing banks interrelate—recall the opening discussion of chapter 2. In this way, it is not so much that different temporalities are bridged by means of various media, with their respective durabilities; it is that different senses of temporality, and their relevant scales, are produced by different durabilities (and the institutions, imaginaries, and infrastructures that sustain them). Kockelman (2007b, 2017c), and Kockelman and Bernstein (2013), take up such issues at length.

6. Note, then, that materiality is not just scale-independent (but dimension-bound); it is also dimension-independent. That is, you can't even talk about degrees of materiality.

7. Indeed, in the case of traditional definitions of materiality, that whatest of whats, archaeologists settled on the whoest of whos: the human body, naked as the day it was born, and thus seemingly shorne of its accessories, and thus seemingly unmediated. That is, classic definitions of materiality smuggle along with themselves the most seemingly vulnerable of humans—that which is minimally accessoried to go the distance, except by digging down. That said, if technique is as important to media as technology, then there has never been an unmediated hand or eye, brain or tongue, or even a naked body, as long as there has been habit, skill, social relations, and so forth.

8. Home sapiens is really *homo scalar*. But I understand that the use of a particular scale is reflexive: along a certain scale (prehistory) we can presume a certain scale (the media equivalent of nudity) such that the 'modern' (posthistory) gets constituted as that which seems to be scale-free.

9. Causality has many meanings. Here we are using it to refer to something like secondness, as opposed to thirdness. The real point, however, is that such categories are best understood as poles of a (multidimensional) continuum rather than positions in a (monodimensional) opposition.

10. Recall our discussion of Heidegger's notion of references in chapter 3.

11. For the sake of contrast we are radically simplifying the details of semiotic processes. Recall Figure 1.1. For example, once astrophysicists find earth-like planets, they will need to take into account all the various semiotic grounds as well. Such grounds become relevant wherever there are life forms, or even the possibility of life frames. And, to be sure, such grounds are key for understanding any epistemic formation's account of any kind of object, no matter how non-lively. For any epistemic formation is itself a frame of life. For research that resonates with these claims, see the particularly important work of Helmreich (2016) and Messeri (2016); and see Kockelman (2011a) for the relation between life forms and life frames, and their relation to semiotic processes.

12. Recall our discussion of source-dependent channels, and self-channeling channels, in chapter 2; such issues hold for interpretant-sign relations as much as signer-intepreter relations.

13. Performative utterances (Austin 1962), which bring into being the states of affairs they represent, most obviously evince such an object type.

14. See Buehler (1982 [1934]) on deictics and the deictic field. For our purposes what is important is that the deictic field is, in some sense, a space of already available paths. The deictic just tells you which one to take; but the path itself exists prior to the deictic, and does the most work in getting you to the destination.

15. Key work in this tradition includes Sperber and Wilson (1986) and Tomasello (2008). Kockelman (2013a, chapter 5) reviews this literature. And Kockelman (2005) reviews the enormous literature on common ground.

16. Also constraining the analyst's inferences, of course, are a whole bunch of relatively backgrounded assumptions about the patient's early years and subsequent biography in relation to the causal ontology of psychoanalysis.

17. As Peirce put it: "Finally, no present actual thought (which is a mere feeling) has any meaning, any intellectual value; for this lies not in what is actually thought, but in what this thought may be connected with in representation by subsequent thoughts; so that the meaning of a thought is altogether something virtual. . . . At no instant in my state of mind is there cognition or representation, but in the relation of my states of mind at different instants there is" (quoted in Skagestad 1998). William James made very similar claims in his account of the ideal self, or *I*, as opposed to the empirical self, or *Me*. And we could say the same thing of semiotic agents per se.

18. Freud even offered a theory of the virtual, drawn from the physics of optics: while the image seen in a mirror is virtual, the image on one's retina is real. As Freud put it: "Everything that can be an object of our perception is virtual, like the image produced in a telescope by the passage of light rays. If we continue this comparison, the censorship between the two systems would correspond to the refraction of a ray of light as it passes over into a new medium" (1999, 404). Note, then, that while Freud contrasted the virtual with the real, following a tradition in the physics of optics, other theorists of the virtual do not make such a distinction. Rather, they contrast the virtual with the actual (as opposed to the real), as per the ideas of Deleuze. Or, as per the ideas of Peirce, they contrast the virtual with the non-virtual (where labeling something virtual or non-virtual doesn't commit one to its reality per se). Finally, note that, in this quote, Freud seems to be saying that all objects, in our perception of them, are 'virtual'; whereas the physicist's account of virtual versus real images would say that, in visual perception, the object on our retina (as opposed to the object in a mirror) is real.

19. *Virtus*, in its original sense, is arguably closest to Aristotle's notion of efficient cause; we are here playing with the possibilities.

20. For example, the non-virtual substance may lack some property that the virtual substance has, and so it may be the lack of a property (say, a corrupting alloy) that constitutes its realness.

Chapter 6

1. While many entities and agents are usually framed as sieves, an important question that often arises is this: What does the concept (or metaphor) of a sieve itself sieve? That is, what kinds of processes are, and are not, sieves. Kockelman (2011a) take up the important relation between sieving and serendipity, and the relation between sieving and serendipity, on the one hand, and selection and significance, on the other. It argues that all four concepts are necessary to understand the multitude of multiverses. That said, this chapter and

the next try to push sieving as far into the other three domains as possible and to show the scales at which it is privileged. Equally useful would be to stress how the other domains push back and, at certain other scales, are themselves privileged. Kockelman (2013a), for example, foregrounds significance and selection.

2. Indeed, many sieving processes involve question-answer sequences, and involve multiple and extensive semiotic processes along the way—grading students, passing through customs, seeking asylum, selecting juries, and so forth. And so both those asking questions and those answering, or those expressing signs and those interpreting them, have opportunities to change their values, beliefs, questions, answers, signs, interpretants, and so forth, as the sequence proceeds, in order to better determine who or what should be accepted or rejected.

3. Note, then, even though most binary devices of the stereotypic sort, as we will see below, are really complicated sieving devices, there is nothing inherently 'binary' about sieves per se: many sieve in a more or less, or graded fashion; and many sieve into more than two types.

4. However you want to frame such distinctions, and if you want to frame them at all.

5. Phrased another way, while the input-output relation is deterministic, the 'meaning' such devices have, and the 'function' they serve, only make sense in terms of the interests of some agent and the features of some object, which are themselves usually only partially determined, and are always dependent on the placement of such a device in a particular context (a context which includes the device's own input).

6. Though, as is well known from information theory, complicated alphabets are not necessary, in that a simple binary alphabet like {0,1} can be used to represent the characters from all other alphabets and, indeed, the strings from all other languages.

7. For intimacy as a metaphor see Gibson (1986 [1979]); Haugeland (1998a); Kockelman (2013a); and Simon (1996).

8. While the scholarship relevant to such concerns is enormous, key works include: Benjamin (1968a); Benkler (2006); Hayles (1999); Kittler (1989 [1986], 1996 [1993]); McLuhan (1996 [1964]); MacKay (1969); Manovich (2001); Mirowski (2001); Suchman (2007); Turing (2004 [1950]); and many of the essays collected in Wardrip-Fruin and Montfort (2003). In linguistic and cultural anthropology, see recent work by Inoue (2006, 2011); Wilf (2013a, 2013bb); Gershon and Manning (2014); Golub (2010); Manning and Gershon (2013); and Seaver (2011, 2015). And see the prescient book by Dibbell (1999), which undertakes the first real ethnography of a virtual world.

9. There is a technical sense of nondeterministic, as used by computer scientists (Sipser 2007), when they describe nondeterministic finite automata, which is not being used here. In particular, such nondeterministic finite automata are equivalent to deterministic finite automata (Rabin and Scott 1959), and so still function as intermediaries as opposed to mediators.

10. While linguistic anthropologists have long been nervous about postulating rules to understand behavior (witness the success of practice-based approaches in anthropology), large collections of such rules can exhibit behaviors that appear—and, thus, for all intensive purposes *are*—highly flexible. (And, indeed, one can write rules for a device that enable it to update its own rules—depending, say, on the environment it finds itself in.)

11. Given our discussion of generativity in chapter 5, this should be seen as highly ironic—especially because a key architect of that paradigm was Noam Chomsky, himself

often offering homage to Wilhelm von Humboldt, both of whom insistently championed the particular genius of *homo sapiens* for symbolic creativity (and moral agency).

12. See, for example, Dreyfus (1991) and Haugeland (1998b).

13. See, for example, Kripke (1982) and Kockelman (1999).

14. Ironically and again recursively, in the domain of cognitive psychology, Chomsky is to Skinner as mediators are to intermediaries, and so he sits on both sides of this contrast depending on whom he is being contrasted with.

15. A key locus for this last distinction was offered by scholars like Tomasello and Call (1997): "The prototype of a cognitive adaptation is a behavior adaptation in which perceptual and behavioral processes (1) are organized flexibly, with the individual organism making decisions among possible courses of action based on an assessment of the current situation in relation to its current goal; and (2) involve some kind of mental representation that goes 'beyond the information given' to direct perception" (8).

16. Needless to say, this definition of agency is meant to be an ideal type: the claim is not that the world conforms to this conception of agency, but rather, by articulating such a conception clearly, we can show all the ways the world does not conform, and thereby revise our conception accordingly.

17. Key works on these three kinds of automata, the history of automata theory more generally, and the nature of programming languages, include: Sussman and Abelson (2001); Bird, Kleine, and Loper (2009); Chomsky (1956); Church (1941); Friedl (2006); Jurafsky and Martin (2008); Kernighan and Ritchie (1988 [1978]); Kleene (1956); McCarthy (1960); McCulloch (1943); Piccinini (2004); Rabin and Scott (1959); Shannon (1949); Sipser (2007); Thompson (1968); and Turing (2004 [1936]). See Kelty (2011) for a particularly rich account of regular expressions.

18. Examples of strings in this language, over a QWERTY alphabet, include: 'abc#abc', '4444#4444', 'davemary#davemary', 'the quick brown fox#the quick brown fox', and so forth.

19. In such cases, one can produce infinitely embeddable constructions, like: 'the cat on the mat behind the door of the house. . .'

20. Left aside are issues related to recognizing versus deciding a language. Famously, and as discussed at length in Sipser (2007), a TM can recognize but not decide a language like {p | p is polynomial with integer roots}.

21. Or, as famously defined by Hilbert, an algorithm is a 'process according to which it can be determined in a finite number of operations' (quoted in Sipser 2007).

22. Or even in the sense that a program may be written once, and run anywhere, as per the well-known slogan of Sun Microsystems to describe the cross-platform utility of their Java programming language.

23. Ironically, Samuel Butler (1872) called such machines 'vapor engines'. And his book was called *Erewhon*—which might be taken to mean 'no ware' as much as 'nowhere'. Nowadays we have hardware, software, spyware and, of course, vaporware (qua highly touted software, or technology, that never actual arrives).

24. Manovich's words for these were automated, numerical representation, dual-encoding, modulation, and variation.

25. Happily, a dictionary informs me that the German word, *(das) Wort*, not only means '(the) word', but also refers to "The native unit of storage on a particular machine.

A word is the largest amount of data that can be handled by the microprocessor in one operation and also, as a rule, is the width of the main data bus. Word sizes of 16 bits and 32 bits [and nowadays 64 bits, I assume] are the most common"; see Interglot Translation Dictionary, http://www.interglot.com/dictionary/de/en/translate/Wort.

26. Many famous interface designers make reference to Whorf. See, for example, Victor (2006) and Englebart (1962). And see Stephenson (1999) for an inspired engagement with Whorf-like ideas.

27. Indeed, such a device is also easily represented by a highly symbolic text, or bit-string. Such a diagram is, in essence, an iconic-index of a transition function.

28. As a recent textbook on deep learning notes, "The true challenge to artificial intelligence proved to be solving the tasks that are easy for people to perform but hard for people to describe formally—problems that we solve intuitively, that feel automatic, like recognizing spoken words or faces in images" (Goodfellow, Bengio and Courville 2016, 1)

29. Kockelman (2014b) takes up several other key topics in this regard—for example, the linguistic anthropology of programming languages, and the need to automate, format, and network languages if one is to study automated, formatted, and networked languages. It also shows the critical relation between these kinds of topics (and techniques) and those that pertain to 'digital anthropology' in its current guise.

30. As we noted in chapter 1, Peirce had made similar claims forty years earlier (Chiu et al. 2005).

31. And not only expert populations of humans, but also lay populations.

32. This is somewhat akin to showing construction types, or form classes, above actual lexical contents. For example, *(the boy who kicked me)*$_{NP}$ *was (my sister's friend)*$_{NP}$.

33. Happily, Wikipedia informs me (as of 6/22/2016) that "The term originates from the Hebrew word *shibbólet* (שִׁבֹּלֶת), which literally means the part of a plant containing grains [think wheat as opposed to chaff], such as an ear of corn or a stalk of grain or, in different contexts, 'stream, torrent' [think rivers with and without their fords and bridges]".

34. Also key are the framing processes that are involved not just in *linking* distinct and potentially distal 'texts' and 'contexts' (across different points in space-time, so to speak), but also in *constituting* any particular 'text' or 'context' (at some particular point in space-time and, indeed, the space-time continuum or 'discretum' itself). See, for example, Halliday and Hasan (1976), Kockelman (2011a; 2013, 202–203), and the essays in the particularly important collection edited by Silverstein and Urban (1996).

Chapter 7

1. It may also scale to include parasites of an economic kind (those who take value from a system without giving) and parasites of a biological kind (those organisms that benefit at the expense of other organisms).

2. As will be seen in what follows, the analytic categories generated in this chapter reflexively apply to this very generation. That is, this chapter is precisely an attempt to develop and delimit (as well as decry and destroy) a particular ontology: a relatively portable set of assumptions regarding the recursive and reflexive, as well as fragile and fraught, entangling of indices, agents, kinds, individuals, and worlds. As such, it is meant to display what it describes, as well as instantiate what it instigates.

3. Spam has been usefully defined by Graham (2004) as "Unsolicited mass email, usually advertising" (249). And this usage of the word (as opposed to referring to a particular brand of tinned ham) is usually traced back to an episode of Monty Python in which Vikings interfere with a conversation by chanting 'spam' over and over again (ibid.). For a careful history and reflection on origins of the word, and its importance to Internet culture, as well as its contrastive relation to the notion of a community more generally, see recent work by Brunton (2010, 2012). And for more work by computer scientists on spam from a Bayesian approach see the original chapter by Graham, as well as related chapters at www.paulgraham.com/antispam.html. While not all spam filters uses Bayesian filtering, or at least not only Baysean filtering (see, for example, www.spamassassin.apache.org), it is the general logic of the approach that interests me.

4. For example, instead of the word index, we might have used a word like sign (icon, symbol, etc.), evidence, qualia, inscription, experience, factor, feature, text, or token. Such an 'index' might be constituted by a single word, a speech act, or an entire interaction; the smell of a rose, or the view from a balcony; something close by, or something far away; and so forth. Similarly, 'individuals' are not necessarily, or even usually, individual people (in the sense of John Smith, Sue Evans, etc.), but can include: a swarm of bees, a swatch of flesh, the Colorado River, a chromosome, or the Pleistocene. And so on, and so forth. These terms were chosen because they seemed to be the least marked. In any case, the important issue is how they are defined; how each of their definitions is necessarily entangled with the others; and how each is frame- (agent-, or ontology-) specific, and so may both scale and shift accordingly.

5. That indices may be reframed as kinds (with their own indices) is, in part, dependent on the kinds of ontological transformations outlined below. In many circumstances, what determines one frame rather than another is the timescale of interest, such that an agent's ability to type indices is relatively fixed, and so it is the judgment of kindedness (from these indices) that is relatively fluid. The fixed/fluid relation may turn on distinctions like hardware versus software or called versus calling function, and so forth.

6. In some sense, this is the generalized equivalent of the parent who not only points something out to a child, but also describes what is being pointed at. And, of course, it is not without performative possibilities: *this is art, that is trash, those are weeds, they are the enemy, I am your friend*, and so forth.

7. For example, your being married, or being named 'Dave', may be more or less independent of my assumptions (as one particular agent) about the world, and hence confronts my individual agency as a social fact (in Durkheim's original sense). This doesn't mean it is independent of all agents' assumptions about the world (indeed, most social kinds are precisely constituted through such socially distributed assumptions, as brought about through such transformative signs). See transformativity #5. Thus, relatively speaking, some particular individual's kindedness may be a function of transformativity #1 from the standpoint of one agent (or group of agents), and yet be a function of transformativity #5 from the standpoint of another agent (or group of agents).

8. A crucial note of caution. Such assumptions are as likely embodied and embedded as they are enminded and encoded. In this way, they too are a part of the world (and vice-versa). For this reason, rather than talking about ontologies and worlds, it is best to talk about *worlded ontologies* and *ontologized worlds*. Kockelman (2013a) analyzes in detail the kinds of complexities that arise in dealing with such assumptions, treating them as

modes of residing in worlds, as much as ways of representing worlds, and as radically distributed socially as well as emergent interactionally.

9. See Peirce (1992 [1878], 1998 [1903], 1998 [1904]) for more on these inferential profiles.

10. Indeed, reflexively speaking, one can watch their sieving activity (as indices) and infer their relatively derivative beliefs and desires (as kinds).

11. See, for example, French (2000) and Saygin, et al. (2001). Crucially, Turing himself (2004 [1950], 453) comes closest to foregrounding the cultural specificity of ontologies, and the kinds of inductions that lead to them, and the kinds of false (or transient) conclusions that can be drawn from them (under the heading 'Arguments from Various Disabilities'). In this way, he noted the importances of issues underlying transformativity #3, even though he, like most subsequent scholars, spent most of his time on transformativity #2. Crucially, all of this is directly related to Butler's (1872) claims in Erewhon: If there was no way we could have predicted the arrival of man by looking at the earth millions of years ago, how could we ever predict the arrival of conscious machines by looking at current machines? As Butler put it, we would deny "any potentiality of consciousness. ... Yet in the course of time consciousness came. Is it not possible then that there may be even yet new *channels* dug out for consciousness [in machines], though we can detect no signs of them at present?" (chapter XXIII; italics added).

12. See, for example, Arendt (1958); Benjamin (1968ab); James (1985); Taylor (1989); and Weber (1978).

13. Readers should no doubt see the critical possibilities present in this scenario. For example, the relation to money, value, coins, storehouses, and tribute economies; the notion of containers and their contents, and ontologies grounded in visible/invisible, or appearance/essence, divides; what happens when urns and coins are replaced by beakers and chemicals (or any other kinds of entities from disparate ethnographic and analytic imaginaries); or when kinds and indices are ontologized in terms of persons rather than things, or strange interminglings; and so forth.

14. To undertake such a sum, one has to be able to not just imagine a particular, and particularly bounded, totality. One often also needs access to an 'avalanche of numbers', such that the likelihoods one uses to reckon are representative of some world—and thus statistical profiles that not only have particular truth values, but also particular use values and exchange values, and so are radically caught up in knowledge, power and profit. This is yet another way where radical forms of enclosure must be presumed, if only provisionally, in order to reckon in particular mathematical ways.

15. Crucially, this linkage of Bayes's Rule and ontological transformativity also allows us to harness the generalizations underlying the mathematics itself—and thus the calculative possibilities offered via a range of mathematical affordances.

16. Three particularly important examples of careful empirical work leading to broad conceptual frameworks in regards to the relation between language, culture, inference, and epistemology are Enfield (2009), Hutchins (1980), and Sidnell (2005). I do not here focus on the linguistic mediation of inference and ontology, as I have foregrounded this process in other work, when the kinds in question are 'mental states' (Kockelman 2010b). And Kockelman (2007a) shows the radically distributed nature of such ontological assumptions, insofar as they constitute modes of representational agency.

17. And, indeed, Bayes's equation per se only applies to transformativity #2.

18. Moreover, the four enclosures described here are just a small sliver of possible modes of objectification. There are other styles of reasoning underlying inference, other forms of mathematics underlying machine learning, other kinds of sieves besides spam filters, and of course other aesthetic sensibilities as to how to suss out the true nature of a suspicious guest (as well as recount and imagine such sussings).

REFERENCES

Agamben, Giorgio. 1998. *Homo Sacer: Sovereign Power and Bare Life.* Stanford, CA: Stanford University Press.

Agha, Asif. 2007. *Language and Social Relations.* Cambridge, UK: Cambridge University Press.

Arendt, Hannah. 1958. *The Human Condition.* Chicago: University of Chicago Press.

Arfken, George B., and Hans Jurgen-Weber. 1995. *Mathematical Methods for Physicists.* 4th edition. San Diego, CA: Academic Press.

Aristotle. 2001a. *Politics.* In *The Basic Works of Aristotle,* edited by Richard McKeon, 1051–1067. The Modern Library. New York: Random House.

Aristotle. 2001b. *Physics.* In *The Basic Works of Aristotle,* edited by Richard McKeon, 240–242. The Modern Library. New York: Random House.

Aristotle. 2001c. *The Categories.* In *The Basic Works of Aristotle,* edited by Richard McKeon, 240–242. The Modern Library. New York: Random House.

Aristotle. 2001d. *Nicomachean Ethics.* In *The Basic Works of Aristotle,* edited by Richard McKeon, 1010–1012. The Modern Library. New York: Random House.

Austin, John. 1962. *How to Do Things with Words.* Oxford: Clarendon.

Bate, Bernard. 2014. "Oratory, Rhetoric, Politics." In *Cambridge Handbook of Linguistic Anthropology,* edited by N. J. Enfield, P. Kockelman, and J. Sidnell, 537–558. Cambridge, UK: Cambridge University Press.

Bateson, Gregory. 1972 [1954]. *Steps To an Ecology of Mind.* New York: Ballantine.

Bazin, André. 1960. "The Ontology of the Photographic Image." *Film Quarterly* 13(4):4–9.

Benjamin, Walter. 1968a. "The Work of Art in the Age of Mechanical Reproduction." In *Illuminations,* edited by Hannah Arendt, 217–252. New York: Schocken.

Benjamin, Walter. 1968b. "Theses on the Philosophy of History." In *Illuminations,* edited by Hannah Arendt, 253–264. New York: Schocken.

Benkler, Yochai. 2006. *The Wealth of Networks.* New Haven, CT: Yale University Press.

Berger, John. 2015. *Portraits: John Berger on Artists.* New York: Verso.

Bergson, Henri. 1988. *Matter and Memory.* New York: Zone.

Bird, Steven, Ewan Kleine, and Edward Loper. 2009. *Natural Language Processing with Python.* Sebastopol, CA: O'Reilly.

Boas, Franz. 1889. "On Alternating Sounds." *American Anthropologist* 2(1):47–53.

Boole, George. 1958 [1854]. *An Investigation of The Laws of Thought.* New York: Dover.

Boyle, James. 1997. *Shamans, Software and Spleens: Law and Construction of the Information Society.* Cambridge, MA: Harvard University Press.

Boyle, James. 2003. "The Second Enclosure Movement and the Construction of the Public Domain." *Law and Contemporary Problems* 66:33–75.

Bourdieu, Pierre. 1992 [1977]. *Outline of a Theory of Practice.* Cambridge, UK: Cambridge University Press.

Braudel, Fernand. 1992. *The Structures of Everyday Life.* Berkeley: University of California Press.

Brillouin, Léon. 1962 [1956]. *Science and Information Theory.* 2nd ed. London: Academic Press.

Brunton, Finn. 2010. "Roar So Wildly: Spam, Technology and Language." *Radical Philosophy* 164:1–7.

Brunton, Finn. 2012. "Constitutive Interference: Spam and Online Communities." *Representations* 117(1):30–58.

Bühler, K. 1982 [1934]. *Sprachtheorie: die Darstellungsfunktion der Sprache.* Stuttgart: Gustav Fisher.

Butler, Samuel. 1872. *Erewhon.* Project Gutenberg.

Ceruzzi, Paul E. 2000. *A History of Modern Computing.* Cambridge, MA: MIT Press.

Chiu, Eugene, Jocelyn Lin, Brok McFerron, Noshirwan Petigara, and Satwiksai Seshasai. 2005. *The Mathematical Theory of Claude Shannon.* Unpublished Manuscript.

Chomsky, Noam. 1956. "Three Models for the Description of Language." *IRE Transactions on Information Theory* (2):113–124.

Chomsky, Noam. 1965 *Aspects of the Theory of Syntax.* Cambridge, MA: MIT Press.

Church, Alonzo. 1941. *The Calculi of Lambda-Conversion.* Princeton, NJ: Princeton University Press.

Clynes, Manfred E., and Nathan S. Kline. 1960. "Cyborgs and Space." *Astronautics,* (September 26–27) 74–76.

Colapietro, Vincent M. 1989. *Peirce's Approach to the Self: A Semiotic Perspective on Human Subjectivity.* Albany: State University of New York Press.

Coleman, Gabriella. 2013. *Coding Freedom: The Ethics and Aesthetics of Hacking.* Princeton, NJ: Princeton University Press.

Crapanzano, Vincent. 1992. *Hermes' Dilemma and Hamlet's Desire.* Cambridge, MA: Harvard University Press.

DeLanda, Manuel. 2011. *Philosophy and Simulation: The Emergence of Synthetic Reason.* London: Continuum.

Deleuze, Gilles. 1991. *Bergsonism.* Translated by Hugh Tomlinson and Barbara Habberjam. New York: Zone.

Deleuze, Gilles. 1992. "Postscript on the Societies of Control." October 59:3–7.

Deleuze, Gilles. 1994 [1968]. *Difference and Repetition.* New York: Columbia University Press.

Dibbell, Julian. 1999. *My Tiny Life.* New York: Henry Holt and Company.

Dixon, R. M. W. 1980. "Speech and Song Styles: Avoidance Styles." In *The Languages of Australia,* by R. M. W. Dixon, 58–68. Cambridge, UK: Cambridge University Press.

Dorogovtsev, S. N., and J. F. F. Mendes. 2003. *Evolution of Networks: From Biological Networks to the Internet and WWW.* Oxford: Oxford University Press.

Douglas, Mary. 1966. *Purity and Danger.* London: Routledge & Kegan Paul.

Dreyfus, Hubert L. 1991. *Being-in-the-World: A Commentary on Heidegger's "Being and Time."* Division 1. Cambridge, MA: MIT Press.

Du Bois, Jack W. 2014. "Towards a Dialogic Syntax." *Cognitive Linguistics* 25(3):359–410.

Dummett, Michael. 1981. *Frege: Philosophy of Language.* Cambridge, MA: Harvard University Press.

Edwards, Paul N. 1996. *The Closed World: Computers and the Politics of Discourse in Cold War America.* Cambridge, MA: MIT Press.

Elyachar, Julia. 2010. "Phatic Labor, Infrastructure, and the Question of Empowerment in Cairo." *American Ethnographer* 37(3):452–464.

Enfield, N. J. 2009. "The Anatomy of Meaning: Speech, Gesture, and Composite Utterances." Cambridge, UK: Cambridge University Press.

Enfield, N. J. 2013. *Relationship Thinking: Agency, Enchrony, and Human Sociality.* Oxford: Oxford University Press.

Engelbart, Douglas C. 1962. "Augmenting Human Intellect." SRI Summary Report AFOSR-3223. Office of Scientific Research. Washington, DC.

Erikson, Jon. 2008. *Hacking: The Art of Exploitation.* San Francisco: No Starch Press.

Essinger, James. 2004. *Jacquard's Web: How a Hand-Loom Led to the Birth of the Information Age.* Oxford: Oxford University Press.

Frege, Gottlob. 1960 [1892]. "On Sense and Reference." In *Translations from the Philosophical Writings of Gottlob Frege,* edited by Peter Geach and Max Black, 56–78. Oxford: Blackwell.

French, Robert M. 2000. "The Turing Test: The First 50 Years." *Trends in Cognitive Science* 4(3):115–122.

Freud, Sigmund. 1999 [1899]. *The Interpretation of Dreams.* Translated by Joyce Crick. Oxford: Oxford University Press.

Friedl, J. 2006. *Mastering Regular Expressions.* Sebastopol, CA: O'Reilly.

Fustel De Coulanges, Numa Denis. 1955 [1873]. *The Ancient City.* New York: Anchor.

Gell, Alfred. 1998. *Art and Agency.* Oxford: Oxford University Press.

Gershon, Illana, and Paul Manning. 2014. "Language and Media." In *The Cambridge Handbook of Linguistic Anthropology*, edited by N. J. Enfield, P. Kockelman, and J. Sidnell, 539–556. Cambridge, UK: Cambridge University Press.

Gibson, James. 1986 [1979]. *The Ecological Approach to Visual Perception.* Boston: Houghton Mifflin.

Ginzburg, Carlo. 1989. "Clues: Roots of an Evidential Paradigm." In *Clues, Myths, and the Historical Method*, by Carlo Ginzburg, 96–125. Baltimore: The Johns Hopkins University Press.

Goffman, Erving. 1959. *The Presentation of Self in Everyday Life.* New York: Doubleday.

Goffman, Erving. 1974. *Frame Analysis.* Boston: Northeastern University Press.

Goffman, Erving. 1981a. "Footing." In *Forms of Talk*, by Erving Goffman, 124–159. Philadelphia: University of Pennsylvania Press.

Goffman, Erving. 1981b. "Replies and Responses." In *Forms of Talk*, by Erving Goffman, 13–56. Philadelphia: University of Pennsylvania Press.

Goffman, Erving. 1983. "The Interaction Order." *American Sociological Review* 48(1):1–17.

Golub, Alexander. 2010. "Being in the World (of Warcraft): Raiding, Realism, and Knowledge Production in a Massively Multiplayer Online Game." *Anthropological Quarterly* 83(1):17–46.

Gombrich, E. H. 1979. *The Sense of Order.* Ithaca, NY: Cornell University Press.

Goodfellow, Ian, Yoshua Bengio, and Aaron Courville. 2016. *Deep Learning.* Cambridge: MIT Press.

Graham, Paul. 2004. *Hackers and Painters.* Sebastopol, CA: O'Reilly.

Greenberg, Joseph. 1980 [1966]. *Language Universals: With Special Reference to Feature Hierarchies.* The Hague: Mouton & Co. 1966.

Grice, H. P. 1989. *Studies in the Ways of Words.* Cambridge, MA: Harvard University Press.

Gumperz, John, and Dell Hymes, eds. 1986 [1972]. *Directions in Sociolinguistics: The Ethnography of Communication.* New York: Basil Blackwell.

Hacking, Ian. 2001. *An Introduction to Probability and Inductive Logic.* Cambridge, UK: Cambridge University Press.

Hacking, Ian. 2002. *Historical Ontology.* Cambridge, UK: Harvard University Press.

Halliday, M. A. K., and Ruqaiya Hasan. 1976. *Cohesion in English.* London: Longman.

Hanks, William F. 1990. *Referential Practice.* Chicago: University of Chicago Press.

Hansen, Mark B. N. 2004. *New Philosophy for New Media.* Cambridge, UK: MIT Press.

Haugeland, John. 1998a. "The Intentionality All-Stars." In *Having Thought: Essays in the Metaphysics of Mind,* by John Haugeland, 127–170. Cambridge, MA: Harvard University Press.

Haugeland, John. 1998b. "Mind Embodied and Embedded." In *Having Thought: Essays in the Metaphysics of Mind,* by John Haugeland, 207–237. Cambridge, MA: Harvard University Press.

Haugeland, John. 1981. "Analog and Analog." *Philosophical Topics* 12(1):213–226.

Hayles, N. Katherine. 1999. *How We Became Posthuman.* Chicago: University of Chicago Press.

Heidegger, Martin. 1977 [1954]. *Basic Writings: From Being and Time (1927) to The Task of Thinking (1964).* New York: HarperCollins.

Heidegger, Martin. 1996 [1927]. *Being and Time.* Translated by Joan Stambaugh. Albany: SUNY University Press.

Heim, Irene, and Angelika Kratzner. 1998. *Semantics in Generative Grammar.* Oxford and Malden, MA: Blackwell.

Helmreich, Stefan. 1998. *Silicon Second Nature: Culturing Artificial Life in a Digital World.* Berkeley: University of California Press.

Helmreich, Stefan. 2016. "Gravity's Reverb: Listening to Space-Time, or Articulating the Sounds of Gravitational-Wave Detection." *Cultural Anthropology* 31(4): 464–492.

Hill, Jane, and Judith Irvine, eds. 1992. *Responsibility and Evidence in Oral Discourse.* Cambridge, UK: Cambridge University Press.

Hill, Jane H., and Bruce Mannheim. 1992. "Language and World View." *Annual Review of Anthropology* 21:381–406.

Hobbes, Thomas. 1994 [1668]. *Leviathan.* Edited by E. M. Curley. Indianapolis, IN: Hackett.

Hutchins, Edwin. 1980. *Culture and Inference.* Cambridge, MA: Harvard University Press.

Hymes, Dell. 1962. "The Ethnography of Speaking." In *Anthropology and Human Behavior,* edited by T. Gladwin and W. C. Sturtevant, 13–53. Washington, DC: Anthropology Society of Washington.

Inoue, Miyako. 2006. *Vicarious Language: Gender and Linguistic Modernity in Japan.* Berkeley: University of California Press.

Inoue, Miyako. 2011. "Stenography and Ventriloquism in Late Nineteenth-Century Japan." *Language & Communication* 31(3):181–190.

Jakobson, Roman. 1990a. "The Speech Event and the Functions of Language," in *On Language,* edited by L. R. Waugh and M. Monville, 69–79. Cambridge, MA: Harvard University Press.

Jakobson, Roman. 1990b. "Shifters and Verbal Categories." In *On Language,* edited by L. R. Waugh and M. Monville, 386–392. Cambridge, MA: Harvard University Press.

James, William. 1985. The Self. In *Psychology: The Briefer Course*, by William James, 43–83. Notre Dame: University of Notre Dame Press.

Jurafsky, Daniel, and James H. Martin. 2008. *Speech and Language Processing*. 2nd ed. Upper Saddle River, NJ: Pearson Prentice Hall.

Kant, Immanuel. 1965 [1781]. *Critique of Pure Reason*. Translated by Norman Smith. New York: St. Martin's Press.

Kant, Immanuel. 2000 [1790]. *Critique of the Power of Judgment*. Translated and edited by Paul Guyer. Cambridge and New York: Cambridge University Press, 2000.

Kay, Alan, and Adele Goldberg. 1977. "Personal Dynamic Media." *Computer* 10:31–41.

Kelty, Christopher M. 2011. "Logical Instruments: Regular Expressions, Artificial Intelligence, and Thinking about Thinking." In *The Search for a Theory of Cognition: Early Mechanisms and New Ideas*, edited by Stefano Franchi and Francesco Bianchini. Amsterdam, New York: Rodopi.

Kelty, Christopher M. 2008. *Two Bits: The Cultural Significance of Free Software*. Durham, NC: Duke University Press.

Kernighan, Brian, and Dennis Ritchie. 1988 [1978]. *The C Programming Language*. 2nd ed. Englewood Cliffs, NJ: Prentice Hall.

Kittler, Friedrich A. 1989 [1986]. *Gramophone, Film, Typewriter*. Stanford, CA: Stanford University Press.

Kittler, Friedrich A. 1996 [1993]. *The History of Communication Media*. Archived at *ctheory.net, Special Issue:* ga 114. Edited by Arthur and Marilouise Kroker. www.ctheory.net/text_file.asp?pick=45.

Kleene, S. C. 1956. "Representations of Events in Nerve Nets and Finite Automata." In *Automata Studies*, edited by C. Shannon and J. McCarthy, 3–41. Princeton, NJ: Princeton University Press.

Kockelman, Paul. 1999. "Poetic Function and Logical Form, Ideal Languages and Forms of Life." *Chicago Anthropology Exchange* 39:34–50.

Kockelman, Paul. 2003. "The Meaning of Interjections among the Q'eqchi' Maya: From Emotive Reaction to Social and Discursive Action." *Cultural Anthropology* 44(4):467–490.

Kockelman, Paul. 2004. "Stance and Subjectivity." *Journal of Linguistic Anthropology* 14(2):127–150.

Kockelman, Paul. 2005. "The Semiotic Stance." *Semiotica* 157:233–304.

Kockelman, Paul. 2006a. "A Semiotic Ontology of the Commodity." *Journal of Linguistic Anthropology* 16(1):76–102.

Kockelman, Paul. 2006b. "Residence in the World: Affordances, Instruments, Actions, Roles, and Identities." *Semiotica* 162(1):19–71.

Kockelman, Paul. 2007a. "Agency: The Relation between Meaning, Power, and Knowledge." Current Anthropology 48(3): 375–401.

Kockelman, Paul. 2007b. "From Status to Contract Revisited: Modality, Temporality, Circulation, and Subjectivity." *Anthropological Theory* 7(2):151–176.

Kockelman, Paul. 2009. "The Complexity of Discourse." *Journal of Quantitative Linguistics* 16(1): 1–39.

Kockelman, Paul. 2010a. *Language, Culture and Mind: Natural Constructions and Social Kinds*. Cambridge, UK: Cambridge University Press.

Kockelman, Paul. 2010b. "Value is Life Under an Interpretation: Existential Commitments, Instrumental Reasons, and Disorienting Metaphors." *Anthropological Theory* 10(1):149–162.

Kockelman, Paul. 2011a. "Biosemiosis, Technocognition, and Sociogenesis: Selection and Significance in a Multiverse of Sieving and Serendipity." *Current Anthropology* 52(5):711–739.

Kockelman, Paul. 2011b. "A Mayan Ontology of Poultry: Selfhood, Affect, Animals, and Ethnography." *Language in Society* 40(4):427–454.

Kockelman, Paul. 2013a. *Agent, Person, Subject, Self: A Theory of Ontology, Interaction, and Infrastructure.* Oxford: Oxford University Press.

Kockelman, Paul. 2013b. "Information is the Enclosure of Meaning: Cybernetics, Semiotics, and Alternative Theories of Information." *Language and Communication* 33(2):115–127.

Kockelman, Paul. 2014a. "Linguistic Anthropology and Critical Theory." In *The Cambridge Handbook of Linguistic Anthropology*, edited by Nick J. Enfield, Paul Kockelman, and Jack Sidnell, 603–625. Cambridge, UK: Cambridge University Press.

Kockelman, Paul. 2014b. "Linguistic Anthropology in the Age of Language Automata." In *The Cambridge Handbook of Linguistic Anthropology*, edited by Nick J. Enfield, Paul Kockelman, and Jack Sidnell, 708–733. Cambridge, UK: Cambridge University Press.

Kockelman, Paul. 2015. "Four Theories of Things: Aristotle, Marx, Heidegger, and Peirce." *Signs in Society* 3(1):153–192.

Kockelman, Paul. 2016a. *The Chicken and the Quetzal. Incommensurate Ontologies and Portable Values in the Cloudforests of Highland Guatemala.* Durham, NC: Duke University Press.

Kockelman, Paul. 2016b. "Meeting the Universe Two Thirds of the Way." *Signs and Society*: 4(2): 215–243.

Kockelman, Paul. 2017a. "Semiotic Agency." In *Distributed Agency*, edited by N. J. Enfield and Paul Kockelman, 25–38. Oxford: Oxford University Press.

Kockelman, Paul. 2017b. "Gnomic Agency." In *Distributed Agency*, edited by N. J. Enfield and Paul Kockelman, 15–23. Oxford: Oxford University Press.

Kockelman, Paul. 2017c. "Temporality and Replacement among the Maya." *Journal de la Société des Américanistes.*

Kockelman, Paul, and Anya Bernstein. 2012. "Semiotic Technologies, Temporal Reckoning, and the Portability of Meaning: Or, Modern Modes of Temporality—Just How 'Abstract' are They?" *Anthropological Theory* 12(3):320–348.

Kripke, Saul A. 1980. *Naming and Necessity.* Cambridge, MA: Harvard University Press.

Kripke, Saul A. 1982. *Wittgenstein: On Rules and Private Language.* Cambridge, MA: Harvard University Press.

Lakoff, George and Mark Johnson. 1980. *Metaphors We Live By.* Chicago: University of Chicago Press.

Lambrecht, Knud. 1996. *Information Structure and Sentence Form.* Cambridge, UK: Cambridge University Press.

Laplace, Pierre-Simon. 1951 [1820]. *A Philosophical Essay on Probabilities.* New York: Dover.

Larkin, Brian. 2004. "Degraded Images, Distorted Sounds: Nigerian Video and the Infrastructure of Piracy." *Public Culture* 16(2):289–314.

Larkin, Brian. 2008. *Signal and Noise: Media, Infrastructure and Urban Culture in Nigeria.* Durham, NC: Duke University Press.

Latour, Bruno. 2005. *Reassembling the Social.* Oxford: Oxford University Press.

Latour, Bruno. 1988. *The Pasteurization of France.* Cambridge, MA: Harvard University Press.

Lee, Penny. 1996. *The Whorf Theory Complex: A Critical Reconstruction.* Amsterdam: John Benjamins.

Lessig, Lawrence 2006. *Code: Version 2.0.* New York: Basic Books.

Levi-Strauss, Claude. 1969 [1949]. *The Elementary Structures of Kinship.* Boston: Beacon.

Litman, Jessica. 2000. *Digital Copyright: Protecting Intellectual Property on the Internet.* New York: Prometheus.

Lucy, John A. 1992a. *Language, Diversity, and Thought.* Cambridge, UK: Cambridge University Press.

Lucy, John A. 1992b. *Grammatical Categories and Cognition.* Cambridge, UK: Cambridge University Press.

Lucy, John A., ed. 1993. *Reflexive Language: Reported Speech and Metapragmatics.* Cambridge, UK: Cambridge University Press.

MacKay, Donald M. 1969a. *Information, Mechanism, and Meaning.* Cambridge, MA: MIT Press.

MacKay, Donald M. 1969b. "Measuring Information." In *Information, Mechanism and Meaning*, by Donald MacKay, 9–18. Cambridge, MA: MIT Press.

MacKay, Donald M. 1969c [1960]. "Meaning and Mechanism." In *Information, Mechanism and Meaning*, by Donald MacKay, 19–38. Cambridge, MA: MIT Press.

MacKay, Donald M. 1969d [1950]. "In Search of Basic Symbols." In *Information, Mechanism and Meaning*, by Donald MacKay, 41–55. Cambridge, MA: MIT Press.

MacKay, Donald M. 1969e [1956]. "Operational Aspects of Some Fundamental Concepts of Human Communication." In *Information, Mechanism and Meaning*, by Donald MacKay, 56–78. Cambridge, MA: MIT Press.

MacKay, Donald M. 1969f [1956]. "The Place of 'Meaning' in the Theory of Information." In *Information, Mechanism and Meaning*, by Donald MacKay, 79–83. Cambridge, MA: MIT Press.

MacKay, Donald M. 1969g [1964]. "Communication and Meaning—a Functional Approach." In *Information, Mechanism and Meaning*, by Donald MacKay, 105–119. Cambridge, MA: MIT Press.

MacKay, Donald M. 1969h [1951]. "The Nomenclature of Information Theory with Postscript on Structural Information-Content and Optical Resolution." In *Information, Mechanism and Meaning*, by Donald MacKay, 165–189. Cambridge, MA: MIT Press.

Malinowski, Bronisław. 1922. *Argonauts of the Western Pacific.* London: Routledge.

Malinowski, Bronisław. 1936. "The Problem of Meaning in Primitive Languages." In *The Meaning of Meaning*, edited by C. K. Ogden and A. I. Richards, 296–336. New York: Harcourt, Brace.

Manning, Paul, and Ilana Gershon. 2013. "Animating Interaction." *Hau: Journal of Ethnographic Theory* 3(3):107–137.

Manovich, Lev. 2001. *The Language of New Media.* Cambridge: MIT Press.

Marx, Karl. 1967 [1867]. *Capital.* Volume 1. Edited by Frederick Engels. New York: International Publishers.

Massumi, Brian. 2002. *Parables for the Virtual.* Durham, NC: Duke University Press.

McCarthy, John. 1960. "Recursive Functions of Symbolic Expressions and Their Computation by Machine." *Communications of the ACM* 3(4):184–195.

McCulloch, Warren S., and Walter Pitts. 1943. "A Logical Calculus of the Ideas Immanent in Nervous Activity." *Bulletin of Mathematic Biophysics* 5:24–56.

McGrayne, Sharon Bertsch. 2011. *The Theory That Would Not Die: How Bayes' Rule Cracked the Enigma Code, Hunted Down Russian Submarines, and Emerged Triumphant from Two Centuries of Controversy.* New Haven, CT: Yale University Press.

McLuhan, Marshall. 1996 [1964]. *Understanding Media.* New York: McGraw Hill.

Mead, George Herbert. 1934. *Mind, Self, and Society from the Standpoint of a Social Behavioralist.* Edited by Charles S. Morris. Chicago: University of Chicago Press.

Messeri, Lisa. 2016. Placing Outer Space: An Earthly Ethnography of Other Worlds. Durham, NC: Duke University Press.

Mill, John Stuart 2002 [1843]. *A System of Logic.* Honolulu: University Press of the Pacific.

Mirowski, Phillip. 2001. *Machine Dreams: Economics Becomes a Cyborg Science.* Cambridge, UK: Cambridge University Press.

Moody, Glyn. 2001. *Rebel Code: Linux and the Open Source Revolution.* New York Basic Books.

Munn, Nancy. 1992. *The Fame of Gawa.* Durham, NC: Duke University Press.

Nietzsche, Friedrich. 1967 [1887]. *On The Genealogy of Morals* and *Ecce Homo.* Translated by Walter Kaufmann. New York: Vintage.

Parmentier, Richard J. 1994. *Signs in Society: Studies in Semiotic Anthropology.* Bloomington: Indiana University Press.

Peirce, Charles Sanders. 1887. "Logical Machines." *American Journal of Psychology* 1(1):165–170.

Peirce, Charles Sanders. 1902. Entry on "Virtual." In *Dictionary of Philosophy and Psychology.* Vol. 2, edited by James Mark Baldwin, 763. New York: Macmillan, 1902. Reprinted in *Charles Sanders Peirce, Collected Papers.* Vol. 6. [1935] 1958, edited by Harles Hartshorne, Paul Weiss, and Arthur Burks, 372. Cambridge, MA: The Belknap Press of the Harvard University Press.

Peirce, Charles Sanders. 1955a. "Logic as Semiotic: The Theory of Signs." In *Philosophical Writings of Peirce,* edited by Justus Buchler, pp. 98–119. New York: Dover Publications.

Peirce, Charles Sanders. 1955b. "The Principles of Phenomenology." In *Philosophical Writings of Peirce,* edited by Justus Buchler, 74–97. New York: Dover.

Peirce, Charles Sanders. 1955c. "Pragmatism in Retrospect: A Last Formulation." In *Philosophical Writings of Peirce,* edited by Justus Buchler, 269–289. New York: Dover.

Peirce, Charles Sanders. 1992 [1867]. "On a New List of Categories." In *The Essential Peirce,* Vol. 1 1867–1893, edited by Nathan Hauser and Christian Kloesel, 1–10. Bloomington: Indiana University Press.

Peirce, Charles Sanders. 1992 [1878]. "Deduction, Induction, and Hypothesis." In *The Essential Peirce.* Vol. 1, edited by Nathan Houser and Christian Kloesel, 186–199. Bloomington: Indiana University Press

Peirce, Charles Sanders. 1998 [1903]. "Nomenclature and Divisions of Triadic Relations So Far As They Are Determined." In *The Essential Peirce,* Vol. 2 (1893–1913), edited by Nathan Hauser and Christian Kloesel, 289–299. Bloomington: Indiana University Press.

Peirce, Charles Sanders. 1998 [1903]. "Pragmatism as the Logic of Abduction." In *The Essential Peirce*, Volume 2, edited by Nathan Houser and Christian Kloesel, 226–241. Bloomington: Indiana University Press.

Peirce, Charles Sanders. 1998 [1904]. "New Elements." In *The Essential Peirce,* Vol. 2 (1893–1913), edited by Nathan Hauser and Christian Kloesel, 300–324. Bloomington: Indiana University Press. Petzold, Charles. 2000. *Code: The Hidden Language of Computer Hardware and Software.* Redmond, WA: Microsoft Press.

Piccinini, G. 2004. "The First Computational theory of Mind and Brain." *Synthese* 141(2):175–215.

Polanyi, Karl 1957. *The Great Transformation.* Boston: Beacon.

Putnam, Hilary. 1975. "The Meaning of 'Meaning'." In *Philosophical Papers: Mind, Language and Reality*, Vol. 2, by Hilary Putnam, 215–271. Cambridge, UK: Cambridge University Press.

M. O. Rabin, and D. Scott. 1959. "Finite Automata and their Decision Problems." *IBM Journal of Research and Development* 3(2):114–125.

Quine, W. O. 1969. *Ontological Relativity and Other Essays.* New York: Columbia University Press.

Reif, Phillip. 1965. *Fundamentals of Statistical and Thermal Physics.* New York: McGraw-Hill.

Sacks, Harvey, Emmanuel Schegloff, and Gail Jefferson. 1974. "A Simplest Systematics for the Organization of Turn-Taking for Conversation." *Language* 50(4):696–735.

Sahlins, Marshall. 1972. *Stone Age Economics.* Chicago: Aldine-Atherton.

Sapir, Edward. 1949 [1924]. "The Grammarian and His Language." In *Selected Writings in Language, Culture, and Personality*, edited by David G. Mandelbaum, 150–159. Berkeley: University of California Press.

Sapir, Edward. 1985 [1945]. "Grading: A Study in Semantics." In *Selected Writings in Language, Culture, and Personality,* edited by David G. Mandelbaum, 122–149. Berkeley: University of California Press.

Sapir, Edward. 1985 [1927]. "The Unconscious Patterning of Behavior in Society." In *Selected Writings in Language, Culture, and Personality*, edited by David G. Mandelbaum, 544–559. Berkeley: University of California Press.

Sapir, Edward. 1985 [1933]. "Language." In *Selected Writings in Language, Culture, and Personality*, edited by David G. Mandelbaum, 7–32. Berkeley: University of California Press.

Saussure, Ferdinand de. 1983 [1916]. *Course in General Linguistics.* La Salle, Illinois: Open Court Press.

Saygin, Ayse Pinar, Ilyas Cicekli, and Varol Akman. 2001. "Turing Test: 50 Years Later." *Minds and Machines* 10(4): 463–518.

Schmitt, Carl. 1996 [1932]. *The Concept of the Political.* Chicago: University of Chicago Press.

Schrödinger, Ernst. 1944. *What is Life?* New York: Dover.

Scott, James C. 1985. *Weapons of the Weak: Everyday Forms of Peasant Resistance.* New Haven, CT: Yale University Press.

Seaver, Nick. 2015. "The Nice Thing about Context is That Everyone Has It." *Media, Culture and Society* 37(7):1101–1109.

Seaver, Nick. 2011. "This is Not a Copy": Mechanical Fidelity and the Re-Enacting Piano. In *Special Issue: The Sense Of Sound*. Edited by Rey Chow and James A. Steintrager. *Differences: A Journal of Feminist Cultural Studies* 22(2–3):54–73.

Serres, Michael. 2007 [1980]. *The Parasite*. Minneapolis: Minnesota Press.

Shannon, Claude E. 1937. "A Symbolic Analysis of Relay and Switching Circuits." Unpublished PhD diss., Massachusetts Institute of Technology.

Shannon, Claude E. 1946. "Communication Theory of Secrecy Systems" which first appeared in a confidential report entitled A Mathematical Theory of Cryptography and dated Sept.1, 1946.

Shannon, Claude E. 1948. "A Mathematical Theory of Communication." *The Bell System Technical Journal* 27:379–423.

Shannon, Claude E., and Warren Weaver. 1963 [1949]. *The Mathematical Theory of Communication*. Illinois: University of Illinois Press.

Sidnell, Jack. 2005. *Talk and Practical Epistemology*. Amsterdam: J. Benjamins.

Silverstein, Michael. 1976. "Shifters, Linguistic Categories and Cultural Description." In *Meaning in Anthropology*, edited by K. Basso and H. Selby, 11–55. Albuquerque, NM: University of New Mexico Press.

Silverstein, Michael. 1984. "On the Pragmatic 'Poetry' of Prose: Parallelism, Repetition, and Cohesive Structure in the Time Course of Dyadic Conversation." In *Meaning, Form, and Use in Context: Linguistic Applications*. Georgetown University Round Table on Languages and Linguistics, 1984. Edited by Deborah Schiffrin, 181–199. Washington, DC: Georgetown University Press.

Silverstein Michael, and Greg Urban, eds. 1996. *Natural Histories of Discourse*. Chicago: University of Chicago.

Simon, Herbert A. 1996. *The Sciences of the Artificial*. Cambridge, MA: MIT Press.

Simondon, Gilbert. 1980 [1958]. On the Mode of Existence of Technical Objects. Translated by Ninian Mellamphy. University of Western Ontario. Paris: Aubier, Editions Montaigne.

Sipser, Michael. 2007. *Introduction to the Theory of Computation*. New Delhi: Cengage Learning.

Skagestad, Peter. 1998. "Peirce, Virtuality, and Semiotic." Paper presented at Proceedings of Twentieth World Congress of Philosophy. Boston, MA.

Sperber, Dan, and Diedre Wilson. 1986. *Relevance*. Oxford: Blackwell.

Stallman, Richard M. 2010. *Free Software, Free Society: Selected Essays of Richard M. Stallman*. 2nd ed. Boston: Soho Books.

Star, Susan Leigh. 1999. "The Ethnography of Infrastructure." *American Behavioral Scientist* 43(3): 377–391.

Star, Susan, and James Griesemer. 1989. "Institutional Ecology, 'Translations' and Boundary Objects: Amateurs and Professionals in Berkeley's Museum of Vertebrate Zoology, 1907–1939." Social Studies of Science 19(3): 387–420.

Stephenson, Neal. 1999. *In the Beginning Was the Command Line*. New York: Avon Books.

Stiegler, Bernard. 1998. *Technics and Time, 1: The Fault of Epimetheus*. Stanford: Stanford University Press.

Strogatz, Steven H. 1994. *Nonlinear Dynamics and Chaos*. Cambridge, MA: Perseus.

Suchman, Lucy A. 2007. *Human-Machine Reconfigurations*. Cambridge, UK: Cambridge University Press.

Sussman, Gerald Jay, and Hal Abelson. 2001. *The Structure of and Interpretation of Computer Programs.* Cambridge, MA: MIT Press.

Tambiah, Stanley. 1968. "The Magic Power of Words." *Man* 3(2):175–208.

Tannen, Deborah. 1987. "Repetition in Conversation: Towards a Poetics of Talk." *Language* 63(3):574–605.

Tarski, Alfred. 1944. "The Semantical Concept of Truth and the Foundations of Semantics." *Philosophy and Phenomenological Research* 4:341–375.

Taylor, Charles. 1989. *Sources of the Self.* Cambridge, MA: Harvard University Press.

Tedlock, Dennis, and Bruce Mannheim, eds. 1995. *The Dialogic Emergence of Culture.* Champaign-Urbana: University of Illinois Press.

Thompson, Ken. 1968. "Programming Techniques: Regular Expression Search Algorithm." *Communications of the ACM* 11(6):419–422.

Tomasello, Michael, and Josep Call. 1997. *Primate Cognition.* Oxford: Oxford University Press.

Tomasello, Michael 2008. Origins of Human Communication. Cambridge, MA: MIT Press.

Turing, Alan. 2004 [1936]. "On Computable Numbers, with an Application to the *Entscheidungs* problem." In *The Essential Turing*, edited by B. Jack Copeland, 58–90. Oxford: Oxford University Press.

Turing, Alan. 2004 [1950]. "Computing Machinery and Intelligence." In *The Essential Turing*, edited by B. Jack Copeland, 433–464. Oxford: Oxford University Press.

Van Valin, Robert D., Jr., and Randy J. LaPolla. 1997. *Syntax: Structure, Meaning and Function.* Cambridge: Cambridge University Press.

Varro, Marcus Terentius. 1938 [43 bc]. *On the Latin Language.* Translated by Roland G. Kent. Cambridge, MA: Harvard University Press.

Veblen, Thorstein. 1899. *The Theory of the Leisure Class.* New York: MacMillan.

Victor, Bret. 2006. "Magic Ink: Information Software and the Graphical Interface."

von Humboldt, Alexander. 1999. *On Language.* Cambridge, UK: Cambridge University Press.

von Neumann, John, and Oskar Morgenstern. 1944. *Theory of Games and Economic Behavior.* Princeton, NJ: Princeton University Press.

von Schnitzler, Antina. 2008. "Citizenship Prepaid: Water, Calculability, and Techno-Politics in South Africa." *Journal of Southern African Studies* 34(4):899–917.

Wardrip-Fruin, Noah, and Nick Montfort, editors. 2003. *The New Media Reader.* Cambridge, MA: MIT Press.

Weber, Max. 1949. *The Methodology of the Social Sciences.* Glencoe, IL: Free Press.

Weber, Max. 1976. *The Protestant Ethic and the Spirit of Capitalism.* New York: Scribner's.

Weber, Max. 1978. *Economy and Society.* Berkeley: University of California Press.

Whorf, Benjamin L. 1956 [1937]. "Grammatical Categories." In *Language, Thought, and Reality*, edited by John B. Carroll, 87–101. Cambridge, MA: The MIT Press.

Whorf, Benjamin L. 1956 [1939]. "The Relation of Habitual Thought and Behavior to Language." In *Language, Thought, and Reality*, edited by John B. Carroll, 134–159. Cambridge, MA: The MIT Press.

Wilf, Eitan Y. 2013a. "From Media Technologies That Reproduce Seconds to Media Technologies That Reproduce Thirds: A Peircean Perspective on Stylistic Fidelity and Style-Reproducing Computerized Algorithms." *Signs and Society* 1(2): 185–211.

Wilf, Eitan Y. 2013b. "Toward an Anthropology of Computer-Mediated, Algorithmic Forms of Sociality." *Current Anthropology* 54(6):716–739.

Wiener, Norbert. 1948. *Cybernetics: Or, Control and Communication in the Animal and the Machine.* Cambridge, MA: MIT Press.

Wittgenstein, Ludwig. 1961 [1921]. *Tractatus Logico-Philosophicus.* London: Routledge and Kegan Paul.

Wittgenstein, Ludwig. 1958 [1953]. *Philosophical Investigations.* New York: MacMillan.

Zimmerman, Phillip. 1995. *The Official PGP User's Guide.* Cambridge: MIT Press.

INDEX

abduction, 119–121, 181, 190–191. *See also* hypothesis
accept, 143
accountability, 9, 31, 105, 138, 149, 202
actor network theory, 22, 36, 38, 40, 47, 199
affect, 96–97
affordance, 14, 17–18, 51–52, 56–57, 66, 75–76, 133, 141, 157, 164, 213
Agamben, Giorgio, 23, 80, 204
agency, 3, 9, 14, 24, 31–32, 42, 43, 50, 63, 81–83, 96–97, 106–107, 110, 116–117, 124, 135–138, 141, 148–150, 161, 163–164, 175, 189, 192, 194, 210
Agha, Asif, 177
algorithm, 24, 154, 156, 162–163, 182–183, 210
algorithmic ineffability, 25, 180–183
alphabet, 143
archeology, 23, 109–117, 207
Arendt, Hannah, 172, 184
argument, 20, 99–102, 105–106, 206
Aristotle, 5, 49, 51, 76, 134, 137–138, 161, 204
art history, 194
assayal, 136, 185, 188. *See also* trial
astrophysics, 116
aura, 11, 124–125, 138, 150, 184
Austin, John, 49–50, 207
authenticity, 124–125, 138, 161
authority, 124–125
autism, 198
automata, 11, 146–147
automating, 1, 19

bad ontology, 194
Bates, Bernard, 151
Bateson, Gregory, 81–82, 114, 140, 199
Bayes' Rule, 24, 173, 186, 188–189
Bayesian anthropology, 173, 186–191
Bazin, André, 207
beautiful, 108
belief, 95–96, 105, 182
Benjamin, Walter, 11, 124–125, 138, 184, 203
Benkler, Yochai, 100, 209
big L, 112
black box, 11, 24, 37, 143, 146, 159
Boas, Franz, 27, 67, 72, 124, 128, 140
Boltzmann, Ludwig, 155

boundary object, 163
Bourdieu, Pierre, 6, 45
Boyle, James, 93, 107
Braudel, Fernand, 51
bridge, 2, 18, 21–22, 24, 27–29, 77, 80, 112, 160, 165
Brunton, Finn, 212
Buehler, Karl, 208
Butler, Samuel, 210, 213

capitalist, 51
causality, 113, 134, 137–138
channel, 3, 27–28, 29–31, 33–34, 37–38, 55–59, 61, 68–70, 106, 130, 200, 202, 203, 213
channel-addressing signer, 42–48
Chomsky, Noam, 122, 147, 154, 209–210
Church-Turing Thesis, 154
circle, 9–16, 18, 21
citation, 79–80, 100. *See also* reference
code, 3, 40–42
Colapietro, Vincent, 198
combination, 56, 74–75, 130
commodity, 17, 91, 186, 193
commons, 9, 11, 80
computation, 1, 158–160
computer science, 2, 24
computer-mediated interaction, 8
connotation, 98–99, 101–105
contact, 199
context-free grammar, 153–154, 157
copy, 122, 124
coupling, 63–64, 66, 70, 124, 149, 180, 202
critical theory, 107, 125–126, 164–168
cybernetics, 11, 22, 42–43, 62–63, 134, 161, 203

database, 206
data-mining, 186
death, 72, 109
deduction, 181, 190–191
deep learning, 211
degree of freedom, 22, 59–61, 92–93, 202–203
DeLanda, Manuel, 126–127, 129
Deleuze, Gilles, 23, 74, 107–108, 125–131
denotation, 98–99, 101–105
desire, 193–194
determinism, 146–147, 159, 209